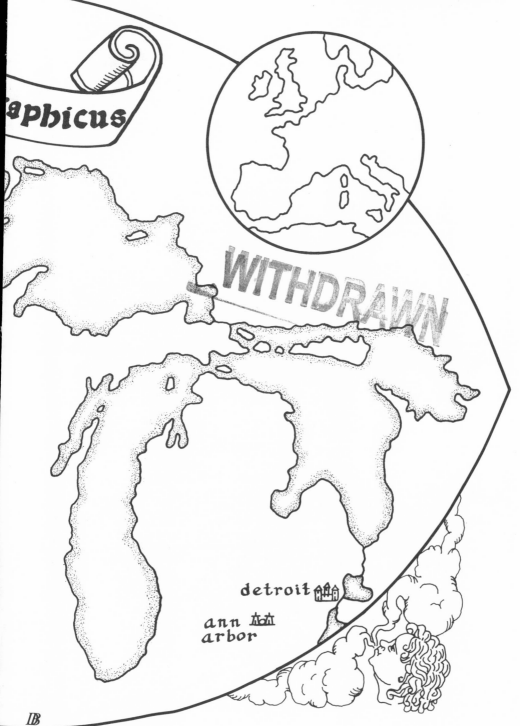

aphicus

detroit

ann
arbor

A BOOK FOR JACK

Words To, By and About

JOHN PARKER,

Curator of the James Ford Bell Library,
University of Minnesota

PUBLISHED IN SPRING, 1991

MINNEAPOLIS/ST. PAUL

ASSOCIATES OF THE JAMES FORD BELL LIBRARY,
1991

ISBN number 0-9601798-2-8

This book is printed in an edition of 750 copies. Edited by Carol Urness.
Production by Irving B. Kreidberg.

Published by the Associates of the James Ford Bell Library,
University of Minnesota, 472 Wilson Library, 309 19th Avenue South,
Minneapolis, Minnesota 55455.

Table of Contents

Preface: Elizabeth Savage, President of the Associates
of the James Ford Bell Library, vii

Part I. Essays

Carol Urness, The Early History of the James Ford Bell Library, 3

Pat Parker, A Very Special Time, 19

Jackie Cherryhomes, Dear Dad, 22

Sarah Parker, Dad, 24

Charles Parker, Memories from the Oldest Brother, 26

Herb Parker, A Parker, 27

Bill Parker, Well Done, 29

Dick and LaJean Anderson, An Exciting Time, 31

Georgia C. Haugh, The Discovery of Jack Parker, 34

Ralph Hopp, Jack as Friend and Colleague, 36

Irv Kreidberg, High Standards, 38

Brad Oftelie, Here's A Story, 39

Carol Urness, Colleague and Partner, 41

Part II. Selections from John Parker's Writings and Speeches

James Ford Bell and His Books, Introduction by Bernie Muck, 57

Travel Literature, Introduction by Maynard Hasselquist, 65

Keeping Bees, Introduction by Elizabeth Savage, 79

A Sermon, Introduction by Pat Jones, 87

China Journal, Introduction by Curt Roy, 92

Old Men, Old Books, Introduction by Ken Nebenzahl, 112

Book Collecting as a Way of Life, Introduction by Bill Laird, 123

Red Canaries and a Cage too Small, Introduction by Tom Shaughnessy, 134

Selected Publications by John Parker, 144

Part III. The Letters

Letters appear on pages 149–249

Part IV. The Associates of the James Ford Bell Library

Mary Whitehead, A History of the Associates, 253

Vicki Zobel, A Chronology of the Associates, 261

List of Members, 270

A Letter from the Editor, 282

Preface

This book has been put together at the suggestion of Jack Parker's friends, who wanted to honor him on his retirement as curator of the James Ford Bell Library. Their letters are their appraisals of a rare man. To say Mr. Bell knew how to pick men for the job goes without saying, and we feel sure he would be particularly pleased by his library today. It was his idea and the nucleus of his books that created the James Ford Bell Library, as he wanted his collection preserved in one place; he would be delighted by Jack Parker's scholarly enhancement and enlargement of the collection. Jack's scholarship, integrity and modest charm have had an influence on our Minnesota and on his colleagues in far-flung parts of the world. The book world, especially, but as we all know his interests took in much more. His travels to China and his pursuit of the early Jesuit missionaries there, to the Arctic for Eskimos and Indians, and always to Europe for additions to the collection, are all part of his life. If exploring and the voyages of merchant explorers are the field of the James Ford Bell Library, we are now exploring the work and life of creative Jack Parker.

ELIZABETH Z. SAVAGE, PRESIDENT
ASSOCIATES OF THE JAMES FORD BELL LIBRARY
SEPTEMBER 3, 1990

Part I. ESSAYS

The Early History of the
James Ford Bell Library

BY Carol Urness

A small book can easily be overlooked in the reference collection kept in the Reading Room of the James Ford Bell Library. (This is not the vault area, where we never overlook anything, big or small if we can help it, but the "modern" reference collection in the Reading Room. It has dictionaries, bibliographies, catalogs, etc. in it). One of the books in this collection is *Canadiana and French Americana in the Library of J.C. McCoy*, published in a limited edition of 350 copies in 1931. The copy is inscribed on 23 September 1932 at Villa d'Andon, Grasse, France, from James Comly McCoy to Mr. Bell. Someone has gone through this book and indicated which of the titles listed are found in the University Library ("U. of M.") or in Mr. Bell's Library ("Bell" or "JFB" or "X"). This book, and another by Mr. McCoy, *Jesuit Relations of Canada, 1632–1673*, published in Paris in 1937, are rare and should probably be in the vault. The *Jesuit Relations* contains a letter from Daniel L. McCoy, son of J.C. McCoy, presenting a copy of the book to Mr. Bell. The author, J.C. McCoy, died in 1934, when his last book was in press.

Knowing Mr. McCoy must have been a real pleasure for James Ford Bell. Both were midwesterners (McCoy was born in Illinois in 1862) who were fascinated by books about early travel to North America. Both collected Jesuit books and studied them carefully. In the introduction to his *Jesuit Relations* bibliography, Mr. McCoy acknowledges the help of J.F. Bell. In a letter to the son, Daniel, Mr. Bell records his feelings about the bibliography and writes "Somehow, as I note point by point, laboriously and faith-

3

fully established through the years, I still feel that I am reading
one of your father's friendly letters. We had a pleasant correspondence and I am sad in its loss. I felt that I knew him very well."
In time Mr. Bell bought the collection of *Jesuit Relations* that Mr.
McCoy had assembled, combining the two great collections. But
that is getting ahead of the story . . .

Mr. Bell's fascination with collecting the *Jesuit Relations* is understandable. In terms of content, these annual reports from the
Jesuit missions in North America to the Order at home in France
describe North American peoples, their customs, languages, family and social life, as well as the region's natural resources and geography. These small books were best sellers of their day, over
much of the seventeenth century. Like many other once common
books, they are exceedingly rare today. Also, because they were
published hastily in variant editions, they are a challenge to any
collector. At the time he met Mr. McCoy, James Ford Bell
(1879–1961) was in his early fifties; he kept collecting *Jesuit Relations* seriously for the rest of his life.

It would be very interesting to know if the two of them discussed Biard's *Relation* of 1616, a book that keeps appearing off
and on in the story of Mr. Bell and his Library. Pierre Biard lived
in New France (Acadia) for two years, as part of the first French
attempt to establish a mission in North America. Biard's book is
not one of the annual reports of the Jesuits, which came later, but
it is the earliest report on North America written by a Jesuit. Biard also reveals something of his own personality when he writes
about the progress of the mission "Everywhere, in France as in
Canada, it is necessary to sow before reaping, and to plant before
gathering, and not to be so avaricious or impatient as to wish, like
userers, the profit at the same time as the loan." Mr. McCoy did
not have a copy of the Biard book, and the two collectors might
well have discussed it. Mr. Bell collected many books besides the
Jesuit Relations, of course, as will be seen in this brief early history of the James Ford Bell Library.

The records that remain from Mr. Bell's acquisitions in the
1930s and 40s, show that he was a careful, discriminating buyer.
He enjoyed the pursuit of a rare book, that is clear. He also was
demanding in the condition of the books he purchased, something
that continues in the James Ford Bell Library today. The records

and correspondence about his purchases, kept in the University Archives, show that he was a fine bookman. Near the end of World War II, apparently, Mr. Bell was thinking seriously about his book collection and what he should do with it.

On a Saturday in January, 1945, the Dean of the Graduate School at the University of Minnesota, Theodore C. Blegen, went to see Mr. Bell's Library at 200 Chamber of Commerce building, Minneapolis. Dean Blegen, a well-known historian, was impressed. In a letter to Mr. Bell of 17 January 1945 he wrote "I am not ordinarily given to the use of superlatives, but my enthusiasm for the collection of books that you have built up does not permit anything but superlatives." In the same letter "I believe that I am stating only the simple truth (and not indulging in any exaggeration) when I say that your books are the finest collection I have ever seen." Dean Blegen did not waste an opportunity, continuing further "I am going to take the liberty of saying frankly to you that I want to see this collection preserved under your name in the library of the University of Minnesota. It is not only that it would greatly add to the glory and distinction of the University and its library, but that, preserved as an entity and enriched further in years to come, it would be a tremendous inspiration and help to the faculty and selected students and scholars." And Dean Blegen goes on to point out that an organization called the Friends of the University Library has just been formed. "My ideal is to have this great library of ours *ringed* about with friends who will gladly come to our aid in enlarging the riches of the library whenever it is necessary for us to go outside the usual sources of University income for such a purpose." (Ideals of administrators — as well as librarians — seldom change!)

Mr. Bell clearly was pleased with the visit also. To Dean Blegen he wrote in return, "It was a real pleasure to show you the books. I sensed in you an appreciation and enjoyment that is rare." Mr. Bell was modest about the size of the collection, with the statement that "One cannot, without the greatest stretch of imagination, claim that it is a comprehensive collection, but at least it can serve as the nucleus and, I hope, the inspiration to others similarly minded to build here on our prairies something that can vie in quality at least with the best anywhere." While he wanted his Library to stay in Minnesota, he wanted even more to be sure that it would not remain static. If that were to be its fate, he wrote, he would rather see it sold.

Mr. Bell's abilities as a collector did not go unnoticed in other quarters. In April of 1945, E.W. McDiarmid, Director of the Division of Library Instruction, wrote to Mr. Bell, stating that the curriculum was being revised with an eye toward offering extension courses for librarians and "interested persons" in the area. Would Mr. Bell like to teach a course in book collecting? Mr. Bell answered "If I were at liberty to engage my time on the fixed schedule which would be necessary, or if I had the time available, I should be delighted, but I assure you that I am struggling now, with advancing years, to relieve myself of responsibilities and it would be out of the question for me to undertake it." At the time Mr. Bell was 66 years old.

Ms. Annabelle Johnson, Mr. Bell's secretary, aided him in his book collecting for years, as the correspondence shows. The notes they exchanged on the letters to book dealers indicate that she was very much involved in helping him. In addition, Mr. Frank K. Walter, the Librarian Emeritus, collated and described books in the little library, though in the summer of 1945 he became ill and could no longer continue this work. A superb cataloger from the University Library staff, Ms. Virginia Doneghy, took over in his place. The catalog published in 1950 is *Jesuit Relations and Other Americana in the Library of James F. Bell*, and is called the Walter-Doneghy catalog. The University of Minnesota Press published this model bibliography. The lengthy collations given in it, the paginations, the information on illustrations and maps, plus the citations to scholarly studies and the heavy use of illustrations — all of these things make the catalog an ideal bibliography but incredibly difficult to produce. We have never tried such an elaborate catalog again.

Mr. Bell wrote a foreword to the catalog, indicating, "To possess an original is to know the authentic environment of the author and the spirit of his times." He compared collecting such works to hunting, noting that "The pursuit of such works in a field of shrinking supply has a peculiar fascination that is attuned to man's love for rare things. . . . The collector must understand what he wants and why he wants it. Every new success fires his total effort with increasing knowledge and understanding and a resulting satisfaction and fulfillment." And he wrote, "To collect one must become a wanderer, if not both physically and mentally, at least mentally, roving everywhere, enlarging the field of acquaintance and contact." The *Jesuit Relations* formed the heart of Mr. Bell's collection and of the catalog describing it.

On 23 January 1950, Mr. Bell wrote a letter to the New York book dealer Edward Eberstadt. In describing his collecting he notes that to this point he has limited it to the "fundamental discoveries" of North America. "Beyond this I have confined my efforts to the approaches to what we call the Northwest through the three main arteries of the Hudson's Bay, the St. Lawrence, and the Mississippi." He further notes that "My collection is not large but I have confined myself to buying important things, and only in prime condition. Unless I can have what seems to be a perfect copy, I would prefer to go without." The high standards of the Library were established very early.

Painstaking research was done on the *Jesuit Relations* for the catalog, some of it by Mr. Bell's office staff. Mrs. Bertha Berg Jespersen, for example, examined each of Mr. Bell's books with great care and made extensive notes. Her material was most valuable when it came to preparing descriptions of the books for the catalog. Mr. Bell also had some research assistance from Mr. Lawrence Wroth, Librarian of the John Carter Brown Library, who also had extensive experience with the *Jesuit Relations*. Mr. Wroth had studied the McCoy collection, and wrote a preface to the 1937 published catalog of it. In a memo of 23 June 1952 Annabelle Johnson wrote to Mr. Bell: "Did Mr. Tree [Roland Tree, of the bookselling firm of Henry Stevens and Co.] tell you he thinks a case of Scotch would be better than a fee to Dr. Wroth, inasmuch as the latter would turn money over to the library. Do you wish us to do anything about this?" There is a penciled note from Mr. Bell in response, indicating it was already taken care of: "Sent Scotch."

The publication of the catalog caused a stir. In a letter of 16 October 1950 to Mr. Bell, James T. Babb, the Librarian of Yale University Library, wrote: "I took it [the catalog] home last evening and read it through fairly carefully. I do congratulate you on this fine volume. I particularly envy you the collection of Jesuit Relations. We have almost none of them in their original form here at Yale. I have always understood that your library will eventually go to the University of Minnesota, and if this is so they are to be greatly congratulated. If it is not so I should be happy to take the train to Minneapolis immediately." There was a man who knew how to get books for a library! Mr. Bell answered "Apparently the necessity of your coming out immediately is not indicated!" But he invited Babb to visit any time.

After the publication of the catalog, negotiations between Mr. Bell and the University continued. As he wrote to President J.L. Morrill on 3 June 1952, it was his "earnest desire" that the collection should go to the University, but he did not want the Library to die. A rather elaborate program was outlined, whereby the collection was to be kept in trust for the University but not deeded fully to it for ten years after his death, during which time Mr. Bell's three sons would be trustees. For its part the University should "show an interest in keeping the collection alive and making reasonable additions thereto. . . . " The concern and love for his books is evident in the same letter. He wrote, "I have never desired to have my name connected with the things in which I have taken an active interest, always feeling that it militated against the support from others who might not be particularly interested in magnifying somebody else's name. However, since these books all bear my bookplate and the library has been known as the Bell Collection I should like in this instance to have the name retained." Mr. Bell's own very serious commitment to building the collection was clear. Between mid-1950 and mid-1953 he spent the sum of $146,675.75 on books to add to it, according to a report made by cataloger Virginia Doneghy.

Shortly before the Library was to move to the University, the question of its name was raised, apparently. On 24 July 1953 Annabelle Johnson wrote "He is inclined toward 'The James Ford Bell Library.' He feels that the use of words like 'collection,' 'Americana,' or 'Western Hemisphere Exploration' might restrict its future scope." She added, "As you know, Mr. Bell is up in the wilds of Canada. . . . " No doubt because of the small number of books that were involved, the name settled on was the "James Ford Bell Collection." The name was changed to "James Ford Bell Library" after the Museum of Natural History was named for Mr. Bell. The confusion was just too much: too many of the books coming from dealers ended up in the museum building. Besides, somebody tried to deliver live worms to us "to feed your birds." One time the curators almost had dual cardiac failures when the original edition of a book by Bartolomé de Las Casas, a Spanish priest who defended the Indians in the New World, was left over-night in a hallway mailbox outside an office in the museum.

Mr. Bell couldn't do everything himself. As the time neared for the collection to be transferred to the University Library, more than a room and a vault were needed. So in May, 1953, the position of principal librarian was established for the Curator of the James Ford Bell Collection. This was job number 4830, which had a beginning salary of $370 per month; a maximum for it was $420 a month. The new appointment was to be at the minimum salary, according to the notice.

On Tuesday, 21 April 1953, Mr. John Parker visited the Library "in connection with the curatorship of the James Ford Bell Collection." At the time he was employed as the assistant manuscripts librarian at the William L. Clements Library at the University of Michigan, where he was a graduate student. He had served in the Army Air Corps in India and the South Pacific from 1943–46. (Mr. Bell probably liked that — planes were a subject that fascinated him and he had considered building a library on the subject of airline routes and the development of modern trade). During the interview Mr. Bell asked the candidate if he knew where to buy a Biard. Although he didn't, Jack was hired. He was to begin his new position on September 1, 1953.

An article in the *Langdon Republican* (North Dakota) newspaper carried the heading "Jack Parker Receives High Curator Position at U of Minnesota." It noted that Jack, son of Mr. and Mrs. P.C. Parker of Nekoma, was hired to be the curator of the collection, which "is a recent acquisition of the University library and consists of many rare books relating particularly to the early exploration of northeastern North America." Jack, it continued, graduated from Jamestown College and then earned a master's degree in history at Wayne State University at Detroit. He was taking graduate courses in library science at Michigan. In June he was going to New York and Washington, D.C., to visit libraries and book dealers. The article concludes "Before going to Minneapolis, Mr. and Mrs. Parker will visit his family at Nekoma and Mrs. Parker's parents, Mr. and Mrs. R.J. Falstad, at Garrison."

They arrived on the scene in time to participate in the big dedication of the James Ford Bell Library, which was held on 30 October 1953. Five speakers: Stanley Pargellis of The Newberry Library, Colton Storm of the Western Reserve Historical Society, Louis B. Wright from the Folger Shakespeare Library, plus Mr. Bell and Dean Blegen — inaugurated the Library. In 1954 their remarks were published by the University of Minnesota Press as *Book Collecting and Scholarship.* This book is now a collector's item. The text was set in Linotype Janson, printed by Lund Press, bound by A.J. Dahl Company, and — most importantly — was designed by Jane McCarthy. A very nice beginning, indeed, for the Library.

Mr. Bell spoke about book collecting and said, "It is, I think, man's insatiable appetite for experience. He wishes to live not only his own life but the lives of many other men as well, particularly the lives of men whose preoccupations are similar to his own. . . . One seeks those objects which reflect his interests. He awakens to the possessive urge to gather them about him. He treasures them for those qualities which bespeak his interest, often far better than his own words. They form the historical background of his present cultural environment. He, in effect, becomes a collector." And later, "As I look back on the genesis of this effort and seek a reasonable explanation, there is a recurring thought that it concerns itself with *trade*. Being in trade, I was perhaps influenced, without knowing I was influenced, by this environment."

"Trade, to me, is an expression of the world's economy of living. Each individual seeks to live, and to live advantageously. His needs may not be fully satisfied with what is immediately available. If he has a surplus of things of his own production, he uses it as a medium to secure other things from those who have an available supply. . . . "

"Trade in itself is basically a selfish interest. Trade knows no border, no kin, no breed, no loyalty nor patriotism or sentiment. Trade goes on regardless of wars, riots and commotions. Trade seeks avenues of advantage even as between enemies. Always it seeks that which serves its interests best . . . "

"In this rather embryonic collection of gleanings from the wealth of the past, I have tried to gather together the basic items of trade and subsequent exploration which led to the discovery of this country. It is my hope that the collection may be expanded along the lines which depict the progress of trade as it touched upon the shores of this country and found herein already-established trade routes which led man on to traverse the width and breadth of this continent and contributed to its development and continuing success . . . "

" . . . I am happy to offer for their use certain fragments of time bound up in books. This collection does not loom large in the light of other great libraries. And yet, everything must have a beginning, and the great libraries in other parts of the world, as well as here, were once small both in extent and purpose. What I have has been carefully chosen and is, I think, of a quality and an extent at least to form the nucleus of a library which — with the interest and help of the FRIENDS OF THE LIBRARY and others in the community — may some day take its place with the others both in its extent and the values it offers. May it help to make the generations of students that will pass through this university good trustees for posterity of the boldness, confidence, vision and wisdom which these books contain as gifts from the past!"

When the celebrations were over, after the speeches and the big dinner and the reporters, it was time to turn a generous gift into an operating Library. Before long a problem was brewing and Jack wrote to Mr. Bell, who was in Georgia at the time, about it. In a letter of 5 February 1954 Jack wrote: "In the three months that we have been functioning as a library our concern has been primarily with the acquisition of books and the organization of them into a useful scholarly resource." A friend of Mr. Bell's had come to the Library, suggesting that he "and other speakers" could promote the Library to business and professional groups, at luncheon clubs and other civic groups. The "romantic" aspects of the book should be emphasized. Jack reported that he had not said "no" right away, but rather had wanted time to think it over — and apparently, the more he thought it over the less appealing the thought was. In his letter he said, "I feel that when the Library is being talked about, it should be someone who is familiar with the books that does the talking." Furthermore, he added " . . . the most exciting and romantic thing about any book is the story it tells, and the historical circumstances that surrounded its author at its writing." Jack added that he thought the Library should work through the Friends of the Library in its efforts to raise funds.

Mr. Bell's answer to the letter, dated 14 February 1954, is interesting. He admits that his friend is "an enthusiast" and "I do agree with him to the extent that the city should take pride in building up around this nucleus a great collection, but just how to do it is another matter. Like yourself, I find it a little difficult to see the procedure in his terms." And "Your thought that we should rely upon the Friends of the Library is perfectly sound, but at the same time unless there is someone who is going to take a real initiative in the matter and give some time, thought and effort to it, I am afraid the most we will get will be wishful thinking." He agrees " . . . when the library is being talked about, it should be someone who is familiar with the books that does the talking. However, this, like most all efforts, requires a certain amount of dramatization." And he concludes "Just at the moment I don't believe we have found ourselves and know just what course to follow. Therefore, while it is well to keep the matter in mind and to turn over various thoughts which occur in connection with it, let's wait awhile before we come to a decision." Good advice.

The Library was rather often in the limelight. It was just a year old, in the fall of 1954, when the Martin Waldseemüller "globe map" became part of the collection. This map, printed in gores so it could be cut out and shaped into a globe, is *very* rare. The reason, of course, is that in 1507, when it was printed, most people *did* cut it out and paste it on a wooden ball to make a globe. Saving globes for several centuries is not easy. The map has the name "America" on it for the first time. The Waldseemüller map is the most commonly reproduced single item in the Library. It appears in all kinds of books, and students often see it reproduced in their history textbooks. Thus students from distant places were made aware of this new Library at the University of Minnesota.

Students on campus also became aware of it rather quickly. Jack must have been a little proud to write to Mr. Bell on 21 October 1954 that "I am sorry that I did not feel free to discuss the Kelmscott Press books or the Spanish map with you more freely on the phone Monday. At the moment you called I was speaking

to Professor Krey's class in Historical Method, and with all fifteen
of them sitting in on the conversation, I did not feel that I could
discuss it as frankly as I would like to have done." Early in 1956
he sent a description of an English book that had become available for purchase and wrote to Mr. Bell, "I am currently spending
my free time working on a thesis for the University of Michigan
on English travel and trade literature of the sixteenth and seventeenth centuries. I try to separate my own interests from those of
the Collection as a whole when considering such books as this
one. This is not always easy to do. . . . "

In the spring of the same year he sent a memorandum to Mr.
Bell and Dr. Edward (Ned) Stanford, Director of Libraries. The
subject: "The Scope of the James Ford Bell Collection." It begins,
"After three years of considering the type of collection which we
wish to build at the University of Minnesota, and after three trips
abroad in search of materials, it now seems both possible and
desirable to set forth clearly, for ourselves and for persons who
will in the future be associated with the Bell Collection, the types
of materials which we consider pertinent to a collection devoted
to the history of trade." And thus the first "conspectus," as we now
call a collection development plan, of the Library was created.
The annual report of that year (1955–56) described four categories which sound familiar: "1. Purchasing and cataloging
materials for the Collection; 2. Preparing publications from the
Collection; 3. Making materials from the Collection available to
students through exhibits and research; 4. Publicizing the Collection among various interested groups in the area." A total of 568
items were added to the Collection during the year. The supple-
ment to the Walter-Doneghy *Jesuit Relations* catalog, *The James
Ford Bell Collection, A List of Additions, 1951–1955* was published as was the little book by Sergio J. Pacifici titled *Copy of a
letter of the King of Portugal sent to the King of Castile concerning the voyage and success of India*. Twenty groups visited the Library during the fiscal year. Circulation was up, too, as students
and faculty members became more aware of the Library's
resources. In short, the Curator was busy.

On 26 February 1957 Jack wrote a memorandum to Dr. Stanford, Director of the University Libraries. The subject was:
"Work to be undertaken by prospective assistant in Bell Room."

He notes how his work has changed over the four years he had been there. In the first year he had spent 75 per cent of his time in work relating to the Library. That first year 114 items had been added to the Library. About 750 items would be added in 1956–57, and "In looking over this year's work, I would estimate that I am working on the purchase and describing of books about 25 per cent of the time. . . . " And he added "I recognize the fact that I am becoming an administrator of a Collection with many facets, and I must know something about all of them. I am most concerned with the fact that I am spending a lot of time on public relations at the expense of time spent learning about the books we are buying. . . . In the long run the excellence of my public relations will be directly proportional to the degree to which I know what I am talking about." And he concludes, "We must either restrict our activities, admit to a lower quality of work, or expand the staff." Dr. Stanford naturally supported the last alternative, and Vsevolod (Steve) Slessarev became Assistant Curator later that year. Steve was working on his Ph.D. in medieval history at the University of Wisconsin.

The summer of 1958 held a major disappointment for Mr. Bell when he did not get the Antonio Pigafetta manuscript account of the voyage of Ferdinand Magellan. Pigafetta was in the crew and his account of the circumnavigation of 1519–22 would have been a stellar item in the Library. At the auction, someone else got the manuscript. In a tape recording of 9 July 1958 Mr. Bell admitted, "I was terribly disappointed about losing the Pigafetta item. . . . If there is another real item, Jack will have to go over himself and attend the auction, with discretionary powers that I would not think of permitting to an ordinary bidder." He asked Jack to find out who the bidder was and to offer the selling price plus a 10% commission. The effort was futile—Yale got the Pigafetta.

Some comments Mr. Bell made on this same tape about the general economy are interesting: "Certainly prices are reaching the sky in all things. I am truly worried about the effects of increased inflation, which seems inevitable. If it really goes wild, as it did in Germany, it will wipe us all out. It was a terrible occasion. I remember so well the fact that a twenty dollar bill got I do not know how many million marks. I went out to dinner that

night and matched with a party of three and lost the match. As
I recall it, the dinner cost me forty million marks, which was
about all the money I had on me despite the fact that every pocket
was filled and I carried some extra in a bundle wrapped up in
newspaper."

"They had a very peculiar way of making poor paper which
disintegrated shortly after it went into use and therefore the
government was saved the problem of reclaiming it."

"All this goes to show what might happen in case things go on
unrestricted and unrestrained."

Shortly after this Mr. Bell wrote to Jack about the progress of
the Library. "My sincere and heartfelt congratulations to you as
we approach the fifth anniversary! I am deeply appreciative of
the superb job you have done in building the library to its present
status, and I know this feeling on my part is shared by the officials
of the University and by all those who have had knowledge of the
accomplishments you have effected." At the fifth anniversary, in
October of 1958, the James Ford Bell Collection, after a beginning of some 600 volumes, held over four thousand books, maps,
manuscripts, documents, broadsides and pamphlets. More importantly, the quality of the Library was well recognized. Of
course, it still did not have the 1616 book by Biard, even though
Jack kept looking for it . . .

On 10 September 1959, Mr. Bell wrote to Jack that "It would
be nice if we could get the Biard, but like yourself I will believe
it when we have it in hand!" The Italian bookseller, Mrs. Marzoli, had been asked to search for it. Later in September Mr. Bell
mentioned it again, this time stating "It would be a matter of
satisfaction to have the Biard," and in the same letter, "On the
matter of the Biard, somehow or other I feel at last we shall fill
in this item we have so long sought." He was disappointed once
again — the elusive Biard remained beyond reach that year.

Jack was noted for the quality of his public appearances before
various groups. In April, 1959, Mr. Bell congratulated him on
one of them, and added "I am wondering if it is feasible and practical to extend a general invitation to the public, either through
the newspapers or otherwise, to attend an evening with the books
and hear one of your fine talks. Probably this suggestion is not
compatible with the policy of the Library, but it arises from the

thought, 'Why hide your light under a bushel?' At least, in the commercial world we like to have it standing outside." Jack went on another book buying trip that year. In August Mr. Bell wrote rather wistfully, "As the time approaches for your departure, I am filled with deeper regret that my age and physical state will not permit me to accompany you and to enjoy some of the interesting experiences that lie ahead." Back home again, Jack was soon involved with a television series about the Library.

Early in 1960 Jack wrote to Mr. Bell, enclosing some book descriptions with the comment "It is good to get back to writing reports of this type again. . . . " A backlog of sixty undescribed items purchased by the Trust had accumulated. Steve Slessarev, Jack writes, is busy preparing a paper for the International Congress on the History of Exploration to be held in Lisbon in September. He will attend, he notes, but gave up the idea of writing a paper because of the television series. (This meeting had another result, by the way, which was the formation of the Society for the History of Discoveries – Jack, Steve, Thomas Goldstein and Wilcomb Washburn were the official founders of the SHD. The idea for it is rumored to have arisen over a bottle of wine).

Throughout their correspondence, Jack always opened his letters "Dear Mr. Bell," closed them "Respectfully," and signed them first, "John Parker" and then, beginning sometime in 1957, "Jack." Mr. Bell's closing was always "Sincerely" and usually his opening was "Dear Mr. Parker" though there was a period when he addressed letters simply "Dear Parker." On 30 March 1960 Mr. Bell wrote "Dear Dr. Parker, I can't resist the urge to be among those who have the privilege now of addressing you with that title. I know the occasion marks a most important milestone in the work to which you have devoted yourself so splendidly and with such high recognition. We are indeed happy for you and offer you our most sincere congratulations." Mr. Bell always addressed his letters to "Dr. Parker" after that.

During the summer of 1960 Jack was again buying books in Europe. This time he also took a leave to work on his book about Emanuel van Meteren. He wrote to Mr. Bell late in August: "Coming toward the end of this trip I cannot but reflect on the condition of the book trade this year. I have seen fewer spectacular things than on any previous trip. In fact, no one has shown me

a book worth $5,000. . . . My own feeling is that we must step
out now and then to pick up the spectacular item when it is
clearly in our field, but that to a research library it is not often
that one item will be worth more to us in the long run than a
dozen or more books or manuscripts with good content but less
publicity value." And then in closing, "We have had a most
happy summer here, and will remember it all our lives. I could
not imagine a nicer moment than one I had yesterday as Jacque-
lyn and I looked out over the countryside from the top of Windsor
Castle's tower. There have been many wonderful experiences,
both of work and recreation which we will not forget." The rest
was good, for once at home, the pace was hectic. Steve had taken
a teaching position in Ohio and had not yet been replaced. There
was the Library to run, books to be purchased and described, students to help . . .

Jack cataloged twenty-one items in December. On 13 January
1961 Mr. Bell wrote to him, "It seems to me that you are working
under considerable pressure these days, with the programs and
the annual report, as well as the book reports. Don't be concerned
if you fall a little behind in any one of these categories. There will
be plenty of time to catch up later." Mr. Bell probably knew he
was wasting his breath! In his next letter Jack describes the format
of a catalog which he and Mr. Bell had often discussed.

A description is made for every book added to the James Ford
Bell Library, a practice which originated in these early days
when Mr. Bell couldn't always come to the Library to see them.
Jack wrote descriptions of the books for Mr. Bell's information.
Some of the book descriptions are lengthy; some are rather short.
All are in the Library and form a special source of information on
the items in the collection. Some of this information was to be
used in the "annual report" of the Library. As Jack stated in a letter of 24 January 1961, "To call something an 'annual report' kills
off a lot of its appeal. . . . " After discussions, the title decided
upon was *The Merchant Explorer*. The goal was "to make a readable review of some of our significant acquisitions." Mr. Bell, in
a letter of 6 February 1961 writes, "Like yourself, I think we
should try to depart as much as we can from the academic or normal Annual Report. Let's make it a readable review." This goal
was attained with the first volume, published in 1961, and *The*

Merchant Explorer is still the favorite publication of the Library for many people.

On 24 February 1961 James Ford Bell wrote a letter to President O. Meredith Wilson about the Library. He wrote, "my ambitions are to see it grow and take on added lustre, and I hope that part of this will be possible during my lifetime, and that it will continue long thereafter." He never had the satisfaction of seeing the Biard added to the Library. He was able to watch his Library take root and flourish and show great promise at the University of Minnesota before his death in May, 1961.

NOTE: Much of the above information came from records in the University Archives, Walter Library, University of Minnesota. The help of Penelope Krosch and her staff is greatly appreciated.

A Very Special Time

BY Patricia Parker

Upon the occasion of a retirement, it seems that most of us are inclined to look back over that part of the retiree's career that puts us in the picture. When the retiree is one's spouse and the career being celebrated is encompassed by a marriage of even longer duration, it becomes extremely difficult to know what to focus on in a brief essay such as this. I have found myself increasingly thinking about the beginning of Jack's career at the James Ford Bell Library as his retirement approaches. It was a very special time in our lives for many reasons, not the least of which was the opportunity it gave us to travel and meet new people. Particularly, this was the time we met many of the antiquarian bookdealers who were to play a continuing role in the development of the Bell Library in subsequent years. So I would like to mark Jack's retirement by recollecting some of the people in the booktrade we met during those first few years. It is easy to call these people to mind after all this time not only because they introduced us to an exciting world where the pursuit of a highly prized book could occupy one's complete attention; more importantly, I remember them because they became our friends.

A visit to our attic is a great way to revive memories of these first years in Jack's career at the Bell Library. Among the memorabilia stored there are the beautifully embroidered postcards (now a thing of the past) that Jack mailed home from cities in Spain and Portugal during a bookbuying trip; a small stuffed owl aptly named Mr. Hakluyt that one of our daughters was given by

Professor David Quinn of the University of Liverpool; a smocked red and yellow baby dress from Paris; trolls accumulated when Jack was in Norway buying books from Asbjorn Lunge-Larsen and Claes Nyegaard; a delicate miniature Sante Maria that marked a visit with Telles da Sylva in Lisbon; a 1953 playbill from a New York theatre.

It's the playbill that takes me back to the very beginning. It's hard for me to believe it was thirty-seven years ago that Jack and I went to New York for the first time, making the trip from Ann Arbor in our old Ford car. A first visit to New York, particularly for a Midwesterner, is an experience never to be forgotten. In our case, the purpose of the trip made it especially memorable. Jack had just accepted the job of Curator of the James Ford Bell Library at the University of Minnesota; he was to start September 1. Before we made the move to Minneapolis, we decided to go to New York to meet some of the antiquarian bookdealers Jack would be doing business with. Because I'm also a librarian, I think I looked forward to the trip as much as Jack did.

I met Mr. H.P. Kraus on that first trip to New York. What a great introduction that was to the antiquarian bookseller's world! Mr. Kraus had the ability to make a couple of novices feel at ease in very impressive and potentially intimidating surroundings. I have very fond memories of this and subsequent visits with Mr. Kraus over the years. He came to Minneapolis several times and, reflecting back on these visits, what I remember best are the wonderful conversations we had. Mr. Kraus described the goings-on in the world of rare books in a way that I found irresistible. I'm sure it was his keen sense of bibliographic intrigue, as well as his scholarship that made these conversations so delightful.

London is the city I associate most with Jack's book-buying trips during those early years in the James Ford Bell Library. Several times we made the trip to London as a family and this gave me the opportunity to get acquainted with well-known English antiquarian bookdealers. Among them were Lionel and Philip Robinson. I remember very vividly their beautifully appointed Pall Mall shop and their warm hospitality. Recalling their stories about how they got started in the booktrade makes me realize again what a privilege it was for me to get to know the Robinson brothers.

I also met Tony Hobson on one of our early trips to London. He invited us to attend an antiquarian book sale at Sotheby's and I recall the table that was set aside for the important booksellers who were attending the sale. This was also the first time I had seen bidders communicating with an auctioneer by using obscure hand gestures that to the uninitiated were extremely hard to follow. It was in London that I first met Miss Winnie Myers, one of the best autograph dealers in the business. Winnie very quickly became a good family friend. Our children loved her because she related to them in a very special way — I think it was her playful sense of humor and her tremendous appreciation of childhood that endeared her to them. I bought my Robert Scott manuscripts from Winnie years ago; today, when I look at them I am once again reminded of the wonderful times we had together.

Dr. and Mrs. Ernst Weil were also among those first friends we made in London. One of my favorite recollections is of the time Jack and I, along with our two young daughters, were invited to tea at the Weils' handsome Hampstead Garden Suburb home. Sarah and Jackie sat absolutely speechless before a bowl of enormous strawberries while Jack and I enjoyed being in the company of two people whom we both admired very much. We saw the Weils often that summer because we had rented a house within easy walking distance.

I also traveled to the Continent with Jack on several book-buying trips during those early years and that gave me an opportunity to meet rare book dealers in Holland, Switzerland, France, Portugal and Italy. I'll always remember my first meeting with Mrs. Carla Marzoli at her home in Milan. That was the beginning of a friendship that has continued to the present time. Nico and Nanny Israel are among our dearest friends in the booktrade. When I think of Amsterdam, I immediately think of the Israels and the good times we've had together in that beautiful city. We have had another long association with a family we first met through Jack's work; the Lunge-Larsens. Jack met Asbjorn on his first book-buying trip to Scandinavia; Asbjorn and Berit welcomed him into their home in Oslo and a close friendship between our families has continued ever since. Our children exchanged visits as they were growing up and I was fortunate to have Lise Lunge-Larsen as a student of mine at Augsburg College. We were saddened by both Berit's and Asbjorn's deaths but we find ourselves taking great pride in the success their daughter Lise is having as a storyteller whose special skill lies in the telling of Norwegian tales. As Lise once told me, she first read these tales in a beautiful first edition in her father's library. As I have been writing this brief reminiscence, the names and faces of other bookseller friends have emerged as well — the list of people I've come to know and like in the book trade is a very long list indeed. There are the Nebenzahls, Ken and Josie; Jacques Vellekoop, Michel Sinelnikoff, Hugo Brant Corstius, and many more. Jack has always seemed to enjoy having his family share in his professional life — the people, the places, the acquisition of beautiful books. Because this has been the case, I have truly enjoyed and appreciated these past thirty-seven years filled with rich experiences and wonderful friendships in the company of a terrific rare-book librarian!

Dear Dad:

BY Jackie Cherryhomes

I've had trouble putting down on the paper what I've been thinking about. I've been told to write down a memory I have about you, but I can't seem to focus on a single memory. Being your daughter has been a 36 year experience — it's been a process and a lifetime of events which all seem to string together into one large event.

From the very beginning you taught me about politics. When I say politics, I don't mean "how to be a politician." I mean the politics of life and the commitment that one must have to one's fellow human beings. You knew the meaning of "do the right thing" long before it was a popular phrase.

I remember watching the returns in the Kennedy/Nixon race at the Bruckensteins' and how important that all was.

Doorknocking for Earl Craig when he ran against Hubert Humphrey, you didn't care that Earl would probably lose. You cared that he stood for the the right ideals. I remember the passion with which you supported McCarthy. He too stood little chance to win, but he stood for the right ideals.

I saw the impact that the Vietnam War had on your life. I watched your pain as the young men we knew either went to Vietnam, to jail or to Canada. I remember the many moratorium marches we hiked in the freezing cold. To this day, I can't put into words the effect these experiences had. I can't explain it, but I believe my political conscience was formed at the dinner table as we talked about the war.

You taught me that one couldn't sit idly by while one's government was engaged in illegal and immoral actions. One has a responsibility to participate, and so we both participated. You took me to my first precinct caucus — you didn't go back, but turned the "local" politics over to me.

When I ran for class president, you asked me how I was going to win when I wasn't really a member of the popular group. I said I would put together a coalition of "the women, the hippies and the Black kids." I did it and I won. It was at that point that I knew I wanted a career in elected office.

The political conscience you instilled in me helped me through my first election as class president. But the depth of your influence was what helped me through this last difficult year-long pursuit of elected office. All the stamina and fortitude to get through that election, inside me, came from the knowledge that I was "doing the right thing," and that I had a mission. All summer, my standard was: "what would Dad think of this?" If I could tell you about it and look you in the eye, it was the right thing to do. If I couldn't do that, I knew that I'd better rethink my actions.

Dad

BY Sarah Parker

My dad has a really cool job. It didn't matter that as a young girl I never really understood what my dad did for a living. I just knew it was cool. Kim's dad worked at the Pig's Eye Plant, Terry's dad worked at the Post Office and Lisa's dad was a chemist. Their dads all had normal jobs — jobs you could describe. My dad's job defied description.

He had this terrific office with these tall old red velveteen chairs. There were old maps everywhere and he had a huge vault that held a letter Christopher Columbus wrote. There was no comparison. My dad had the greatest job of all, even if I didn't understand it.

When a teacher would ask the inevitable, "And Sarah, what does your father do for a living?" I would dutifully reply, "He's the Curator of the James Ford Bell Library." The teachers often looked as bewildered as my friends when I spouted off this rehearsed response. Fortunately they never asked me to elaborate. I don't think I could have.

To be truthful, I'm not sure even today I fully understand just what it is my father has been doing all these years. I still get a bit tongue-tied with explanations of my father's occupation. I know he is a scholar, a librarian, a historian, an author and a teacher. But to me he is so much more than that. He's a great dad.

You see, long ago when I decided I would never get a handle on his occupation, I focused my attention on what I knew best — John Parker as a father. Sure I knew he wrote books and travelled across Europe. I knew he was extremely intelligent and widely respected. But to me the greatest thing about my dad was that he was *my* dad.

Many people know him for his academic achievements. I know him for his ability to make gardens grow and bees buzz. I know John Parker as a gardener, a storyteller, a beekeeper and a philosopher. While he was busy securing that one-of-a-kind book from a far away land, he was also teaching me how to plant potatoes.

My dad is summers at Waupagasset Family Camp, singing

songs and catching frogs. My dad is Sunday afternoons at Cooke Hall shooting hoops and teaching me the infamous "hook shot." My dad is late night talks about broken teenage hearts, passing on poignant philosophies of life.

We had a lot of adventures with dad. Train trips across Portugal with live chickens pecking at my heels. We ate strange food and dared not ask what it was. We toured the Swiss Alps and the English countryside. We swam in the ocean and explored great palaces. I am grateful for all those experiences. But not every adventure was to an exotic land. There were numerous trips to North Dakota. We camped in Canada, we rode rides in Disneyland. We paddled canoes across Lake Itasca. In fact, of all the places in the world we have shared, Lake Itasca is still my favorite. I suspect it is his as well.

Through all the adventures, I never stop to think of my dad as "John Parker, Curator of the James Ford Bell Library." He is my dad. He writes books, he also plants tulips. He is held in high regard by booksellers and beekeepers alike. I have long respected him for that balance.

As an adult, when I stop by to see my dad in his office, I know the magic is still there. The same red velveteen chairs, same maps, same dad sitting behind what I believe to be the world's first typewriter, piles of files all around. I know my dad has made tremendous contributions to the James Ford Bell Library. I know he will be missed. I also know I am not worried about John Parker in retirement. It simply means he will have more time to do the things I know and love him for. More flowers to plant, more photography, more time for adventures. Who knows, maybe he'll even brush up on that "hook shot." These are the kinds of things that in my eyes have made him a vital and interesting man. Perhaps the best thing about his retirement is that I no longer have to struggle to explain what it is my dad does for a living. I can simply say, "He's an all 'round great guy, a true friend, and the best dad a girl could ever hope for." You see, many of you can call him a colleague, some can call him a close friend. I have the privilege of calling John Parker, Curator of the James Ford Bell Library, "Dad."

Memories from the Oldest Brother

BY Charles Parker

I remember Jack as a quiet, easy going, mild tempered and contented little boy. He was always able to find ways to entertain himself while the rest of us were complaining of nothing to do. He loved to cut out pictures of cars and in those days there were a lot of pictures in magazines of the different makes and models. He had several cigar boxes full of paper cars. He would race them across the linoleum rug in the dining room. The rug had a pattern of small squares. He had a spinner with zero to five numbers, he would then spin and move until one would make it across the room and back. Four of his favorite cars were the Stutz, Packard, Cadillac, and Marmon.

The year Jack started school he became ill. No one knew what was wrong. He became very listless and wanted to sleep all the time. When he was awake he had double vision. The doctor finally concluded that it was a type of sleeping sickness. Every day we would check his vision by holding up one finger but he always saw two. This went on for two or three weeks; one morning Dad checked him by holding up one finger and Jack saw only one! It was a joyous day in the Parker household.

Jack loved to read and always had books around him. He also got a guitar and began to learn a few chords. He enjoyed strumming this guitar and made up little ditties much to the dislike of his sister Cathryn and little brother Bill. He liked to tease them in a good natured way.

We were involved in farming and as soon as Jack was old enough and big enough he was assigned to help do some farm work. He was never too enthusiastic about this part of life but he always had a theory that if you could do your work like milking cows, shocking grain, pitching hay, etc. and think about something enjoyable the time would pass quickly and then it was not all that bad. One of the highlights of his farming days was getting a bicycle for helping shock a field of rye. Dad told him that if the field made 20 bushels per acre he would buy him a bike. The field made 21 so Jack got the bike.

Jack was always careful and conservative with his money and

a good thing as Herb and I were always a little short; he would then lend us a quarter or fifty cents when we were broke. Of course, we always paid it back.

When Jack was a senior in high school he and I had a very close call and only a miracle saved us. Jack came out to the farm to help me haul hay for the livestock on Saturday, March 15, 1941. It was a beautiful spring-like day, but it began snowing quite heavily. After doing our evening chores we were going to Nekoma with the neighbors. We left in a jumper (covered sleigh). We got about a mile and a half down the road when we heard a terrible noise. A snowstorm had hit! We didn't know what to do but decided to try to turn around and find our way back to the neighbor's house. The reins on the harness broke so we had to lead the horses. The visibility was zero and we had over a mile to go. We struggled against the wind and finally got to the neighbor's house. There we stayed until the next day. After a few days they reported that 72 people had perished in this storm. We were thankful to be alive!

Jack went to college after high school graduation and then into the service so he wasn't home much after that.

Now we are happy to say that Jack comes to visit us at least twice a year and we always look forward to his visits.

Jack has lived a good life, has done an excellent job in his chosen field of work, and has been a good husband and father. I am very proud to call him my brother.

A Parker

BY Herb Parker

"At last you have a Parker." Mother told a story many, many times about the lady who came to visit her each time she had a new baby — Cathryn, Charles, me — but according to her, none of us looked like a Parker. She visited again when Jack was born and her first statement was "at last you have a Parker." Percival John was called Jack, and that was a good decision our parents made.

I don't remember much about Jack until he was about three or four years old and was gone most of the winter living at Wimbledon with Grandma and Grandpa Kribbs. I do remember the excitement at our place the day they brought him back, and the love we other kids had for him.

In about the 5th or 6th grade Jack became seriously ill, and the whole family was deeply concerned; I'm not sure, but I think it was diagnosed as encephalitis, and it seemed as though he was in bed for a long time. My personal opinion has always been that this illness kept him from being an excellent athlete; he no longer had the same quickness and speed.

On the farm we were quite a work force — Dad, Charles, Jack and me. Bill was too young at this time to be of any help; he liked to tease and irritate Jack by stealing his cap and running and the like. One day when he was being especially obnoxious Jack chased him down and threw him in the water trough. I recall the summer we had an acre of corn and an acre of potatoes, and we hoed most of the summer. Jack and I were on the work force while Dad and Charles seemed to be into administration and management. We'd all start together in the morning, but after a couple of hours Dad and Charles would have to go to Langdon or somewhere, so Jack and I spent many hours together hoeing. We could have cultivated like others were doing, but Dad liked to do things the way they did it back in Ontario when he was a boy. Jack's observation was that "it's no wonder the Canadians are so far behind." Another summer had a fence building project when we dug the post holes by hand and strung the barbed wire. We had an old Model T pickup with us which could not climb the hills in low, so we had to go up the hills in reverse gear.

Jack was a poet of sorts, and most of his poetry and songs were aimed at teasing Cathryn and Bill. He was the best student in our family and seemed to enjoy books and studying, so it is not surprising that Jackie Parker became Dr. John Parker.

Sports and music were very important in our lives at Nekoma High School. Gerald Watne and Fern Wanek were excellent examples for us, and as coaches they were a wonderful influence. Mother was a fine musician and taught us to love and appreciate music, and Lillian Berggren organized a Mickey Mouse band,

and later the Knights of Melody dance band, which was a real joy to Charles, Jack, and me and a number of our good friends. As the school superintendent, Dad was supportive of sports and music, but always made it clear that academics came first.

With these and many other memories so vivid, it just doesn't seem possible that it is now time for Jack's retirement, but we can all say "well done." I know our family is proud and pleased that "at last we had a Parker."

Well Done

BY Bill Parker

Greetings and welcome to your new earned vocation: retirement, from your first bed partner for ten of your 18 years at home. Sure was nice to have a permanent bedroom after Charles and Herb moved out of the nest, wasn't it?

I believe our relationship in our early years at home was rather typical of brothers who were eight years difference in age. I was a nuisance and you were the big brother. Your ability to strum the guitar and make up songs about the girls I didn't like used to drive me crazy but I'd try and get even by telling Dad something on you! I figured I got even pretty well when you were a sophomore in high school and I told Dad you didn't like the Commercial Law Course he was teaching! I knew Dad wouldn't let that lie! and he didn't.

There are a lot of incidents I remember. When we would gang up on Cathryn or when mother would ask us to get a pail of coal and you and I would cut cards to see who would go after the coal. We would keep cutting cards until the fire was about out and mother would end up getting the coal herself! The most memorable event was that summer day when you were painting the wagon and I was taking your cap and running off with it and you had had it with me. You chased me all over the farm yard and caught me and threw me in the full water trough! You had threatened many times but I never figured you would do it!

I recall vividly the day in February 1943 when you went off to the Air Force. It was probably the most emotional experience that had taken place in our household. We were all very patriotic at that time in life and I recall every Thursday night writing a letter to you. That summer came and all of a sudden at 12 I became a young man taking over the farm jobs that you had previously done. Your return from the Air Force in December of 1945 was a joyous occasion. I recall, you hardly recognized me!

Jack, you always brought a lot of pride to the family. You were the student of the Parkers. You were the only one to graduate as an honor student from high school (quite an achievement, considering the way Dad graded). You won a speech contest in your first semester at Jamestown College. Mom and Dad were very proud. I recall Dad and I going down to Jamestown to attend the program when you were inducted into Who's Who in College and Universities. You were a hard act to follow at Jamestown College. I recall when I started at Jamestown College, I registered in one of Bill Wesley's classes and he told me how glad he was to have a Parker in his class again! I knew I was in trouble, so I dropped the course!

Arliss and I have enjoyed our visits with you and Pat when we come to Minneapolis. We wish you both the very best in your new found vocation. You have served your community, your country, your creator, your vocation, and your family in a very honorable manner in your sixty-eight years. To borrow a phrase of our Dad's, *"Well done thou good and faithful servant."*

An Exciting Time

BY T.R. (Dick) and LaJean Anderson

(Note: Dick died in the summer of 1989. LaJean found notes he had written in 1978, and she edited and transcribed them for this book.)

When I joined the Bell office in January of 1947, Mr. Bell had been collecting books for many years but over the past fifteen years had decided to concentrate his collection in the field of the history of trade. The collection itself was already a significant one. Like most collections, it was running out of room at Bellford, Mr. Bell's home at Wayzata. And plans were being formulated to establish a permanent home, one where great books, maps, and manuscripts, etc. would have excellent care, be properly cataloged, and would be turned into a useful living library, available to scholars from all over the world.

Mr. Bell was an outstanding businessman, but also had the great capacity to excel in other fields. He had been the respected benefactor of the Bell Natural History Museum and of the Delta Waterfowl Research Station. He assembled a collection of early American and English silver, including an original tea set by Paul Revere which is now housed at the Minneapolis Institute of Arts.

However, his interest turned to the Bell Library in later years. He was a graduate of the University of Minnesota and a Regent for many years, so he chose the University of Minnesota as the home of his rare book collection.

On October 30, 1953 — 25 years ago, I had the pleasure to attend the dedication ceremony of the James Ford Bell Library. At that time five essays were presented, (in addition to his own), on scholarship and book collecting. Shortly thereafter these essays were published by the University of Minnesota Press. For anyone interested in book collecting I can recommend them heartily for reading.

The basic principles of establishing a good collection are set forth very clearly; among my favorites is his advice to hold out for the very best.

Shortly after joining the Bell office, I invited several investment brokers to Minneapolis, and Mr. Bell gave a private party for us.

31

I came a little early to help introduce the group. When I entered the room, I noticed, to my astonishment, one of Mr. Bell's recently acquired rare books lying on the coffee table. Having recently signed the check in payment of this book, I was very surprised to see it lying there unguarded.

When everyone was assembled around the coffee table, Mr. Bell casually picked up the book and said it was a 1477 Marco Polo. Then he gave a little talk about it, and passed it around for everyone to touch and look it over, which worried me even more. He then said that this book and others in his collection were all to be used and not left in a vault somewhere, that a reasonable amount of use of any book was good for it, that books are damaged by war, fire, storms, water, etc., but rarely ever by ordinary use.

Like all book collections, his reached the point where it became necessary to find a permanent home for the books. He considered a separate building for the books but decided that the books would find better use if they were housed near a bigger library. Having graduated from the University of Minnesota and having served as a Regent of the University of Minnesota, he finally chose the University of Minnesota as the home of his collection.

It was an exciting time for me in assisting with the relations with the University officials. Mr. Bell agreed to provide a reading room and he imported the fine furniture from England and the unusually rare panelling through a New York City firm.

He also provided a permanent separate trust for the University of Minnesota, in his name, to be used for the benefit of the Bell Library. The result was a fine room, an air-conditioned storage room and workroom for students from the University and other colleges and universities.

The next part of the program was to find a curator to complete the cataloging and to assist in finding new books, purchasing additional books, trips to booksellers in Europe, etc.

Mr. Bell was a most successful businessman. He founded General Mills Inc. in 1928, establishing a young business all based on very high principles and ethics. He was a real leader and was able to attract very highly qualified men in his business activities.

In his other programs he found Dr. Albert Hochbaum and then Peter Ward for his outdoor program in Delta, Manitoba, outstanding men at the JFB Museum of Natural History, and one of the best of all, Curator John Parker, who had the great ability to do many things.

About three weeks after I joined Mr. Bell, he had just returned from a business meeting in New York. I went to see him and asked him for a further explanation of what my job was to be—he said, "Young man, there is a very big job to be done here, and it will be just what you can make of it." I don't know if he said that to Jack Parker, in that way, but he surely did turn him loose right from the beginning, as he did all the rest of us.

Jack is a self starter, has great creativity, and is an excellent writer, having authored many pamphlets, several books and has edited many others.

He has continued to add outstanding books, manuscripts and maps to the Bell collection. He has invited many world scholars who have used the library; he has made the library understandable and enjoyable to all of us non-scholars. He has established the policy and framework of the administration of the library so that Mr. Bell's wish that the library be useful and available to all [has been fulfilled.] And he has pressed for a successor whom we rely on to carry on those same principles.

One of the books that Mr. Bell always tried to obtain, but was unable to do so was the Biard. But a couple of years ago Jack found a copy. This book was the first volume of the Jesuit Relations and that meant that the library now has all 72 volumes of this unusual and very rare set of books written by the early Jesuit Missionaries to North America.

I had pledged with Mr. Bell to help perpetuate the library after his death.

The Discovery of Jack Parker

BY Georgia C. Haugh

Jack Parker had several right beginnings, it seems to me. One of these was his first step in his library career when he came to the University of Michigan to get a degree in Library Science. The next one brought him to the Clements Library at the University, a library rich in rare materials in American history.

One fortuitous day when we were seeking a qualified half-time student assistant, I was sent over to look at the possibilities in the School of Library Science. The Director, Mr. Rudolph Gjelsness, handed me a thick pile of applications. Midway, up popped Jack's résumé with its solid array of credentials. Nice picture, too. I couldn't help noticing that Jack began his upward progression with a degree from my own alma mater, Jamestown College, a liberal arts college in North Dakota. I exclaimed that Jamestown College specialized in recruiting valedictorians who also happened to be stellar basketball players just as in this case. Mr. Gjelsness, a graduate of the University of North Dakota, beamed approval. In fact, he may have led me to this particular sheet. No further recommendations were sought.

Thus, it came about that Jack joined our staff. Under the capable leadership of Colton Storm, Director, and the skillful direction and notable example of William Ewing, Curator of Manuscripts, he quickly developed expertise in the handling of the special material in our library as we had expected he would.

Then, just at the right time, near the end of Jack's studies in 1953, Colton Storm was asked, while attending an A.L.A. convention, for suggestions for the position of director of the Bell Collection at the University of Minnesota. Bill Ewing and I concurred heartily in his recommendation of Jack and true to form he came through the interview there with flying colors. And so, Jack returned north on his greatest venture.

I am certain that Colton Storm (deceased Oct. 1988) and Bill Ewing (retired as I am) and others who worked with Jack such as Chris Brun, Head of Rare Books and Special Collections at the University of California, Santa Barbara, and friends like Mrs.

Joyce Bonk now a valued member of the staff, have shared my feelings of almost familial pride in his brilliant career.

With admiration we have observed his special ability to master challenging situations with grace and wisdom. Possibly, other routes than the one sketched above would have led him to the same destination, or to another one of similar nature. Only the stars will know.

A personal note: After Jack came to Clements Library, I discovered that his father and my father both had emigrated from the same area in Ontario to North Dakota as did many others in the early years of the century—another decision in new directions.

I believe Jack's parents were among the earliest graduates of Jamestown College. Next, Herb preceded Jack as a graduate also, and their future wives were students there. My brother who lives in Minot has kept me apprised of Herb's successes as Dean and coach at Dakota Northwestern University. The football field is named for him. At a Jamestown College reunion in 1983, I watched Herb's induction into the Athletic Hall of Fame.

My husband and I hope that the new, somewhat more leisurely, life will bring Pat and Jack back for a visit to Ann Arbor where we are still in the "new" house they visited in its earliest stages. They would be astonished at the many changes in the city. Admittedly though, no city can surpass the Twin Cities in appeal to a North Dakotan, another correct piece in the almost predestined matching of the right person with the right job.

We know you will enjoy your New World, Jack.

Jack as Friend and Colleague

BY Ralph Hopp

My acquaintance with Jack Parker began in 1953 when we both assumed our positions in the University of Minnesota Libraries — he on September 1 and I on July 1. The coincidence of appointments, to some extent, establishes a peculiar type of bond that carries down through the years. Be that as it may, the Hopp and Parker families have nurtured a personal relationship that goes more deeply than the accident of appointment. The Parkers had no children when we first knew them. We shared the thrill of each new Parker baby as she arrived, first Jackie, then Sarah. Sometime along the way our families began the custom of sharing Christmas and/or Thanksgiving, and that custom carries forward even to this day.

These holiday celebrations were characterized by bounteous dinners, followed by the singing of ballads and Christmas songs, accompanied by two or more guitars — Jack's, mine, and sometimes my son Tom's or daughter Susan's. The highlights of these sessions inevitably were Jack singing his family's favorite tear-jerking ballad, "Old Shep," followed by my singing a unique little children's song which my father taught me when I was a child, a song whose title I never knew but which told the story of a boy trying to shoot a cuckoo bird with his bow and arrow, only to be frustrated when the bird flew away.

Jack is a unique combination of scholar and common man. He appears at ease in conversations about such disparate subjects as honeybees, baseball, birding, gardening, classical history, rare books, printing (he has his own press), country music, to name but a few examples. He is a skilled lecturer, guaranteed to be interesting regardless of the abstractness of the subject. Likewise, he has written and published several important books, as well as numerous periodic bookish articles and reports which always are interesting reading regardless of the level of erudition of the reader.

Knowing Jack's position in the Library as being off the beaten path, so to speak, that is, serving a very specialized clientele in quarters appropriate to scholarly research, one might expect a certain attitude of seclusion on his part. Jack was never one to isolate himself when it came time to deliberate on matters of staff organization, faculty status for professional librarians, search committees for vacancies, or controversial decisions on promotions. Jack willingly accepted tough assignments, often chairing important committees whose work might be challenged. He was a strong supporter of due process. It might be said that he was consistently a friend of the "underdog," always making certain that justice prevailed. As chairman of some of the critical committees he occasionally would be called upon to give testimony, explaining the rationale for the decisions of such committees. Despite the fact that sometimes such reviews became quite controversial and testifying became at best uncomfortable, Jack nevertheless dutifully accepted such assignments. He could be counted on as an impartial, fair-minded chairman. As a library faculty member he spoke out when the situation called for debate. Several times he served in the University Senate, representing the University Libraries.

Professionally Jack is widely known and respected as an expert in rare books and manuscripts. He repeatedly has taught summer classes on rare books at Columbia University Library School. Others no doubt will document more extensively the many contributions he has made in his service as teacher, lecturer and author.

As he enters retirement my wife Dorothy and I wish Jack and Pat many more productive and exciting years. We cannot visualize Jack as retired and we fully expect he will likely continue his activities, with the primary change being that now he is non-salaried.

High Standards

BY Irv Kreidberg

If the year 1954 were transposed to 1471, and Jack Parker walked into the printing office of William Caxton instead of the North Central Publishing Company, Jack would have felt perfectly at home.

He would have found the scrupulous use of materials to set forth the printed word. Intelligence and skill applied to the printer's art would have satisfied Jack that his work scheduled for printing would be given the highest standards of typographic art and design.

It was this attention to quality that identified Jack with the publishing program of the James Ford Bell Library. The first printed piece called "The James Ford Bell Room" told about the collection, the setting in the University Library, and the use the Bell Library would be put to by scholars.

The collection was described as "outstanding for the high quality of its contents as well as for the importance of its subject material."

Jack never lost sight of those high standards. From the beginning he committed design to Jane McCarthy, production manager of the University of Minnesota Press, and one of America's gifted designers. The key word was "care" in establishing top standards of typographic excellence.

The combination of two highly disciplined talents — Jane in design and Jack in history — made it a delight for the printer to satisfy the maxim that an author's work should be read.

The French philosopher Paul Valéry put it this way:

> "The mind of the writer is seen
> as in a mirror which the
> printing press provides. If the
> paper and ink are in accord, if the
> type is clear, if the composition
> is well looked after, the
> adjustment of line perfect, and
> the sheet well printed, the author

feels his language and his style
anew. He sees himself reclothed
with honors which are perhaps
not due him.
"He thinks he hears a clearer,
firmer voice than his own,
a voice faultlessly pure,
articulating his words,
dangerously detaching each one.
Everything weak, arbitrary,
pompous which he wrote
speaks too clearly and too loud.
"To be magnificently printed
is indeed a very precious and a
lastingly important tribute."

The printer's art aiming at perfection and the designer and historian dedicated to high and exact standards in the presentation of knowledge are goals that stand for all to admire. To have participated with Jack Parker in this commitment to excellence is a privilege that I will always cherish.

Here's A Story

BY Brad Oftelie

I remember visiting Jack on Seabury Avenue shortly after his surgery. It was major surgery and it showed. Jack was grey, frail even. I was met at the door by Pat.
"Come in," she said.
Jack got slowly up and came over.
"Doesn't he look great?" Pat anxiously asked.
What could I say? What could I say about this man?

I walked into the James Ford Bell Library an inexperienced student looking for Walter Bigge's account of Sir Francis Drake's voyage to the West Indies. I was handed a book published in 1589. The thought of that did not strike my undergraduate mind. I never questioned the book's survival through four hundred years and how it came to be available at the University of Minnesota. Nor did I think about the people who cared enough about it to ensure its survival. I was stunned by its illustrations and fold-out maps and I remember thinking, "Now here's a story." A story indeed! I went on to finish my paper on Drake, said goodbye to the James Ford Bell Library, and graduated.

Later, much later, after a night of preparing sandwiches in a Minneapolis cafe, I wrote down on a sheet of paper those places that I wanted to spend some time. I put the James Ford Bell Library at the top of my list.

They put me to work oiling books. Beautiful books. A month later I was working on a permanent part-time position. I was fascinated by the place, by the work.

I remember the day Jack said to me, "Brad, we're going to simplify these acquisition accounts." And we did.

Other projects followed. The files were reorganized. I was given the enjoyable task of reshelving the backlog and searching preliminary catalog copy for it. Last, and most fun of all, was the job of taking an inventory of the entire collection. That meant handling every piece. It was a wonderful assignment.

I understood then that it is important to conserve the past and that I wanted to do my part. I left Minneapolis to attend Library School. What followed were long, lonely days. On one of those long days a letter arrived. It arrived at a time when a person needs a letter from home. In a long handwritten letter Jack spoke to me. He was contemplating, thinking of the future and how much there is left to do. That letter was all I needed.

Jack has inspired many people; I am but one on a long list, and really, what more can you do for someone but inspire them? James Ford Bell's inspiration, his "Bound Fragments of Time" speak today. They speak today because people care enough to collect the past and make it known to the rest of the world. Our generation and those to follow will understand what has been collected in the Bell Library.

I have come to know Jack Parker as a friend. A good friend. That day I arrived on Seabury Avenue I was there to pick up a basket full of potatoes Jack had grown that summer before his surgery. I was out there with him in his garage, he was bundled up tight against the autumn chill. And as tired as he was that day, looking at him I could not help but think of all he has brought, not only to my life, but to others as well, and of all he has accomplished. I also could not help but think of all he has left to do.

Colleague and Partner

BY Carol Urness

Memories usually are not accurate. On the other hand, they are often quite vivid and sometimes more fun than reality. The following is not a factual account of working with John Parker in the James Ford Bell Library. I have, rather, put down memories of some good times — and bad ones — that we have had in the Library. Jack has been the Library's Curator since its beginning. It is difficult to imagine the Library without him. Now it is good to think about the past. In the James Ford Bell Library I have been privileged to share efforts with an outstanding colleague in a fine collection (and the other way around). Here are a few early memories . . .

The people in the auditorium waited expectantly. The meeting at the Royal Geographical Society during the summer of 1964 was under way. Dr. John Parker was about to give a paper. In September I was to begin a position as Assistant Curator of the University of Minnesota's James Ford Bell Library, where he was Curator. In my library positions in Reference and Interlibrary Loans I knew him slightly. In my own research I had used the James Ford Bell Library, but my experience with rare books was so limited that when I first entered the Bell Room I thought the books were kept hidden behind the wooden walls! At the Royal Geographical Society we talked briefly before the session; he seemed surprised that I had in tow a Frenchman who spoke no English. I had found the latter in front of the building and figured out that he wanted to attend the RGS meeting. Jack and I exchanged greetings. Soon it was time for his lecture.

The lights dimmed. "First slide," Jack said. There was the unmistakable sound of breaking glass, and the slide appeared on the screen with a great crack across it. The medieval map was difficult enough to decipher without the crack. "Never mind," Jack said calmly. "The other slide will be sufficient." There was a pause and scurrying with the machine. Another crack was heard. The second slide was also broken. Jack gave his paper. This was grace under pressure, a trait I was to see often in the years to come . . .

I don't remember much about the rest of the day, and in fact I am not sure that the above is even close to an accurate telling of the story. We had lunch at an Italian restaurant, with the traditional red-and-white checkered tablecloths. When the bill came we split it. I remember he said, "This is different for me. I've never worked with a woman before." And he said, "Call me Jack." With my head spinning from papers given on subjects I had not known existed, and some in French besides, I tried to nod. I spent part of the rest of the summer wondering what I had gotten into, and especially, how I would ever manage to call him "Jack." This was Dr. Parker, who knew everything about old books; the Dr. Parker who wrote books and gave television lectures. He and his wife Pat danced together gracefully at a staff party — sort of the Library Fred Astaire and Ginger Rogers — and they impressed all of us. Their two perfect and charming little daughters, Jackie and Sarah, were the best behaved children at the annual staff holiday party. And I was supposed to call him "Jack."

At the time I didn't know that Jack was apparently somewhat intimidated by my imminent arrival on the scene. He spent a good deal of time and effort getting the Bell Library rearranged and the stacks in order. A book of Library procedures was prepared for my use. (This is still the only book of procedures that we have). My first day in the Library was memorable, because he met me with a curt "Where have you been?" I responded in the same vein with, "What do you mean?" We went on from there. He expected me on September 1; my appointment began the Tuesday after Labor Day. This was not a very auspicious beginning. Once we figured out the source of the confusion and talked it over, we both felt much better. Looking back, it may have been a good way to start. When we turned to the Library everything was fine. (However, I think I dropped a book that day.)

We both had plenty to do. Jack is a good teacher and I soon found myself acquainted with the world of antiquarian books and book dealers. Letters, phone calls, books, maps, and manuscripts arrived from all over Europe and many places in North America. If nothing else, it was a good geography lesson. Jack encouraged me to spend time looking at the books in the Library, getting familiar with them. I loved the books. My work in identifying obscure publications of all kinds for Interlibrary Loans proved useful, and before too long I could look at a seventeenth-century Dutch book without obvious terror. I started assisting with the compilation of the Library's *List of Additions*, which served as another good introduction to the philosophy and the holdings of the Library.

Through that publication, as well as the Library's monograph series, I was soon involved with modern books produced by the University of Minnesota Press, and worked with people like the legendary book designer Jane McCarthy and the superb editor Jeanne Sinnen. Jane insisted on nothing less than perfection for the physical appearance of a book. Jeanne was just as insistent about content. "I have known a number of authors who said nothing at great length" she said. Jane and Jack established the standards and formats for various publications of the Associates. In these days I first encountered Irving B. Kreidberg, the printer who produced marvelous publications to meet the demanding specifications of the above, Jane in particular.

The public outreach of the James Ford Bell Library expanded with the development of the Associates organization. The first meeting of the "incorporators and directors" was held on December 30, 1963. Invitations to membership went out in 1964, exactly a year later. The first issue of the Associates' newsletter, *The Manifest* appeared in February of 1965. The publications and programs developed in the beginning have continued to this day. At this distance I wonder how we managed it all! We learned many lessons the hard way in the process. For example, think of the membership card used for the Associates today. The card has space to indicate whether the annual membership is for Mr. and Mrs., Mr., Mrs., Miss, or Ms. That seems elementary enough. From the outset the Associates have sponsored some evening lectures at the Library. President and Mrs. O. Meredith Wilson attended one of these lectures. The next day the President's secretary called. At the meeting Mrs. Wilson had greeted some friend and asked him where his wife was that evening. "She wasn't invited," was the reply. In those days membership cards did not have the categories noted above, and apparently Mr. Somebody thought his wife could not be a member or attend meetings. I can still see Jack pacing back and forth in the stacks, saying "damn it, damn it." Listing the hazards of running an organization would be an interesting, nearly endless project.

Hazards aside, the Associates have been a source of great joy for us. They have always provided a forum for activities and relationships beyond the campus. We have never asked people what satisfaction they find in membership. We have tried to make sure that membership includes good publications and programs. Beyond that we are simply grateful that so many people believe in what the James Ford Bell Library is doing. Many Associates are not from the Twin Cities. So far as we know they have not been at the Library, or even on the University of Minnesota campus. And they have been Associates for years.

Local Associates have had many good times together at the lectures and seminars. From the beginning we have been blessed with people dedicated to the organization. For example, one of the first Directors of the Associates, Maynard Hasselquist, drafted the constitution that founded the organization. This constitution, by the way, has often been imitated by other library friends organizations. Maynard is the only "incorporator" who remains a Director. He and his wife, Lorraine, have been loyal Associates since 1963.

When T.R. (Dick) Anderson died in the summer of 1989 we lost one of the incorporators. As a legal and financial consultant for James Ford Bell, Dick wrote all of the documents establishing the Library at the University. Caring for the trust and endowment funds for long term support for the Library were his concern from the beginning. He was a pillar of the Associates. We will miss him. At one meeting, years ago, the finances of the Associates were under discussion. Dick stood up. All that he said was "Let's put more money in the coffers." And more money came in! Dick is remembered in a special way by the T.R. Anderson Acquisitions Fund, which he established.

Dick and his wife LaJean attended Library functions of every sort faithfully and enthusiastically. A favorite memory of him was at an auction the Library sponsored. Dick and Elmer L. Andersen began bidding over an old law book. The price rose and rose. The book sellers in the audience were stunned. Memory fails as to whether Andersen or Anderson finally bought the book. Both bidders had a good time, obviously, and also contributed to the "coffers" again! There were many auctions and book fairs — some were great successes, others were not. The best ones were the ones characterized by spirited bidding. One former Director, Mitch Goldstein, a map collector and lawyer who died in 1980, knew how to put excitement into bidding. He loved auctions and seldom let anyone get away with too big a bargain!

The sum of contributions of all kinds made by the Associates to the James Ford Bell Library is just overwhelming. The time donated by the officers and directors is an obvious example. Bill Laird (now aided by an assistant treasurer, Bernie Muck) has kept track of the Associates' finances for decades. Elizabeth (Betty) Savage has graciously handled the presidency. Both, we trust, will continue! The history of the Associates included in this book indicates some of the debts the Library has to many people.

Memories of those early years recall scenes, like vignettes. One favorite is of Mrs. John S. Dalrymple, one of Minnesota's most cultured and distinguished people. (The term "grande dame," in its best sense, fit her). Mrs. Dalrymple, who died in 1980, was tall, with a beauty that only age and experience gives. Her grey hair was always perfect. Her speech was eloquent and she wore her clothes and jewelry with a natural grace. Furthermore — surely without intending it — she intimidated some of us just by her bearing. She attended the second James Ford Bell Lecture, when Vincent H.D.P. Cassidy was the speaker. Vince, who died recently, was a medieval historian at the University of Akron. He was, more importantly, a free spirit who reveled in poetry and wrote plays more often than history texts. His history writings have a lilt to them, not common these days. We worried just a bit if Vince would remember to come to the lecture, and if so, would remember that he was giving it, and if so, that he really would give it instead of reading poetry. He gave a superb lecture. The scene we remember, though, was at the reception, when we looked across the room to see them: Mrs. Dalrymple and Professor Cassidy. Vince's rather shabby pockets were filled with spilled tobacco and cigarette papers. We watched him roll a lumpy ciga- rette while he talked with Mrs. Dalrymple. Truly a meeting of two cultures! And while we watched she started smoking that funny cigarette — "It wasn't bad," she declared later.

Many Associates (both men and women) have provided food and drink for meetings — and over the years that has added up to great savings for the coffers. Of the Associates, Marge Kreidberg has comforted us with food the most, often using historic recipes from her publications with the Minnesota Historical Society. In the early years Mrs. Walter U. (Irene) Hauser, who also wrote a cookbook, brought many wonderful treats to the meetings. She was also a Director from 1965 to 1973. The Hausers had a very busy schedule of social events, for Mr. Hauser was the Honorary Consul for the Federal Republic of Germany for Minnesota, North Dakota, and South Dakota.

Sometimes Mr. Hauser fell asleep during our programs (at the time this practice was hard to understand, but these days, with occasional unplanned naps during a concert, lecture or a play, understanding has come). When Jack and I were on the program we made it a sort of test to see if we could keep Mr. Hauser awake — no doubt our programs were improved by the more ener- getic body movements and voice inflections. Probably we kept the evenings shorter, too, something everybody appreciated. The best times were often after the programs, when the coffee and goodies were consumed and we talked to each other. And then af- terwards it was time to go home. One night Mr. Hauser said, with a delightful twinkle in his eyes, "Irene has begun her goodbyes.

It should be about half an hour." We watched, and he was right. Oh, how we miss them — and others, too — from the past! The Associates kept us (and still keep us) from turning inward too much or from being content to stay within the campus boundaries.

In the mid-1960s the University was expanding to the "West Bank." A new library was to be constructed there, spacious, modern, air conditioned. The plans called for the installation of the James Ford Bell Library on the fourth floor, in space beyond imagination by comparison to what we had in Walter Library. We would have a real exhibit area and a reading room, both shared with the Department of Special Collections. (Until this time the Bell Room itself was our only reading room). The Bell Room was dismantled, moved, and reassembled in a somewhat different format in the new library, a process that caused some concern. In the fall of 1967 Jack took a quarter leave to work on his book on Jonathan Carver. As he wrote in *The Manifest* of February 1968 "We came to work in January following a three month leave of absence to find ourselves presiding over a near ruin. The James Ford Bell Library will become part of the University's new Wilson Library on the west bank of Father Hennepin's river later this year. Unlike other departments scheduled to move into the new building, we have to take our walls and ceiling with us."

One noon Jack and I walked over to see the area that would house the Bell Room. The ceiling was in and the columns on the side wall were in place. Otherwise the scene was pretty much concrete dust and plastic sheeting and noise, and it was hard to imagine what the room would be like in a new setting. It is hard now to remember the room as it was in Walter Library! Later we watched and worried as men used saws to cut the Elizabethan fireplace into individual blocks. We crossed our fingers as one man made a pattern on a piece of paper, numbering each chunk of the fireplace on its back with crayon and placing the same number on the correct space on the paper. Later the big chandelier hanging from the ceiling was carefully lowered and two strong men lugged it onto a wooden frame for the journey across the river. The ruin in Walter was complete. Moving the room was not our problem. The movers took care of that.

More than anything else we worried about moving the books. What was the safest way to do that? In the end we decided to handle the preparations ourselves. Every book in the collection was separately wrapped, some of the more fragile ones with two different kinds of paper. The call number of each was put on its package. The packages were placed, in order by call number, into boxes and then the boxes were taped shut. This seemed like an endless task—indeed our student assistants piddled around with it until Jack decided to take a hand. He began wrapping books himself, and following his example we all rather quickly became involved and developed into expert wrappers. I learned much from working with Jack, not the least of which is that any big task, undertaken at a reasonable pace with steady effort, will surely get done. He may have learned this as a kid hoeing potatoes in North Dakota. "Never look ahead or behind," he said once. "Look down and keep hoeing." We managed to have fun with the move. And one day the boxes were all unpacked and the library was back on the shelves—looking a little small in the new space. We were close to friends in the History and Geography Departments again. The official dedication of the O. Meredith Wilson Library was held 13 May 1969.

We didn't stop going back across the river, of course. In the late sixties and early seventies we crossed the Mississippi often to attend Senate meetings. Jack and I were both Senators from the University Libraries. At the time the University Senate was in the middle of controversies. Rather than the more usual matters of approving the schedule for holidays and sporting events, the Senate was a center of political discussions. Anti-war protestors attended and sometimes disrupted the meetings; proposals relating to the war were presented on the Senate's floor. Some fundamental issues were raised. Should the Senate be involved in politics? Could the Senate ignore issues that were tearing the University apart? What was just? What was right?

In those difficult days we went to some memorable meetings. Going back and reading the student newspaper, *The Minnesota Daily*, would put a chronological framework on the events and bring them into sharper focus, but the scattered, jumbled memories are sufficient. It helped me that Jack was there to share those times, just as we shared the happier ones. At one Senate meeting a speaker became so irate that she threw the microphone over her shoulder at the audience as hard as she could. That turned out to be pretty hard, and I can still remember the thing whizzing past us like a grenade. At this same meeting, I believe, a "kangaroo court" was convened to try President Malcolm Moos. That meeting broke up in chaos, with several people taken for safety through the tunnel system away from the area. Jack and I picked our way gingerly out the front door, stepping over protestors who wore bandages and had painted their bodies symbolically red. It was inevitable that at one of the meetings a resolution to close the University was placed on the Senate floor. Strong arguments were presented: on the one side Senators argued that it was immoral to pretend we could have "business as usual" in education at a time of crisis; opposing Senators argued just as strenuously that closing the University would be the immoral act. At the end of the debate a roll-call vote was taken. The Senate voted to keep the University at its business of education, but the vote was close and there were violent feelings on both sides. It was a hard day. An even more difficult day came later, when we walked to the East Bank for a meeting, only to find the main mall churning with protestors confronting police who were wearing gas masks and had leashes attached to large dogs. That was terrifying. In terms of what many people have suffered for their beliefs in their lives, our experiences were minor. In the context of our institution dedicated to reason and to learning, the effect was quite different. Unbelievable.

No matter what else happened we kept building the Library. We both love acquisitions. We made trips to Europe and Canada to see booksellers — the one of us left at the Library alternately feeling cheated out of discovering treasures and relieved not to have to worry about lost luggage or plane schedules. It was fun to be the one going from city to city on the hunt; it was also good — and sometimes more powerful — to be the one back at the Library plotting the progress of the trip and receiving the descriptions to choose from. Each role had its advantages.

We had some advantages in our buying: the collection was small enough so that there were (and still are) "gaps" to be filled, and large enough so we could build meaningfully on what we owned. We had sufficient funds from the endowment, foundation, and Associates to keep our position as a force in the trade, but not so much that we could ever be careless in our purchasing.

Maintaining a balance between the expensive "exhibit type" books — quite often Americana or books of famous travelers — and the bread-and-butter things that are less showy and more valuable for research is most important. We need some of each. Buying is never dull. Our focus is unchanged; we stick to materials dating from 1400–1800 that describe European relations and trade with the "outside" world. Books predominate, but we do purchase manuscripts and maps when they are important for our subject focus.

We won't forget the arrival of the Hastings manuscripts! This huge collection came to the Library in the fall of 1965, and the bindings on the volumes were dirty and falling apart. As Jack said in the *Manifest*, "at present they do not attract people with clean hands." The subject of the papers, Warren Hastings, had a successful career with the East India Company and had risen from a position as a clerk to the top of the Company. He became the center of controversy for his actions as Governor General of India. In 1788 he went on trial, charged with "high crimes and misdemeanors." The prosecution sought his impeachment. The trial caused quite a sensation in England. Publications about it show the interest and the intensity of the debate, for what seemed to be on trial was the whole concept of empire. At times lords and ladies stood in line to get seats to witness the trial, and to hear such speakers at it as Richard Brinsley Sheridan. Finally, in 1795, the House of Lords came back with the verdict of not guilty. We ended up with the entire defense brief; manuscript writing on great folio sheets of paper in fifty-four volumes. The paper was fine, but the bindings were in pieces. First the set needed a "clean up" by a hand vacuum cleaner to get rid of all the loose dust, dirt and pieces of binding that were in the pages; then the volumes were rebound for use. The hand vacuum droned on for days, with the students and our secretary in charge.

Every now and then a purchase was so spectacular that a celebration was in order — and sometimes we had one. I remember one of my first big purchases, in 1967, very well. It was the *Navigatio Septentrionalis* of Jens Munk, published in Copenhagen in 1624. The English and French had made many voyages in search of the Northwest Passage. This book describes the only Danish voyage in search of it. Jens Munk sailed with his crew in the summer of 1619, heading westward for China and the East Indies. He sailed across Hudson Bay and reached the present site of Churchill, Manitoba. There his ship was caught fast in the ice. During the winter the crew members began to die of scurvy. It was a horrid scene. All but three of the sixty-five crew members died. The living were too weak to dispose of the bodies of the dead. By the time the birds came north that spring, the three survivors were resigned to death. Instead, they recovered enough health to sail for home, led by Munk. Their story can hardly be beaten for sheer drama. With our strong holdings on the search for a Northwest Passage, and on northern explorations in general, we couldn't pass up that book! I authorized payment of the bill as usual. The price was given in dollars on the invoice. However, the accountant processing it assumed that it must be in Norwegian kroner since the bookseller, Claes Nyegaard, is Norwegian. (Also, because it was a pretty big number). So the accountant converted the sum. That meant the bookseller got about one-eighth of the amount due. Claes was polite, but wrote: "The book is a bargain, but not quite *that* good a bargain." The next time we saw the book for sale was in 1984, when it appeared in the 100th anniversary catalog of Damms Antikvariat, Oslo, the firm headed by Claes. We didn't look back to compare the price.

In the beginning I worried a lot about prices. I ordered a book from Switzerland once, only to find it listed at a much lower cost in an English bookseller's catalog. I was sick about it. Jack said "don't worry." The Swiss bookseller wrote to tell me that the book was sold to someone else. I rushed off an order to the English bookseller. That copy was also sold. It was about five years before I saw another copy of the book, this time at about the combined price of the two copies we had missed earlier. We got the book this time, and it was a bargain because it is important to the Library. The bottom line — and it took awhile to learn it — is that the right price to pay for any book, map or manuscript is what it is worth to the Library, not to the market.

Booksellers who know our subject field often write to us when something very special comes their way. That happened in 1983, when Nico Israel of Amsterdam wrote to offer us the first Dutch edition of *Itinerario, voyage ofte schipvaert* . . . by Jan Huygen van Linschoten. I remember we read the letter and talked

about it in Jack's office. Linschoten, born in 1563, was a Dutch-
man who traveled to Spain in 1579 and then went to Portugal for
several years. He sailed to India as accountant for the newly-
appointed Archbishop of Goa in April of 1583. He remained there
in the heart of Portuguese India for about five years. He was especially fascinated by trade in the Indian Ocean. He returned home
in 1592 and in 1595–96 published a book on his travels and obser-
vations on trade in the Indian Ocean. The book, among other
things, was a sort of guide for the Dutch to use in voyages of the
newly-formed Dutch East India Company. We had to make some
choices. Since the book is fundamental to our Library, it didn't
take too long to decide that we would go after it. We had almost
given up hope of ever obtaining a copy. It is one more jewel in
the Library.

Building the James Ford Bell Library was not the only job. We
wanted it to be used, whether by the people who showed up in
person at the Library, or those who wrote to us or asked for help
through the Interlibrary Loan system. If we could help the latter
by providing a microfilm or xerox copy of what they needed, we
made one if it could be done safely. Sometimes we have only one
letter or Interlibrary Loan request, which we answer and that is
the end of it. At other times we are much involved in research on
behalf of people who never get to the Library. We like to see the
most inexperienced users, the undergraduates — usually history or
geography majors — learn to use the Library. They often say
things like "Is this real?" when they see an old book! The Library
has never had "lots" of readers nor would we be able to accommodate them if we did. We have had good readers, people who have
worked in the Library day after day, perhaps using only one book
or one manuscript. For many of them, the Library has been essential to their research. The time spent in it, for them, is one of
their good experiences at the University. That is enough for us.

In addition to the "users" of the Library we have had the pleasure of teaching our own students. Jack started teaching in the Library School while the James Ford Bell Library was still in
Walter Library. After the move to Wilson Library, the two of us
began teaching "Descriptive Bibliography" together. The class
was directed toward the most advanced and competent students
in the Library School. As the class was always scheduled for Fri-

day afternoons in spring quarter, only the most dedicated students were attracted to it. In ten weeks the students were given an introduction to the world of rare books, specifically by doing research on and writing about one author's book. The book had to be one that was published in several languages, and sometimes in more than one edition in a particular language. Students compared the different editions from the standpoint of both intellectual content and physical appearance. In the process, students learned something about early printing and illustrating, about signatures and bindings. They also studied the people related to the book — the patrons, printers, editors, translators, illustrators. And they compared the content of the different editions, determining what changes were made — and why, if possible — from one edition to the next. And the students wrote papers based on their research, and gave reports in class. They worked hard and enthusiastically.

Even though we did not spend much time revising lectures, each year new readings were added and the content was somewhat different. A day or so before each class we would look at the notes and decide who would "do" the first hour and who "got" the second. In spite of the fact that we taught it every spring, we never tired of the class. In the first week we warned the class that this was "a seminar in bibliographical research and writing" with the whole library as the laboratory for it. They would get "weekly problems related to each other and to the total problem of the course, which is an understanding of both the physical and intellectual aspects of a book." The students wrote their papers week by week. By the end of the course the students had produced fine research papers, and we were proud of them. The students seemed to profit from the class, and many of them have kept in touch in some way or another. Former students have become Associates and one, Bernadette (Bernie) Pyter Muck, who was one of the students, is now a Director of the Associates.

Our experiences teaching in the History Department and the Honors Division have been similarly rewarding. Since 1973 we have taught the "Expansion of Europe" course together with Professor Paul Bamford of the History Department. This two-quarter course is a laboratory course, with the James Ford Bell Library as the lab. Through research on materials in the Library, students learn to read older type and handwriting. They learn to see the older sources in the context of the time in which they were created. Students specialize enough to become true experts on something—a single document or event. Students sometimes translate materials from foreign languages. They learn to write footnotes and to edit a document. We always learn along with them.

Every class is different. Each is special. I remember the time we assigned a seventeenth century English manuscript letter to Joel Rutchick. That class might well have been the one where the undergraduate students were so good that they kept outshining the graduate students. When the class met for the second time, the students sat around the table in the Reading Room and gave their progress reports on their newly-acquired research projects. They were progressing beautifully. Then Joel spoke. "I couldn't read a word of my letter," he said flatly. We felt guilty for giving him such a terrible document. Not too long after, with a little help, he read it all and wrote a fine paper. The students have been good for us. In that class students learn much that helps them in research and writing. As a result of it, some of them have written their theses or dissertations based on research begun in the course. On our side the profit is equally obvious—the chance to see what we build daily put to its very best use!

Memories, Jack—very good ones. There are so many more, so many about the students and about the staff we have had in the James Ford Bell Library. We have been fortunate. And there were events not mentioned, like the conference on the American Revolution and the meetings of the Society for the History of Discoveries. Many, many good memories. Thank you for being such a wonderful friend and colleague. If we could, I'd like to go back in time and place to that Italian restaurant. And I'd buy the lunch. Otherwise, I wouldn't change anything.

Part II. SELECTIONS FROM WRITINGS
AND SPEECHES

James Ford Bell and His Books

BY John Parker

INTRODUCTION BY BERNIE MUCK

In this introductory chapter to *The World for a Marketplace*, Dr. Parker describes his relationship with James Ford Bell, the founder of the library that bears his name. Jack wrote the book to celebrate the 25th anniversary of the Bell Library. It is fitting that this chapter be included in a book celebrating Jack's career, since Jack has so well carried out Mr. Bell's vision of a library that would "tell the story" of European expansion.

My relationship with Jack also began at the Library, when I was beginning my graduate work in library science. Over the next few years, I had the fortune to work with Jack in the library and to study under him both at work and in class. During those years, I, of course, learned much about rare books and about European expansion. I also learned the art of book indexing. But Dr. Parker also taught me two other things. First, I learned that my new employer would regularly treat the most commonplace work as worthy of recognition. Much of the work I performed in the library was mundane but Dr. Parker never treated it that way. Instead, he always expressed his thanks for the everyday tasks of typing, proofing, and filing. Second, he encouraged the Library staff, and later I learned, the Associates, to develop their skills to help the Library. Prior to coming to the University, I had taken some Latin but no modern languages. Soon Jack was having me catalog Spanish commercial documents — a task that, on its face, was a ridiculous assignment. Jack correctly felt that my Latin combined with embryonic cataloging skills were equal to the task. Jack also encouraged me to index books, starting with the proofing of an index of the Library's holdings. Soon, I was in-

57

dexing books published by the Library which, to an indexer, were a challenge in that they frequently included the copy of an original manuscript. I no longer work in a library or use my Latin, and my last index
was that for *The World for a Marketplace* but I have tried to remember
Jack's other lessons in my job as manager.

Since leaving the Bell Library as an employee and student, Jack has
made sure that I have not left the Library itself. So I have had the continued good luck to see him regularly at Board meetings of the Associates
and at Associates dinners and meetings. He continues to impress me with
his love of all facets of books — from their contents to their indexes to their
endpapers to their covers. And, of course, he continues to "tell the story"
of the Bell Library in any medium to any audience that he feels will
bring new students and Associates to its collection.

It has now been over twenty years since I first ventured into the woodpanelled world of the Bell Library. In those years, I have made the transition from "Dr. Parker" to "Jack" and have introduced my children to
"Dr. Parker!" Now they, too, have enjoyed the diverse activities of the
Associates that Jack has encouraged — book fairs, the Columbus play, the
art of woodblock printing. I look forward to them reading Jack's written
work, starting with *The World for a Marketplace*.

"A library like that will have a great story to tell." These words
were spoken often by James Ford Bell as he contemplated the development of his library. It was not the story of acquiring books
and manuscripts that he was anticipating; it was their contents — their memories as he saw it — the record of human experience committed to paper and ink. "Bound fragments of
time," he called them in his address on October 30, 1953, when
he entrusted his personal library to the University of Minnesota,
where he envisioned its continued growth and the opportunity to
tell its story.

The narrative he proposed had its plot well-outlined in his
mind: the story of western civilization's expansion through the
driving force of commercial impetus. By no means unaware of the
other forces at work, such as science, religion, and simple human
curiosity, James Ford Bell saw these as related to and used by the
acquisitive tendencies of western civilization during the centuries
that its explorers discovered continents and oceans, enabling merchants and their royal patrons to establish trade routes, steadily
reaching out into numerous regional economies, linking them to-

gether, and eventually creating a world economy dominated by Europeans.

The total effect of creating a world marketplace is beyond the grasp of anyone: the exchange of goods, of technologies, of languages; the impact of one civilization upon another; the impressions Europeans made abroad; the impressions of non- Europeans that were developed; the emergence of institutions for managing trade in a foreign land; the means of planting and developing colonies; the provision for workers to till the soil and harvest the crops; the impact of competing producers upon European economies; the philosophical rationale for all of this: for whose good was it being done?

The history of European expansion is an immensely complex story, and in building a library which would "tell" that story Mr. Bell knew that he was undertaking something that would never be done completely and definitively. And that is one reason it fascinated him. He delighted in looking for basic causes and forces, and then following them wherever they led, usually into new areas of inquiry. And in every area there was a memory of human experiences chronicled in books and manuscripts. These original sources were for him the ingredients basic to an understanding of history.

As a fisherman he had to know the full life cycle of his prey, its natural enemies, its feeding habits. And he had to understand his own fishing equipment — so much so that he often made it himself. As a hunter he was primarily interested in the migration and nesting habits of birds. A miller and merchant by profession, it was said of him by his colleagues that he, more than anyone of his profession, fully understood the whole enterprise — the chemistry of grain and flour and baking, the machinery of the mill, the marketing of the product, and the consumers' attitude toward it.

It was no narrow mercantile education that produced such a breadth of outlook upon his business or upon the world about him. He was as much at home in a duck blind in Manitoba as he was in a London bookstore or a museum in Rome. He brought this kind of sophistication to book collecting, which he saw as "an invaluable aid to man's memory of events past and present." It started when he was a child, according to his own account. Born

in 1879, he was not sufficiently robust as a child to engage in some
of the more vigorous boyhood activities, so his mother, Sallie
Montgomery Bell, read to him frequently, instilling in him a love
for literature and for the books that communicated literature. His
formal education took him in quite another direction, since he
majored in chemistry at the University of Minnesota, fully aware
of chemistry's importance in the milling business to which he
aspired. His father, James Stroud Bell, who had come to this city
in 1888 from Pennsylvania, was by this time a prominent person
in the Minneapolis milling industry. But a specialty in chemistry
did not tie James Ford Bell down to a laboratory. Soon he was on
the road as a salesman on his first step into the milling and mercantile world. International business, war, and humanitarianism
came together in his life during World War I, when he served
with Herbert Hoover in the U.S. Government's Food Administration.

Back in Minnesota after the war, James Ford Bell set about
building a giant milling empire, General Mills, but in those years
he was also buying books, experimenting with his own taste as he
acquired first editions of Shakespeare's works, the poems of
Robert Burns, some Caxton imprints, and a number of editions
of Franklin's *Poor Richard's Almanack*.

The Minnesota merchant with time for books gradually came
to ask of his business the same question he asked about all other
subjects. How did it begin? How did merchandising start in Minnesota and where can we find out? His collecting turned to those
questions and in finding answers he was on his way to acquiring
one of the most complete collections known of the *Jesuit Relations*
of New France, and other accounts of French penetration of the
North American interior. These could not be collected without a
similar interest in the sources for the English fur trade in the heart
of the continent, which found expression in the formation and development of the Hudson's Bay Company. During the 1930s,
when every businessman in America was trying to keep his company solvent, James Ford Bell was doing this and finding time to
lay the foundations for a library. With a larger view perhaps beginning to intrude on his local historical interest, he acquired in
these years such items as a Columbus *Letter* and a first edition of
Marco Polo's *Travels*.

Inevitably it became apparent that North America could not be studied apart from the rest of the world. The earliest approaches to Canada were searches for an Atlantic route to Asia, and were contemporary to voyages made to India via the Cape of Good Hope. The Minneapolis merchant knew that East Indian spices and Chinese porcelains were more basic to Europe's commercial interests than were North American beaver, however exciting the latter might be to the history of this continent. There was no geographical beginning or end that could be prescribed for this subject of commercial expansion that did not break down before the question, "How did it begin?" The Corte Real voyages to Labrador, Vespucci in South America, Magellan reaching the Pacific — these were inescapable objects of Mr. Bell's search for beginnings. The books that described them became his prime desiderata. The maps that chronicled the new knowledge that was being added to what was known about the earth's shape, size, and make-up, became increasingly important to him.

Another World War, and in its aftermath the breaking up of European overseas empires and American economic expansion further demonstrated the complexities of the international commercial network, and in Mr. Bell's view made more imperative the need to understand it from its beginnings. That understanding called for more study than one person could give, more collecting of books than a businessman could do in his spare time. The need for an institution to house and to foster the growth of his library became a major concern, as well as the means to make the books and manuscripts available to scholars. The answer to this problem occurred easily in the late 1940s, for Mr. Bell was at that time a member of the Board of Regents of his alma mater, and one of her most enthusiastic patrons. His love of nature had already brought to the University of Minnesota its outstanding Natural History Museum. Now his fascination with the history of mercantile enterprise and its relationship to geographical knowledge and imperial expansion would bring his library to the same campus.

The dedication of the James Ford Bell Library in 1953 was more than a commitment of some six hundred well-chosen volumes to the University of Minnesota. It was also a commitment to the idea that the history of European overseas expansion was to be studied here through the development of a library that would enable students and faculty to tell and to interpret the "story" of that movement of Europeans into the larger world, and their eventual domination of it.

From that date, with James Ford Bell as its patron and I as its curator, the Library became a part of the University of Minnesota. We collected books together for nearly eight years, until Mr. Bell's death in 1961. We traveled abroad, searching out booksellers who might be able to supply what we needed. We visited libraries both public and private. We called on scholars and other collectors. We read books.

In those years we developed a scope for the Library that seemed to satisfy the desire we had to get to the beginnings of our "story" yet not to try to tell the end of it. In all directions there had to be room for growth, for reaching out to acquire a book or manuscript dealing with a related subject or event that we had not thought of. It was not enough to begin with Columbus or Vasco da Gama. We had to find their beginnings as explorers in the books they read, the traditions they inherited. So we reached back into classical antiquity for the most respected geographies of the fifteenth century, and we included the medieval geographers, travelers, and encyclopedists who added new knowledge, or kept alive earlier ideas that came to be used by the navigators of the first generation of the Age of Discovery. Likewise, we found it important to gather the laws of maritime cities, particularly those in the Mediterranean, for examples of commercial legislation that might prove to be important as precedent for newly established overseas trade. We felt that in gathering both the intellectual and mercantile climates of the fifteenth century we would be helping future researchers and ourselves to understand the assumptions with which explorers and colonizers went to Asia, Africa, and the New World in the sixteenth century.

That framework of geographical knowledge, steadily enlarging, making possible ever more expansion of commerce, which in turn opened new and more detailed knowledge of the distant parts of the earth, was to be a basic theme for the sixteenth, seventeenth, and eighteenth centuries. Any geographical text of importance, any account of a voyage of discovery, any report of new lands and peoples and products outside of Western Europe was to be collected. And as governments came to acknowledge special relationships with overseas trade through the formation of trading companies, the establishment of colonies, granting of monopolies, and legislating regulations upon such commerce, the laws, documents, and debates recording these were to be within our sphere also. We determined that the end of the eighteenth century would be a suitable stopping place: American independence, the French Revolution, the voyages of Captain James Cook provided new directions in European colonial history and geographical exploration, justifying a terminal point for our Library.

From one end of this historical spectrum to the other, and throughout its world-wide scope, Mr. Bell's interest ranged with almost equal intensity. If the French in Canada held a particular fascination for him it left room for a lively interest in the early newsletters announcing Portuguese discoveries and trade in India. The classical geographies and their steady modification through the sixteenth century, Dutch colonization in Brazil, the various East India companies, early Arctic exploration, maps of distinction, these and any conceivable subject relating to the expansion of European trade fascinated him. He read booksellers' catalogs voraciously. By the last years of his life we were finding that in Asia and Africa, as had been true in Canada, the merchants were often silent; the missionaries reported what was going on. Their books continued to be essential to us.

We became acquainted with booksellers throughout Europe, Great Britain, the United States, and Canada. On business trips to New York for other purposes Mr. Bell could not resist the book shops. We bought actively but selectively. And the University of Minnesota also contributed significantly to the acquisitions program with a budget from which less expensive items were purchased. Every book that was acquired or considered for purchase was described as to contents and bibliographical detail and reported to Mr. Bell. For every such report I received an acknowledgment — some from his fishing camp in Quebec, some from his farm in Georgia. Almost never was there disagreement, never a criticism for a mistake. After seven years of this library-building, Mr. Bell wanted us to begin "telling the story." We had begun a publications program through the University of Minnesota Press immediately upon the dedication of the Library, whereby we hoped to share our holdings with scholars through a series of facsimiles, translations, and interpretations of items in the Library. But these were written by specialists whose interests did not encompass the span of the Library's holdings. My own knowledge was clearly inadequate to undertake a history of European expansion as reflected in the Library's resources. We agreed to a kind of publication that would begin to interpret the Library in terms of current events, and thus *The Merchant Explorer* was born in the spring of 1961. Our last conversation together was a discussion of the first issue of that publication, which had just come off the press. He liked it and the idea it represented, of continuity between today's news and events of the more distant past.

A realist about all things, James Ford Bell knew that he was starting a Library that would be continued by others. He had funds set aside for continued acquisitions. The James Ford Bell Foundation came into being to give additional support to the Library, which has enabled it to grow steadily, thanks to the generosity of its directors, T.R. Anderson, Charles H. Bell, J. Ford Bell, Jr., Samuel H. Bell, and the late Sally Bell Perry. Their contribution to the quality of the Library is second only to that of its founder.

On this, its twenty-fifth anniversary, the James Ford Bell Library houses some ten thousand items. Its reputation is established as a distinguished collection of primary source materials. Research scholars both resident and distant have found here rare editions, manuscripts, maps, and documents that relate closely to each other and thereby facilitate the researchers' work. Students are instructed in the importance and use of original sources, in distinguishing their important features, in editing texts. Exhibits display the Library's holdings to the public. The Library serves the varied clientele its founder intended it to reach. And it continues to grow, so inevitably the "story" Mr. Bell wanted told gets bigger and more complicated, far beyond the abilities of one person to tell and interpret definitively. I have attempted, however, to tell parts of that story in our most recent publication, *The World for a Marketplace: Episodes in the History of European Expansion.*

Travel Literature

*A speech given by John Parker in the spring of 1989
to the Independent Scholars Forum.*

INTRODUCTION BY MAYNARD HASSELQUIST

It has been said many times "it takes one to know one" — and in this case the reference is to fellow travellers. I must have started serious traveling about the same time as you did, Jack, back in 1959. The reasons for our respective travels were not all that different either — mine was in quest of trade for American business, yours in search of the history of trade as it relates to Colonialism which turned out to be big business. Both of us succeeded in our missions, but both of us also gained much more. We benefited from all the delights which are the entitlements awarded to every traveler in every age and which you have so beautifully analyzed and described in your treatise which follows this preamble.

For me the true joy of travel has been in the friendships I have made the world over and which will remain to be enjoyed for the rest of my days. One such friendship, recently acquired, is indeed like the Jason of old whom you write about. Ah, but my friend's travels take him not to the mythical Golden Fleece, but to the very real and briny depths of the sea where he has found and explored the lost *Titanic* and the German battleship *Bismarck*. The modern Jason is Dr. Robert Ballard of Woods Hole, Massachusetts — today's most prominent and acclaimed oceanographer. Exciting as his discoveries have been however, of even greater consequence is his dedication to making certain that school children can not only share but participate first-hand in the exciting travels and explorations in which he becomes engaged. This he does by means of a new telecommunication media known as telepresence. Through this media students throughout the country can become a part of his scientific undersea voyages by means of two-way communication and even two-way

65

guidance of his mighty robots which are appropriately named "Media" and "Jason." The young students have become modern day Argonauts and are discovering the excitement and thrill of scientific education through simulated travel — travel not otherwise possible.

You will be interested to know, Jack, that Dr. Ballard commissioned me to establish a nonprofit organization for educational and scientific purposes which is known as the Jason Foundation. How remindful that is of the Associates of the James Ford Bell Library, the organization which you and our good friend T. R. Anderson asked me to establish some twenty-five years ago. Interestingly enough also, Ballard's 1990 Jason Voyage held in May of this year, was to the depths of Lake Erie. There for the first time since 1812 it was possible to see the Goddess Diana, whose lovely wooden head was the sculptured bow of the lead warship of the War of 1812. She became the symbol of the project and came alive for the first time for school children here in Minneapolis at the James Ford Bell Museum of Natural History due in large part to the generosity and personal efforts of Bell Family members. We have come full circle, Jack. James Ford Bell, Sr. would be proud of our scientific venture into the future with Ballard just as he was proud of your making his dreams come true in the organization and establishment of his Library. Most of all, however, he would be proud of the importance you have given his work and the untiring efforts you have devoted to his dream these many years after his death. I congratulate you, Jack, and I am pleased to have been part of your history as well as part of the travels which you so skillfully describe.

Written in East Berlin, Germany   9 June 1990

In the sorting out and arranging of disciplines, fields of study, areas of expertise — those boundaries of territories within the province of academe by which we define our fiefdoms — travel literature has resisted labels and boundaries, and indeed seems to have had no permanent home in the academy. Perhaps travel literature should be transient, migratory. But surely it is a part of serious scholarship and I intend to demonstrate that.

The most abundant and consistently high-quality scholarship in the study of travel literature is to be found in the publications of the Hakluyt Society. Founded in London in the mid-nineteenth century, and named for Richard Hakluyt the preeminent collector and publisher of travel narratives in Elizabethan England, the Hakluyt Society issues monographs annually, modern studies of earlier travels. The latest one — I received it only last month — is *The Journal of Rockfort Maguire, 1852–54*, edited by John Bockstoce. It is a journal of two years in the mid-nineteenth century at Pt. Barrow, Alaska. I cite it here because in the preface editor Bockstoce says what I will be trying to say today. "Maguire's journal is more than a priceless ethnographic document: it is also a fascinating account of European men learning to cope with the dual challenges of an exotic environment and a foreign society."

Is that not at the heart of our travels and our writing about them: reporting what we see and learning to cope. And adjusting our cultural predispositions to situations where they may be inconvenient, misunderstood, or merely irrelevant. Waiting to go ashore on a South Pacific island Robert Louis Stevenson mused "what will it be like to be among people who were never ruled by Caesar, never recited Cicero, or read Shakespeare."

In such situations we truly discover our cultural baggage, and more often we reveal it without discovering it ourselves. This observing what is without, and revealing what is within is a constant in the history of travel writing.

Let us go back to the beginning, to the oldest travel tale in our culture, the voyage of the Argonauts; and while it has often been retold, and was put into the form most of us know in the third century B.C., the ingredients of the story go back to at least 1500 B.C. It is a story of adventure in places ill-defined, where persons of this world and the other world mingled easily. But the travelers were very human, displaying what *we* recognize as courage and honor and frivolity because that is what the Greeks called it. And if Jason and his shipmates gave us models of behavior, Apollonius of Rhodes gave us a model of narrative style. We are all to some degree heirs to the Argonauts and to Apollonius. Who would not like to be literary heir to this departure scene as they sail out from Pelias:

> Now when the radiant dawn with bright eyes looked forth upon the high mountain-tops of Pelias and the headlands of the tossing main were swept into clear view before the breeze; in that hour rose up Tiphys, and at once he bade his comrades go aboard and make ready the oars. . . . So they went up upon the benches one after another, as before they had allot-

ted each to his place to row, and sat them down in order beside their gear. And in the midst sat Ancaeus and Hercules,
that mighty man, and nigh to him he set his club, and beneath his tread the ship's keel sank deep. And now were the
cables drawn in, and they poured a cup of mead upon the sea.
And Jason with a tear, turned his eyes away from his fatherland. But they, like young men who range themselves to
dance . . . all together and in time beat the ground with
nimble feet to the sound of the lyre . . . , even so they in
time to the lyre of Orpheus smote with their oars the boister-
ous water of the deep, and the waves went dashing by, while
on this side and on that the dark brine bubbled up in foam,
boiling terribly beneath the might of those strong
men . . . while ever far behind their course was white with
foam, like a track seen over a grassy plain.

A fitting departure for a champion crew of oarsmen setting off
with young Jason to bring back the golden fleece from the distant
land of Colchis, and thus recover from a greedy uncle the right
to rule his kingdom. Throughout the voyage they were tested:
their strength, cunning, loyalty to the goddess Athene, loyalty to
their purpose. Early on they came to Lemnos, an island where in
response to unfaithful husbands the women of the place had slain
every male, and then realized their island would be depopulated
at the end of their generation. So Jason's crew was welcomed, and
behaved well, so well indeed that they could have stayed on per-
manently, and perhaps some would have. But the strong man,
Hercules, stayed with the ship, pleasure's counter-force of duty,
railing at his companions, "No fair fame shall we win from this
long sojourn among strange women; nor will some god of his own
accord take the Golden Fleece and give it to us at our prayer."
And so the oarsmen came back to their ship. Virtue, as defined
by Greeks, triumphed.

So also at the island of the Berbyces where the king challenged
all comers to a boxing match. He had killed most of his opponents. It was not Hercules who stepped forward into the ring. It
was Polydeuces, a young, quick, fearless man. Dodging and
weaving he won the day: skill over brute strength. And later, Jason's capture of the golden fleece, in spite of incredible odds, was
possible when courage, duty, ingenuity, and the love of a good
woman were brought together.

We may never know, or believe, much about the land of Colchis, but we know about Greek values a thousand years before Homer by the way Greeks behaved away from home. And Homer's *Odyssey*, surely the most often published travel story in western culture reinforced such values. Remember that the goal of Odysseus was always to get home to his wife and son. And the wind-blown outward voyage was the result of not going home promptly after the Trojan War. "Come on guys, one more village to sack, one more day of carousing; it won't hurt us; we deserve it." And so the great adventure began.

Those were times, 3,000 to 4,000 years ago, when the patch of earth Homer could know was but a miniscule patch of the imagined total earth. And maritime technology kept it miniscule. Seven days running before a gale took a ship beyond the realm of experience, and fantasy could take over to teach virtue and to entertain. The poet was more in evidence than the teacher, yet Homer had to have some reality about his story to give it credibility, and in addition to Odysseus's humanity Homer gave him a ship that has remained credible all through succeeding time. Here is Odysseus building it:

> He felled twenty trees in all, lopped them clean, smoothed them carefully, and adzed them straight and square. Then he bored them and made them fast to one another with dowells and battens. He laid out the bottom as wide as a good shipwright would for a beamy freighter. He set up close-set ribs, made half-decks fast to them, and finished up by adding side planking . . . The goddess (Calypso) brought him cloth for a sail, and he fashioned a fine one. . . . Putting the craft on rollers, he hauled it down to the sea.

All of this would work in shipbuilding today. But the ship sails to places full of fantasy. There again the ancient Greeks gave us a start in thinking about travels: reality where it is possible, beyond that imagination, hearsay, entertainment, which often reveal the traveler's values as we invent challenges to them. Utopias have ever been a commentary upon the world of experience which falls short of our dreams.

What the Argonauts and *Odyssey* give us therefore is travel as a vehicle for literature, the travelers are carriers of values, not observers of geography. That would change greatly as the Greeks built colonies in the Mediterranean and marched armies to India. The *Historia* of Herodotus, written about 450 B.C., is sometimes called the first travel account into the real world. Here is why: "Assyria possesses a vast number of great cities, whereof the most renowned and strongest was Babylon, whither, after the fall of Nineveh the seat of government had been removed." (Power and politics are present in that statement). Now for some local geography: "The city stands on a broad plain, and it is an exact square, 120 furlongs in length each way. . . . While such is its size, in magnificence there is no other city that approaches to it. It is surrounded . . . by a broad and deep moat, full of water, behind which rises a wall fifty royal cubits in width and two hundred in height." Now lest you Greek readers be wondering about royal cubits, Herodotus adds "the royal cubit is longer by three fingers' breadth than the common cubit."

This is not just a description of Nineveh, although it surely is that in detail. It is also a statement about Greek love for details and specifics, reflecting a culture that would shortly measure the circumference of the earth with great exactness, and spawn critics even of the methods of doing it. It shows a culture ever pushing at the frontiers of what could be learned. Herodotus wrote of the Nile: "I was particularly anxious to learn why the Nile, at the commencement of the summer solstice begins to rise, and continues to increase for a hundred days . . . forthwith retires . . . continuing low during the whole winter. On none of these points could I obtain any explanation from the inhabitants, though I made every inquiry."

It is this relentless sense of inquiry the Greeks took with them in their travels that made them valuable fifteen centuries later. They tried to have it all, so far as their technology would allow. Here is Strabo in the first century A.D.: "He who has elevated his mind, will he be satisfied with anything less than the whole world." And again Strabo, "Every one who undertakes to give an accurate description of a place should be particular to add to its astronomical and geographical relations, explaining carefully its extent, distance, degrees of latitude and climate." And so Eratosthenes measured the circumference of the earth, Ptolemy plotted out all known places on a latitude and longitude grid. Strabo among others described every known place in detail.

How to mount that kind of science on a narrative that sang like Homer? Not easy, but travel writers have tried ever since. And of course that kind of science gave way to other kinds of learning and thinking along the way.

Let us leap through five centuries from Strabo into the religion-dominated mind of western Europe, into the Atlantic travels of an Irish monk, St. Brendan, who was born in 484, and although a real historical person became a mythical traveler, absorbing through time the travels of others (as Odysseus and the Argonauts had done, by the way) into his own undoubted wanderings. The Irish religious quest at sea was for some sacred place — a Land of Promise, Isle of the Blessed. We hear no geography in these voyages, no descriptions of temples or market places, or fortifications and their dimensions. Here is St. Brendan arriving at his long-sought destination:

> For forty days the boat thrust ahead, passing at last into a thick cloud which encircled the island he had sought so long. Emerging from the cloud into light, the monks beheld the Land of Promise. It was warm, fruitful, bathed in seemingly endless autumn sunshine. They disembarked and pushed up country for forty days, viewing the landscape on all sides but never glimpsing a farther sea. Finally they stood on the bank of a great river which glided into the interior. It was too broad and deep to cross. Brendan said they could do no more and would not be able to discover how large the country was.

There is nothing here that we, or Herodotus, would call intellectual curiosity about the world. Indeed, Brendan's objective was to be released from the world. Scholars have ever since wondered where he sailed, and are not helped by the directions Brendan was often given by ancient hermits and talking birds as he went from one island to another.

Not all medieval travel tales are so vague. But many of them are far less interesting. The dominant format of travel narratives from this period is the pilgrimage, and while partaking in the Greek passion for detail and descriptiveness, what was observed and described is often rather dull to our ears. Here, for example, is bishop Willibald, an eighth-century traveler to the Near East:

> As soon as they had obtained leave the travelers went direct to Damascus, a distance of a hundred miles. St. Ananias re-

poses there, and it is in the land of Syria. They remained there
one week. And two miles from the city was a church, on the
spot where St. Paul was first converted, and the Lord said to
him "Saul, Saul, why persecutest thou me?" &c. And after
praying there they went to Galilee to the place where Gabriel
first came to St. Mary and said, "Hail, full of grace," &c. A
church now stands there, and the village which contains the
church is Nazareth. The Christians reportedly bought that
church of the pagans when the latter were about to destroy
it. And having there recommended themselves to the Lord,
they proceeded to the town of Cana, where our Lord turned
water into wine. A large church stands there, and near the al-
tar is still preserved one of the vessels which our Lord com-
manded to be filled with water to be turned into wine. And
the travelers drank wine out of it. They remained there one
day and then continued their journey to Mount Tabor, the
scene of our Lord's transfiguration, where there is now a
monastery and a church . . . "

I am sure you get the idea: an enumerative account by a one-
dimensional mind. After all, the pilgrim had one reason to travel,
one set of inquiries to make, one story to tell. And for most medieval Europeans there was no other reason to travel. Merchandising
was largely local. The roads to and from Rome had declined and
were not safe. The Mediterranean Sea was worse: it was full of
Moslem ships, by definition hostile. Yet the traveling mind was
not entirely confined to churches and shrines. When circum-
stance and technology do not serve, the imagination may, and the
Quest for the Holy Grail, the search for Prester John, and
wonders of the unknown world combed out of Greek and Roman
literature carried readers beyond the drabness of reality. And
then in 1240 reality from beyond the known world came roaring
in with Ghengis Khan.

The door to the outer world thus rudely opened was an invitation and Europe responded with the hope that the unity God intended for all peoples might now be possible by bringing to this
powerful ruler the power of the truth. And its success in conquer-
ing Europe over the previous dozen centuries left no doubt in the
European mind that Christianity was *the* truth. Missionary-
ambassadors went forth with confidence, with some curiosity
(born of the Renaissance then brewing) and with not a little ad-

miration for an empire more vast than Rome had built, a first-
class administration of innumerable peoples all held together
with a firm hand and a pony express communications system that
was efficient and safe. And it was rich. Here is John of Plano Car-
pini who went out to Mongolia as emissary of Pope Innocent IV
in 1245, revealing his own interest in this world's goods as he described what he saw. "They are extremely rich in animals,
camels, oxen, sheep, goats; they have such a number of horses and
mares that I do not believe there are so many in all the rest of the
world. . . . The emperor, the nobles, and other important men
own large quantities of gold and silver, silk, and precious stones
and jewels." Western confidence had some problems when the
Khan, or one of his officials looked down his nose at the gifts these
diplomats brought: "You come from an important man, and you
give so little." But the confidence was born of belief in their religion, and they never doubted their eventual triumph.

This was to be a recurring theme in European travels to Asia:
the material and administrative superiority of the East which
amazingly did not discourage the West, but indeed enhanced its
hope of finding there a rich and powerful ally against the long-
hated Moslems. So Marco Polo, bowled over by well-governed
cities full of merchandize, described them as full of pagans and
idolaters — pejorative terms for people who had everything but
the truth.

European culture rode into the Renaissance on this religious
confidence and on its quest for the wealth of the East. And built
into it was a return to classical writers and their curiosity about
the world with resultant technological advances. With an advancing technology, superior in military and naval terms to most
of the outer world, and a religion defined as the truth, it is not surprising that a major feature of the Renaissance was what one
scholar has called "Latin arrogance." Sixteenth century travel
literature is often disdainful of non-European cultures, except for
their products. Generalizations are difficult for this period, but
where there was opulence to be observed the Europeans were ad-
miring observers. Here is a Portuguese description of the King of
Calicut, 1505.

> The king was lying down on a litter covered by a purple silk
> cloth. From his waist up he was naked, from the waist down

he was clothed with a cloth of cotton, worked with gold and
silver. He had on his head a cap of brocade made like an antique helmet. From his ears hung two pearls as big as hazel-
nuts, one round and the other pear-shaped. He wore two gold
bracelets with many jewels and pearls and an infinite number
of rings on his hands. All those gems were very precious and
of great price. There was also a large chair made completely
of silver. Its armrests and back were of gold with many precious stones. There were twenty trumpets of silver and three
of gold, a third longer than ours and quite loud. In the room
were six moorish lamps of silver and they burned day and
night.

You get the idea of eastern opulence and a covetous West. No
wonder that Columbus had gone from island to island in the West
Indies in search of gold. No wonder that Portugal drained itself
of manpower seeking quick riches in the East.

There was more than wealth to be admired. There was learning, a number of sophisticated cultures. In China the earliest missionaries found themselves in the presence of inquiring and tolerant scholars. Matteo Ricci, the founder of the China mission, was
himself a scholar of great achievement, and he got along well
with his hosts, but he had to withhold complete admiration because of his religion. Here in the early 17th century he describes
one of the cities he visited:

> The people here are thrifty and accustomed to living on little,
> and though they practice a false religion, very many of them
> are strict observers of the Chinese fast. The literati, or edu-
> cated class, are formed into a society and on appointed days,
> certain of the most learned of them hold discussions relative
> to the practice of the various virtues . . . but lacking the
> light of the true faith, they are wandering aimlessly along the
> path of virtue, stray sheep without a shepherd.

From what was perceived to be the other end of the sophistication spectrum — the North American Indian — there was admiration again, but with the same reservation. This time it was admiration for the natural life. Here is Father Pierre Biard in 1616,
writing the first Jesuit account of the Indians of Nova Scotia:

> The nature of our savages (note the possessive) is in itself
> generous and not malicious. They have a rather happy dispo-
> sition and a fair capacity for judging and valuing material

and common things, deducing their reasons with great
nicety, and always seasoning them with some pretty comparison. . . . Generally speaking, they are lighter of build than
we are; but handsome and well-shaped, just as we would be
if we continued in the same condition we were at the age of
twenty-five . . . They are droll fellows . . . and if they
think they have occasion look down on us. . . . You will see
these poor barbarians, notwithstanding their great lack of
government, power, letters, art, and riches, yet holding their
heads so high that they greatly underrate us, regarding themselves as our superiors.

And not without some justification, Father Biard observes, for
he wrote that they did not store up wealth nor fight over the in-
heritance after a death. They lived off the land and had plenty to
eat and to wear. Indeed, he observed that they were probably
happier than most Europeans, except in the matter of the salva-
tion of their souls.

We could not ask for a clearer catalog of 17th century European values: "government, power, literacy, art, riches" — enun-
ciated only because the Indians appeared to lack all of them. How
often we explain ourselves abroad by noting what is lacking in our
hosts.

Staying with Father Biard a moment longer, we gain some insight into the scientific mind of the time, an attempt to interpret
nature in frozen Canada:

The second cause of the cold is . . . the wild and primitive
condition of the land, for this is only a boundless forest, and
the soil cannot be warmed by the sun, either because it has
a hard crust, having never been ploughed, or on account of
the trees which cast upon it a perpetual shade, or because the
snow and water stagnate there for a long time. . . . Whereas, if the land were inhabited and cultivated, from it and
from the dwellings of the inhabitants would arise exhala-
tions, warm and dry fumes; furthermore the sun would find
it prepared to feel its rays, and to scatter the cold and fogs.
For upon the small part which we ploughed, the snow always
melted sooner . . . and from there the fogs usually began to
scatter and disappear.

The Age of Science was yet 150 years away, Newton's *Principia*

about half that distance, so let us hasten there and find Pehr Kalm
in Pennsylvania observing the soil:

> The soil does not seem to be deep in this section, for the upper
> black stratum is hardly two inches. This I had occasion to see
> both in places where the ground is dug up and in such places
> where the water during heavy showers of rain made cuts. The
> upper soil is a dark color and the next a pale hue like bricks.
> I have observed everywhere in America that the depth of the
> upper soil does not by far agree with the computation of some
> people, though we can be almost sure that in some places it
> has never been stirred since the Deluge.

Or let us join a contemporary of Kalm's, Pehr Osbeck, in China
about 1750, observing flowers:

> Torena *Asiatica*: the calyx is pentagonal, erected; its five seg-
> ments are lanceolated, narrow, and shorter than the tube of
> the flower; the corolla is lanceolated; the upper lip is almost
> entire, and reflected; the lower lip has three *laciniae* and is
> bent downward. The filaments are four, shorter than the
> corolla, they are fastened in pairs in the lower lip. . . .

What has happened here? The European traveler has become — if a naturalist — a cataloguer of natural phenomena, seeking relationships between plants, attempting to discover the order
in nature that Newton, Linnaeus, and others were sure could be
found. And if the traveler was a social scientist there was an equal
interest in what natural organizations had emerged among peoples who had not been under European influence. Here is Captain Bougainville in the South Pacific:

> Though the isle is divided into many little districts, each of
> which has its own master, yet there does not seem to be any
> civil war or any private hatred in the isle. It is probable, that
> the people of Tahiti deal amongst each other with unques-
> tioned sincerity. Whether at home or not, by day or night,
> their houses are always open. Everyone gathers fruits from
> the first tree he meets with, or takes some in any house where
> he enters. It would seem as if . . . there was no personal
> property amongst them, and that they all had an equal right
> in those articles. . . .

It is not far from the books of naturalists in the mid-eighteenth
century to the full-fledged, nationally supported scientific expedition, with volumes of scientific data. And as the earth and seas

were scraped for specimens it was inevitable that a Charles Darwin would scrape up the remains of some that no longer existed and ask why. Travel became interested in geological time, noting the rise and fall of land masses as well as empires and civilizations. Oh, there had been ponderings of the Flood, and the chronology of Chinese empires that went through it dry-shod, but it did not come close to what we call science.

Linnaeus, Thomas Jefferson, Sir Joseph Banks, Charles Darwin — they and countless of their contemporaries were about a liberalization, and a liberation of thinking that moved into democracy and mass literacy with a profound effect on travel literature. The book had heretofore been the result of the voyage. A rising market made it the reason for the voyage. It was a good way for journalists to make a living. Unimportant journeys written to the popular taste became common. And that is not to denigrate them. They deserve to be judged as literature, not as discovery.

And a very important newly-liberated group were women, freed to travel and to write about travel. There were almost none in the eighteenth century. There were many in the nineteenth, and they added very significantly to the contemporary view of the world, and our understanding of the cultural filters through which these women saw it.

The papal ambassadors and Ghengis Khan were hardly more unlike than the people of Cincinnati and their visitor, Mrs. Trollope:

> I never saw any people who appeared to live so much without amusement as the Cincinnatians. Billiards are forbidden by law, so are cards. To sell a pack of cards in Ohio subjects the seller to a penalty of fifty dollars. They have no public balls, excepting, I think, six, during the Christmas holydays. They have no concerts. They have no dinner-parties.
>
> They have a theatre, which is, in fact, the only public amusement of this triste little town; but they seem to care little about it, and either from economy or distaste, it is very poorly attended. Ladies are rarely seen there, and by far the larger proportion of females deem it an offence against religion to witness the representation of a play. It is in the churches and chapels of the town that the ladies are to be seen in full costume; and I am tempted to believe that a stranger

from the Continent of Europe would be inclined, on first reconnoitring the city, to suppose that the places of worship were the theatres and cafes of the place. No evening in the week but brings throngs of the young and beautiful to the chapels and meeting-houses, all dressed with care, and sometimes with great pretension; it is there that all display is made, and all fashionable distinction sought. The proportion of gentlemen attending these evening meetings is very small, but often, as might be expected, a sprinkling of smart young clerks makes this sedulous display of ribands and ringlets intelligible and natural. Were it not for the churches, indeed, I think there might be a general bonfire of best bonnets, for I never could discover any other use for them.

The ladies are too actively employed in the interior of their houses to permit much parading in full dress for morning visits. There are no public gardens or lounging shops of fashionable resort, and were it not for public worship, and private tea-drinkings, all the ladies in Cincinnati would be in danger of becoming perfect recluses.

And finally, there was the liberation of all of us to travel where and when we pleased with the coming of the automobile. No one sang of it more sweetly than Edith Wharton:

The motor car has restored the romance of travel. Freeing us from all the compulsions and contacts of the railway, the bondage to fixed hours and the beaten track, the approach to each town through an area of ugliness and desolation created by the railway itself, it has given us back the wonder, the adventure and the novelty which enlivened the way of our posting grandparents. Above all these recovered pleasures must be ranked the delight of taking a town unawares, stealing in on it by back ways and unchronicled paths and surprising it in some intimate aspect of past time. . . .

(*Winged Wheels in France*, 1909).

With both travel and literacy now widely available in the twentieth century what would we do with it? There would be a travel technology beyond the common traveler for awhile, the airplane, and to see the earth, our home forever, from a distance, that gave song to some who wanted to write about a new travel experience. Charles Lindberg in *We* wrote of coming in for his famous landing at Paris: " . . . as I crossed the channel and passed over Cherbourg, France, I had probably seen more of that part of Europe than most native Europeans. The visibility was good and the country could be seen for miles around. People who have taken their first flight often remark that no one knows what the locality he lives in is like until he has seen it from the air." Antoine de St. Exupéry was more flourishing in his descriptions of playing among the clouds. Air travel was in its beginnings a remarkable liberation.

And as flying became common and hardly noteworthy as a basis for travel literature, adventurer-scholars took to ancient technologies to study the oceans and the deserts. Sven Hedin, Thor Heyerdahl, Tim Severin and others retraced old routes, or discovered old routes. We even find a bit of novelty in Paul Theroux who rides trains all over the world. And in reading them we look for what we believe in: authenticity, accuracy, perseverance (no successful travel author ever just gives up and goes home), and we look for words that sing a little. It is not reporting, it is not merely observation. It is literature.

Keeping Bees

INTRODUCTION BY ELIZABETH SAVAGE

Among the mysterious charms of beekeeping are the accoutrements. Whatever Jack Parker feels about his helmet, gloves, smoker and tools — his calm, unhurried manner is what the nervous, excitable bees need. After donning the screen-faced hood, the long heavy canvas gloves, and finally getting dry grass and old rags to burn in the smoker, many beekeepers are in an excitable state themselves. Not Jack though, he'd take his handy wrought iron hive tool, open the hive and hunt for the queen bee — she is markedly bigger which helps. But of course there can be only one queen bee per hive so any interlopers have to be finished off quickly. The honey from the Parker hive not only looks and tastes good but wins blue ribbons annually at the Minnesota State Fair to prove its superiority. An old homily states the bee is more honored than other animals not because she labors but because she labors for others.

For a publishing house that delights in insects to want a booklet on honeybees seems most natural — to a keeper of bees, at least. So its request for some thoughts and feelings, and possibly some information, about the life and activities of honeybees brings this response. I hope my reflections upon the seasons and the response of honeybees to them will convey something of the wonder I feel for these remarkable creatures.

JACK PARKER

To Russ and Winnie Johnson,
the best of beekeepers,
teachers and friends.

TO MAKE A CANDLE

It is December, a time to make candles. For Hanukkah. For Christmas. Hundreds of Decembers have seen candles lighted as symbols of faith, small drops of light scattered around the world, gifts from the honeybee. How does it happen that bees should be builders of candles, givers of light? It could not be otherwise with bees as part of our creation. Wax is as much a part of the honeybee's economy as pollen and honey. In the life of the hive, cells of wax are the womb where the queen places the egg which becomes a bee twenty-one days later. The wax cells are the granary for pollen gathered to feed the larvae. They are the honey storehouse for the colony's survival in winter.

Comb is built as it is needed and in response to nature's provisions. In spring when the first nectar flows in flowers and when cells are needed for brood, the bees build the cells with wax. They also provide a wax covering for each cell containing larvae which is broken open by the emerging young bee.

Which bees are the wax makers? Worker bees only, and among them only during a limited stage of life. From about the twelfth to the eighteenth day of its working life the worker bee may be a builder of comb. Beeswax is secreted in miniscule flakes from between the segments of the bee's abdomen. As the honey flow intensifies in midsummer the need for storage space will be felt, resulting in more wax production. If a bee must retain honey for a long time in its stomach for lack of comb in which to deposit it, wax will begin to secrete from between the abdominal segments.

When it does the bee will remove the particle of wax with a hind leg, transfer it to a foreleg and mandible for working into the wall of the cell. In association with other bees it molds and shapes the wax particles, forming them into the hexagonal comb structure. One cell will be the work of a hundred bees or more.

Some days later when the new-built cells are filled with honey and it is "ripened" to the correct moisture content, the wax-makers will cover it over with a thin capping of wax. It is these cappings, removed and saved by the beekeeper at extracting time that makes the best wax for candles. The comb-building stops with the end of the nectar flow in late summer. Comb built in one season will be useful in the next and for years to come, but the bees will have to repair cells damaged in handling and in extracting, and of course each season new cappings will have to be built by the bees. A new colony of bees in a new hive will have to build comb for brood, for pollen, and for honey production as the season progresses.

And what of the wax-builders in December when we burn our candles, and what of the winter months that follow? Left in their hive out of doors in northern climes, the honeybees cluster together for warmth. The honey they have stored is their source of heat, released through their metabolism. A colony of bees in Minnesota will consume about seventy-five pounds of honey between October and April, and in doing so will have kept the surface of the cluster at about forty-five degrees. The interior of the cluster will be much warmer, as high as ninety-five degrees when brood rearing begins in January. As the external temperature declines the cluster will become more dense, and it will loosen up as the temperature rises, always being less compact at the interior than at the surface where the bees form a tight layer of insulation from one to three inches thick, their bodies kept warm by the heat being transferred from the interior of the cluster.

And all through the winter the cluster will slowly move over the combs where the honey is stored, chipping away the wax cappings to get at their food. It is always dark in a beehive, and as we light our candles we think of that darkness in which is stored the source of the light that glows before us. Light from flowers and sunshine and rain. And we count our blessings.

IN PRAISE OF DANDELIONS

There is a patch of earth that arches slightly above the level of the country road, its flora generally unremarkable. The surrounding wire fence defines some farmer's dream that here cows or sheep might feed. But a different flock comes to this knoll — honeybees. Unencumbered by trees, or too poor to support them, the hill in summer takes the brunt of the sun's rays, receives their blessing in spring. Early in May the sun's glow is matched here by the earth's, a carpet of dandelion blossoms, and the bees come out in force to gather nourishment for their brood.

The queen's egg-laying program has accelerated gradually through the early spring and the larvae have been fed from pollen and honey that were stored in autumn. Pussywillows and popple (quaking aspen) blossoms have provided the first fresh pollen as field bees have ventured out in the warmer afternoons of March and April days. But with dandelions, the only harvest of this impoverished hill, the brood-rearing season gets its momentum.

From more than a mile away they come, honeybees to collect nectar from the much maligned dandelion, but not only nectar. Some are carriers of pollen only. Whatever their purpose, the bees gather on the feathery hairs of their bodies innumerable grains of pollen, some of which do their much-heralded work of pollinating, assuring us and them of more dandelions. But most of the gleaming yellow grains are carefully brushed by the bees' front and middle legs into small pouches, pollen baskets, on the hind legs, placed there of course for that purpose. Returning to the hive these pollen-haulers present a near-comic appearance, like heavily-laden peddlers going about their business.

Their business is to provide food for the brood while it is in its larva stage, and the more plentiful the supply, the more eggs the queen will lay, the ideal being a population explosion to provide an abundance of field bees to bring in nectar later in the season. The returning pollen gatherers unload their cargo in comb cells near those filled with brood. The house bees feed on it, digesting it with a mixture of honey enabling them to secrete from glands in the head a rich substance called royal jelly which is fed to the developing larvae. The dandelion pollen's contribution to this "bee milk" is protein primarily, but it also contains fat, phosphorus and iron. The abundance of these nutrients along with nectar, also supplied by the dandelions, may stimulate the queen to lay 1500 to 2000 eggs per day.

The egg, deposited at the bottom of the comb cell develops into larva after three days, and it is literally bathed in royal jelly for the next three days by the house bees. Then feeding is reduced, except in a cell where a queen is being produced, and the larva begins to develop its wax glands, brood-feeding glands, and other bee-like characteristics. At the end of its six days as larva — nine since the egg was laid — the cell in which it lives is capped over with a thin layer of wax, and the food it has absorbed sustains it through twelve days during which it develops into a complete adult bee and it gnaws away the capping to become a working member of the colony, ready for house bee duties, the first of which is to consume pollen and honey so that it can nurse the new larvae.

House bee, brood nursing status, is not a permanent condition. After eight to ten days the new worker reduces its pollen consumption and its head glands diminish. The pollen-based protein in its body is transferred from them to the wax glands as the worker moves to the wax-building phase of its life, and ultimately the protein goes to the flight muscles as it becomes a field bee.

The foraging bee that was larva when the first dandelion pollen came in will find no blossoms on the hill. Indeed, it will not go there, for it will have learned from other foragers of new sources of pollen. But the hill will have done its work. The bee yard a mile away will be alive with bees, ready for other blossoms that are opening.

TEN DAYS IN JULY

Does it seem remarkable that a single beehive standing at the edge of a grove of trees would weigh one hundred pounds more on July 25 than it weighed on the 15th? More bees? More pollen? Not really. More honey. The phenomenon known as the honey flow is what beekeepers work and wait for all the year 'round. Some years it happens spectacularly. Some years it does not happen at all.

The season may have several minor honey flows: dandelions in early May; wild raspberries a month later, followed perhaps by wild blackberries. But in Minnesota the main flow is clover, alfalfa, sweet clover (yellow and white), and sometimes basswood. Each floral source produces a distinct nectar. Each plant has its own requirements for maximum nectar secretion.

Nectar and pollen are the reasons bees are attracted to flowers. Sight and smell draw bees to the blossoms which are usually the source of nectar secretion. How do the bees know where the flowers are, and that they are producing nectar? In the economy of the honeybee colony some members are explorers, scouts ranging far out from the hive. Finding a floral source, the bee probes the blossom, extends its proboscis into the plant's nectary and sucks out a minute quantity of the sweet liquid. She goes to another blossom, repeats the extraction, and on to another and another — to at least a hundred, often many more. In sweet clover this will take from half an hour to forty-five minutes before the load is completed — a load of from 25 to 70 mg. of nectar, depending upon the richness of the honey flow. The field bee flies back to the hive, it may be a hundred yards; it may be three miles.

She enters the hive and announces her discovery in a series of body motions best described as a waggle dance. The motions indicate the direction and distance to the nectar source. She will deliver her load to house bees and return to the field. Turn-around time for her is from four to five minutes. Other bees will have followed her directions and soon bees are exploding out of the hive, returning, doing their dances, unloading and heading back to the field. More bees will have gotten the message and the volume of traffic at the entrance to the hive increases. Each of the field bees may make ten to twelve trips per day, depending, of course, upon the distance involved.

The returned loads of nectar are transferred from the mandibles of the field bees to the proboscises of house bees who manipulate it to remove some of the moisture — making nectar into honey — before depositing it in the comb cells. It will be necessary to continue removing moisture from the newly-stored honey, and this is done by forcing air through the hive by bees fanning their wings. Nectar coming into the hive will have varying moisture content, as high as 70 per cent. It must be reduced to less than twenty per cent before the bees consider it "ripe" and then they will seal the cells with a thin coating of wax.

Back to that hive at the edge of the woods. By mid-July the colony had a population of about 75,000. Of that number one-third would be field bees. If each of them made ten trips a day — 250,000 flights — and each trip brought in an average of fifty mg. of nectar, they would be bringing in about twenty-five pounds of nectar per day. Continuing the flow for ten days would produce some 250 pounds of nectar brought to the hive. If this nectar was in the range of seventy per cent moisture and it had to be reduced to less than twenty per cent, the net yield would raise the weight of the hive by about a hundred pounds in ten days.

Ten very good days for bees — and for beekeepers.

DEATH, LIFE AND CONTINUITY

"Little honey hath the hive where there are more drones than bees." So ran a commentary on the human community in 1609. Does it matter, a little honey or a lot? Indeed it does. All of that nectar-gathering in summer is for one purpose: continuity of the colony into the next season. Honeybee colonies will see to it that there are not too many drones. And in autumn none at all. When the honeyflow is over, when the fall flowers have ceased to yield nectar, the queen will stop laying eggs. The hive population stabilizes for the coming winter, and the drones will be forced out of the hive. Incapable of providing for themselves in the best of seasons, they quickly starve when ejected.

Symbol of the free-loader, drones are nevertheless an essential part of the colony's life. They are the male bees. Their only function is to fertilize a virgin queen when the occasion requires it. Every afternoon during warm summer days they hover above the bee yard, waiting for a queen on her maiden flight. If one should appear she is fertilized in mid-air by one or more of the drones. She may make several flights on the same day, but this fertilization episode will be the only one she has for the rest of her life. So when there is no possibility for a new queen to be fertilized there is no need for drones, and they are exiled from the colony.

Next spring when a new season starts the workers will prepare drone brood-cells, slightly larger than for workers, and the queen will lay unfertilized eggs in them, and these will emerge as drones twenty-four days later. Their lives will be short, even during the summer, averaging about three weeks, so they must be replaced through the brood-rearing season, but it is all over for them when the frost comes.

Without drones and without brood the colony makes ready for winter. The workers in the colony will be entirely "new bees" in that they have emerged during the summer, for a worker's life span in the nectar-gathering season is limited to about six weeks. Those that have died will have been replaced throughout the summer to provide heat in the hive during winter.

The queen may be the same one that started the colony in the spring. Or she may be a new one, a "supersedure" produced during the summer. When a queen is injured or killed, or loses her fertility she must be replaced if the colony is to survive. In such an emergency the worker bees will select several larvae in the very early stage of development, feed them an especially rich diet of royal jelly, and create for these larvae much enlarged cells for the growth of the new queens, since a queen is considerably longer in body than either workers or drones. After fifteen days of this special care the new queen emerges, and frequently her first act will be to seek out the other queen cells containing adult queens about to emerge. She will tear open the cells of undeveloped queens and allow the workers to destroy them. If indeed another queen has emerged, then the queens will fight until one of them has destroyed the other. She is then ready to leave the hive on her maiden flight, and the drones will be out there waiting for her, hundreds, possibly thousands of them so that her absence from the hive need not be long, her exposure to birds and other hazards being reduced to a minimum. Two or three days later her egg-laying career begins.

So an able queen, together with a large population of workers, and no drones, settle into the frosty autumn weather, equipped to survive the dark cold months if honey enough has been gathered to feed them. "Bees will not freeze, but they will starve" is a beekeeper's adage, an admonition to leave plenty of honey in the hive if there are to be bees there in the spring.

A Sermon

INTRODUCTION BY PAT JONES

Jack Parker has been a member of the Minneapolis Friends Meeting for thirty-five years. He has served the Meeting in many ways. Currently he is a Trustee and a member of the Fundraising Committee for a planned building renovation. Jack is, first of all, though, a cherished person and a gifted speaker in our meetings for worship.

Jack gave this sermon in March 1980. I chose it as an example of his sermons because it was the only one I could find in print! For any of the others we would have had to transcribe from tape, or would have had to search your files, Jack!

The sermon, printed in *The Northern Light*, a newsletter of the Minneapolis Friends Meeting, begins with the following note: One of the delights of our life together at Minneapolis Friends is the shared responsibility of delivering the weekly Sunday message. Practically every Sunday, under the direction of the Ministry and Counsel Committee, a different person from the midst of our membership (and attendership) is invited to share with us from the depths of his or her spiritual life. Besides providing a unique way for us to get to know each other, it is also a concrete expression of our Quaker belief that we are *all* called to be ministers for each other. The following is the message that John Parker shared with us last month; it struck such a responsive chord that many thought that it should be shared with others and for those who were there, that it should be put into print so that we could continue to draw inspiration from John's words.

When Lynne asked me early in February to speak late in March I put my faith in spring, and agreed to speak this day. Spring is an inspiring time, and its arrival has from the beginning of recorded time moved poets and wordsmiths of other kinds of eloquence. I don't know that Quakers have any record of more or better speaking in the spring. But this one will try.

And to speak of peace — or in other words, alternatives to war, is as old as spring. We might justly despair of new thoughts and remain silent in prayer. But the search must not be given up, and we do not know at what time a small seed dropped in the right place, might produce a great tree. Wasn't it Samuel Johnson who as a small boy went climbing a cupboard in search of apples and found a book — thus giving birth to a great literary genius. I doubt that I am planting trees today but would settle gladly for a flower from this garden that has nourished me for a quarter of a century.

We talk endlessly here about peace, and I asked myself as I gathered these thoughts, are we not at peace? Is there a war going on among us? Has there not been less international bloodshed of late — say in the last five years — than at most times in recorded history? Clearly we are legally and politically at peace. But just as clearly we do not have peace in the deeper sense. Like the neighbors of Three Mile Island, they may not be sick with disease, but they are sick with fear. If we have legal peace is it not merely because we are afraid to go to war. Peace by balance of power — or by balance of fear. And that is not peace. Indeed, fear is the opposite of peace.

What then is this peace which we seek? What do *we* mean by peace? I will try a definition of it, and some historical background to illustrate what I mean. Peace, I say, is a *sense of unity among mankind that transcends differences and disagreements among individuals and groups.*

That unity is broken when one person will attempt to destroy another for any cause or reason. Whence comes a sense of unity that is so strong as to prevail against human will and intellect which produces the reasons and causes for destructive conflict. Clearly some strong focal point is needed to hold humanity in such a unity. Can it be fear? I think not, for fear is a variable, never constant. We do not share it equally. The strong have less fear than the weak. The source of unity must apply equally to all humanity.

The focus for unity — or attempted unity — has not always been the same. People have sought for it in various places and by various ways — and I am here speaking only of attempts at unity within the Christian community. There surely are others outside of it. Paul was saying to the Corinthian Christian community that the unity among them was derived from the *source* of their individual gifts "there are varieties of working, but the *same God* who inspires them in every one." And "For by *one spirit* are we all baptized into *one body* — Jews or Greeks, slaves or free — and all were made to drink of *one spirit*."

Such was the unity of humanity as perceived and preached by and to early Christians. But it was not adequate to persuade Christians to desist from killing people (including each other) for one cause or another. The height of this heresy was reached in the Crusades a thousand years after Christ's mission on earth, when whole armies were raised in the name of Christ to go out and kill other human beings. Logically enough, it was this height of folly which brought forth a good argument against it.

St. Francis of Assisi, in the 13th century, reflected the revival of learning which was taking place. He held to the belief of his time that the world would come to an end shortly, but before it could do so God would see to it that all of humanity had a chance to come to unity and be saved from damnation. And of course, to Christians like St. Francis this was the great opportunity — to be the agent of unity. How to do it? Not merely by preaching, but by learning — education — intercultural understanding must precede conversion. It was, therefore, incumbent upon Christians who would labor for human unity under God to learn the history, languages, and cultural characteristics of other people. Then, meeting them in the intellectual arena of discussion and debate, the non-Christians would perceive their own errors and accept truth. For all people, St. Francis believed, have an equal desire for truth. In short, the unity of humanity would come in the search for, and acceptance of truth.

In this spirit was the modern missionary movement born. It was built upon by various religious orders and denominations. But it did not succeed in its objective. Why? It had enemies. Precisely at the time the Franciscans were preaching unity, Europe was evolving into a state of intense disunity, organized disunity, for the modern state was being born. Loyalty to humanity was to become secondary to a political loyalty, or a cultural loyalty. And the learning that gave such hope to St. Francis produced all sorts of scholars — but that same intellectual energy produced gunpowder, accurate artillery and other means of destruction. The ships that carried missionaries out to India and China and Africa on their unifying missions carried as well European rivalries, which no less infected the missionaries. They became Spanish or French or Portuguese missionaries rather than merely Christian. So the hope for unity through the search for and acceptance of truth was shot through with disunity.

But the learning continued, and in many Christians, a hope for unity. The learning of George Fox's time was becoming less dominated by theology. It was the time of Isaac Newton too, and from Newton's law of gravity evolved the hope that in all of nature there were laws, inherent and immutable, which governed the material universe. Then if this be true, said the lawyers and politicians and philosophers, are there not equally laws of nature that govern human behaviour and human governance. It was not hard for Quakers to get involved in this kind of thinking, for we saw in the Inner Light a constant that was akin to the natural laws of the scientists. A hundred years after Fox began preaching, Quakers and others were asking aloud this question "by what law of nature does one person set himself up as the owner of another?" Here was unity at last — all humanity equal in the sight of God, and of other human beings. Quakers led this movement in England, and they had strong influence in France. Pennsylvania was viewed as the model society because of its acceptance of this principle of human equality. Paul's letter to the Corinthians was not outmoded: "slaves or free, all were made to drink of one spirit." There were to be no slaves, otherwise Paul was correct.

So unity was decreed by natural law. It found its way gradually into Civil law, and quibblers with the principle are now becoming rare. But still we have no unity, no peace. What went wrong this time? Again there was an enemy within. The very knowledge which revealed nature's laws enabled us to unlock the earth's treasures, giving us an industrial revolution whereby the accumulation of goods and thereby of wealth became possible for a greater number of people in western Europe. The scramble was on for the control of the earth, for the things that were in it. Knowledge of the natural laws — call it science — could not be contained, nor could the idea of unity through equality, so the struggle for the earth's goods became world-wide. We all wanted more than our share.

And that, Friends, is the essence of our disunity now. This is where we are in 1980, trying to talk about peace while we are scrambling for the diminishing supply of the world's goods — and using a vast amount of what we are gathering up to threaten each other with. Such peace as we have is based on a balance of fear. And fear is the opposite of peace.

Where then is the hope for unity which I have described as the essence of peace? One might try again to preach with Paul's words "by one spirit we are baptized into one body." And it might have effect among committed Christians. But the world is not Christian. St. Francis would say the message must be in a language the non-Christian can understand. It must encompass concepts basic to other beliefs if it is to gather them with us in unity. And in an age that is heir to 300 years of Newtonian and post Newtonian science, the message of unity must have something of science about it. In my view the unifying message is not very complicated in concept, but it could work. It is simply this. The earth is the only home humanity will ever have. It is *equally* home to *all* of us who live on it. This is a *unity more fundamental even* than belief in God the creator, for the most ardent non-believer in God must believe in the earth as the source of our living. The earth's material nature is undeniable, but that does not lead away from God. No more than the secular learning of St. Francis led him away from God's purpose. But the earth is not just our physical home. Its spiritual nature and value are evident to anyone who searches the earth for such values. For me a colony of bees is a greater wonder by far than Paul's letter to the Corinthians.

May I suggest that Quaker God-centeredness could be achieved through earth-centeredness. Our concern for the poor of the world, and for the spiritual hunger of many of the rich, will be best served through a right sharing of the earth's goods, and by increasing those goods through care of the earth. Could not the John Woolman of our own time, or the William Wilberforce of this new search for unity teach that human dignity is to be found in a more simple and earth-saving and earth-nurturing life style than most of us now practice.

Mother earth has a vast family to feed and clothe and house — and a tremendous distribution problem, hampered above all by human greed.

Quakers could be leaders in solving these problems, just as we were in setting a part of that family free. We would, I believe, be more than ecologists and environmentalists. We would, I am sure, be seekers of the spirit, reaching for the still small voice of God in the earth, the mother of us all. This, I believe, is the direction of peacemakers.

China Journal

INTRODUCTION BY CURT ROY

In the spring of 1982, I had the privilege of traveling to China with Jack Parker. We were with thirty-six Minnesotans in a group organized by the Minnesota Historical Society.

Jack Parker and I were seat mates on the long flight across the Pacific. The seating was cramped and there was a definite shortage of leg space. My petite wife curled up in the seat next to the window, and was soon asleep. But Jack and I chatted through much of the flight.

I was only casually acquainted with Jack Parker before the flight. I was president of the Minnesota Historical Society at the time, and Jack was a member of our Board, but I did not know him well. I learned about his deep interest in China as we flew west.

Jack Parker has a special interest in Matteo Ricci and the other Jesuit missionaries who were in China in the sixteenth and seventeenth centuries. The James Ford Bell Library has a rich collection of the writings of these Jesuits. Jack has given an important lecture at the Boston Public Library in which he described these Jesuit writings as "Windows into China." In his *Journal*, Jack tells of his efforts to find the tomb of Matteo Ricci, and of his satisfaction in finding the site of Ricci's church in Beijing.

Visiting China was a wonderful experience for our entire group. Beijing is a fascinating blend of the old and the new. We saw the Temple of Heaven, Forbidden City, Ming Tombs and the Great Wall. But we also saw crowds of people in blue Mao jackets, vast numbers of bicycles, the mausoleum of Chairman Mao, and the monument in the center of Tiananmen Square. Little did we realize that this square and this monument would be the focal point of the student demonstration in the spring of 1989.

Our visits to Xian, Shanghai, Guilin and Guangzhou (Canton) were wonderful. Jack Parker describes them so well in his *Journal*. When our time in China was ending, we all found it hard to leave. We had seen interesting places, and had experienced the warmth and friendliness of the people. We had grown to be very fond of our guides, and we were distressed that they would not accept even the smallest of gifts as expressions of affection and appreciation.

The *China Journal* is vintage Jack Parker. It is the beautifully phrased writing of a man of letters. Jack describes the places we visited and the things we saw. More than that, it is a very personal account in that he reveals his thoughts and impressions during this very special journey. Jack Parker's *China Journal* is a joy to read. I commend it to you.

MARCH 29–30.

Our giant kite carried us westward in the morning, hastened along by our sun powered shadow that fled across the brown earth of Nebraska, leaped crazily through Colorado's mountains, invited our gaze upon the desert's reds and browns, and then joined us on the man-made green of southern California. In the L.A. airport we fumbled for signs of friendship we might display to each other, most of us still strangers. We shared bits of conversation over coffee, cared for each other's hand baggage to permit nervous little time-wasting shopping trips. Then the shadow took us northward in the late afternoon sun. Fluffy clouds did not hide the Golden Gate, and further north they parted to reveal the rough edge of North America where it splintered and shattered itself upon the ocean. White and gray was our shadow's path along the Alaska coast. And out to sea the Arctic ice-field came down to protect the Aleutian Islands, scattered there like seeds of rock from the pocket of an absent-minded God. Now our shadow released us as the sun sank red and orange in some remote province of Siberia. We coasted through the dark until a vast birthday cake of light invited us down to earth. Bodies out of tune with place and time tried to rejoice in their exhaustion as they settled upon crisp Japanese bedding. But they slept fitfully, pillowed on an unfamiliar meridian.

MARCH 31.

The restorative power of even a disturbed sleep is awesome. From grumpiness we have passed through neutrality of spirit into a state of enthusiasm for the day. Breakfast unites east and west and we have made Tokyo's meridian our own. Aloft once more, we watch our shadow take us across the Sea of Japan, and across the China coast, over the Yellow River. We are in China. From my earliest geography texts I am remembering the vastness of the population. From everything I have read since I conjure teeming millions down there. We land at Beijing. From the window I scan the horizon and see no multitudes. One lone bicyclist in the distance rides into view like an ant on a windowsill across the room. We disembark into an airport building that is like a courthouse on a Saturday afternoon — a few guards, no passengers but ourselves. Baggage is sorted out, money is exchanged at a bustling little desk where abacus beads rattle out computations alongside the silent tools of Texas Instruments.

It is a long ride into Beijing, and now the multitudes emerge — gangs of workers by the roadside, in fields, in orchards, at building projects. Everywhere it seems there is building construction — endless rows of apartments. Our local guide, Mr. Chien, grinds out statistics from his station at the front of the bus: education, bicycles, per capita income, television sets, and we are not listening. We are feeling where we are now, in a totally different society. People pull carts by hand here. They dig ditches with shovels — thousands of them. There are horsedrawn carts full of bricks. The air is full of dust.

In the city the pace quickens, but we slow down and begin to become tourists. The Temple of Heaven is between the airport and our hotel. Mr. Chien's plan for a nice orderly tour under his expert guidance is destroyed at once by thirty-six Minnesotans and their cameras scattering in as many directions in the sunlit temple grounds. Here the emperors just after 1400 built this temple to worship in and to pray, especially for good harvests. Round at the north end and square at the south, the temple grounds spoke of Chinese cosmography — a round heaven, a square earth. The main building is wooden, some 120 feet in height, and brilliantly colored, a photographer's feast. Now it is 5:00 p.m. and we start for our hotel amidst streets alive with bicycles. The riders are dressed in blue. They move like rivers of very orderly humanity, all at about the same speed. How often we note in this first viewing of "the Chinese masses" their apparent good health, their general cleanliness. How very American we are away from home! Dinner is quite splendid, our hotel room a bit dowdy, a Russian built thing from the fifties, a vast complex that reminds us of a college campus. Our baggage arrives, we unpack, for nine hours we sleep in this immensely quiet place.

APRIL 1.

We are like a troop of scouts full of eagerness this morning as we start out our first day in Peking (Beijing). It is cool and cloudy as we get into the bus.

We have become more familiar with each other, but our remaining indecisiveness is quickly minimized as we attend to Mr. Chien's morning propaganda chore. He starts us off with a message about China's progress in recent years as we head for the "Mausoleum of Chairman Mao." In the vast square so often pictured in recent years we unload and take our place near the head of a seemingly endless line of people, four abreast, moving slowly through and out of the mausoleum. We are cautioned not to speak or to take pictures. We move up the steps in silence. I am in the last row of our group. Behind me are what seem to be miles of silent Chinese. We enter the mausoleum through a great hall whose wall is covered with a tapestry of needlepoint, a rural Chinese scene. It must be fifty feet long. We move now in columns of two to the interior room where the body of Mao lies in its crystal casket. An overpowering silence fills the room. Our footsteps are drowned in carpet. We walk, we look, we walk on, out of the room, out of doors, down the steps. No one speaks until we are in the square. Is it a religious experience or an irreligious one? Does any human being deserve this reverence? Must we have someone to revere? Mao led a revolution. He wrote classical poetry. He personified a nation's needs. He made mistakes and has been forgiven. How long will the reverence last, how long will be the line of Chinese filing past before it stops?

The square is full of sunlight now and children and conversation, and photographers. And people shuffling slowly in that endless line to the mausoleum. Across the square from the mausoleum is the Museum of Chinese History, and to this we repaired, already inspired by modern China's spirit. The museum is well done within the obvious limits of a frugal society. Little beyond the objects on display is needed to make the point of great antiquity, great beauty, or importance. Here are cannon cast by Jesuits in the seventeenth century. Here are early Chinese books and scrolls, scientific instruments, and many artifacts from archaeological digs of the past thirty years. A political flavor comes through in the explanations of the guides. There is an extolling of rebel leaders of peasants (and of course we recall some American Revolutionists who were "embattled farmers"). The museum tires out some tender feet, and for half an hour I sit on the steps outdoors and let the people be my museum. How similar their uniforms — not just similar, same. Yet look closely at their faces. How different each is from all the others. This fragment of 900 million, each carrying a different light in the eyes. How humbling to think that I am one of them, one of so vast a human family, which today is what I am.

The tired feet are bussed to a downtown hotel for lunch. New foods include some unusual pears from the Peking area. This is early spring. How was last year's crop so nicely preserved? I didn't find out. After lunch there is some free time. How free? We all wondered at first. We roamed the streets and alleys with cameras, encountered a shoemaker plying his trade. We were waved at by passing cyclists. We "read" billboards, we watched traffic, bought stamps in the hotel, did some shopping. We boarded the bus having broken whatever restraint barriers we had built for ourselves in our minds.

The afternoon took us on a tour of Peking's air raid shelters, a strange performance, largely political I think but demonstrating the preparedness of the city for a Russian attack. Also, for me it was a demonstration of the massive capabilities of the Chinese to move great quantities of earth by hand. The whole city seems to have been rebuilt underground. But business is alive and well in the bowels of the earth below this communist capital. We had tea in a gift shop full of lovely things to buy, placed there for the likes of us.

After dinner we went to a French ballet, "Sylvia," with a Chinese cast. Nice performance, but some of us dozed. It had been a very busy day.

APRIL 2.

This is the day of the Great Wall. It begins with Mr. Chien singing the *Internationale* as part of our morning propaganda exercise, an offense to some of our group, but no one made any overt objection. As our bus moves out through Peking's suburbs into semi-agricultural country, Mr. Chien gives us some views of communes and life therein, which he experienced as part of his re-training and correcting of his former opinions. He makes quite a lot of the fact that each farmer on the commune now has a private plot of land which he is free to cultivate according to his own wishes. This, says Mr. Chien, has improved food supplies remark-ably and is making the farmers "a lot of money". We are being propagandized to be sure, but we are also seeing a lot of food production, and in Mr. Chien's defense let it be noted he does not criticize anyone else's economy, only the system that existed dur-ing the reign of the "gang of four" in China.

It is about forty miles out to the Wall, an interesting trip in its own right for its demonstration of land use. Up in the high lands the most desolate soil gets picked clean of rocks, and patches of garden emerge. Orchards cling to the sides of hills, only a few trees at a time. People are literally hacking out an existence on these mountain slopes. Every field has its pile of manure being spread by hand. All field work in the uplands seems to be done by hand. We did meet a lot of tractors on the road, and other kinds of farm vehicles. Trucks are numerous, but many horse-drawn carts as well. But almost no cars. There are no private cars in China.

The Great Wall is well named. Nothing made by human hands is more impressive in my experience. The Pyramids of Egypt did less for me. They are like monuments to a historical experience. The Wall is the historical experience. We see it creeping over the hills and mountains before we get to the vantage point chosen for us. It is far off to the right. Then it walks over a mountain to the left. And then we are on it, looking off into the mountains and valleys, and we marvel that it was built by people who merely knew how to move pieces of the earth by hand, forced to do so by rulers who were inspired by fear of invasion. One might weep for the volume of human labor so expended in these bleak moun-tains, but we do not. With the brisk wind in our faces we walk in the spring sunlight and I wish only that I could do it alone, at sunrise, feeling the wildness of the land about me, standing sen-tinel with those rocks for a moment of their eternal existence. We boast a little about how far we walked up the steep incline. And we are humble at the thought of those who walked there carrying rocks to build it. As the bus carried us down the mountain again, we found ourselves looking right, left, and upward for one more glance at the piece of the Wall marching across a mountain.

The return trip to Peking took us by way of the Ming Tombs. We came to a broad ravine surrounded by moderate hills, high enough to be a barrier against evil spirits. Here the third Ming emperor, Yong Le, determined to be buried, and twelve others of the dynasty followed him to their separate tombs in this peaceful countryside. One tomb has been excavated fully, that of Wan Li (1573–1620). While pondering the wealth that went into the tomb along with his mortal remains, I was equally impressed with the sheer effort of removing such quantities of earth for this and the other twelve tombs. Was there hate or love in the hearts of those earth movers as they built this place of peace for their emperors? Did they revere their leaders as Mao is revered? To bring us to this valley of tombs a Sacred Way was built, a broad avenue four miles long, lined on either side with white marble statues of immense size. Were they carved there or were they moved there? It does not matter. The stone came from somewhere else. The mind falters at contemplating moving the uncarved stone or statues by hand or animal power.

We return to Peking overcome with impressions of some past spirit and technology that built a Wall, dug mammoth tombs, erected immense statues. Someone among us in dismay at the current state of China said "What have they been doing these last hundred years?" There was no response. We were contemplating what they had been doing four hundred or two thousand years ago.

APRIL 3.

What a beautiful spring day for a stroll in the park, and that is what we did, joining some ten thousand Chinese vacationers in the grounds of the Summer Palace. Begun in the twelfth century as an escape for the royal family from the oppressive atmosphere of the city, the grounds of the Summer Palace are now a public park, containing some 600 acres of which two-thirds of the area is a lake. To Minneapolitans it was much like Lake Nokomis on the Fourth of July — or Como Park to the St. Paul traveler — with children running about eating popsicles and cotton candy, old folks sitting in the sun, young couples boating on the lake. It is a good atmosphere to experience, an island of relaxation in this earnest and puritanical society.

The buildings in the park are impressive for their size and antiquated opulence. Most of us made it to the top of Longevity

Hill — 240 steps — to view the scenery. We walked through a brilliantly decorated passageway for more than 7,000 feet, every inch
of the ceiling painted with birds, dragons, and other traditional
figures. At the lakeshore we admired — or at least wondered at — a
marble boat built by a nineteenth century empress who stole the
money from the navy to do it. We had lunch in a truly elegant
restaurant, and then went for a boat ride on the lake, a real tour-
ist crowd, enjoying it all.

But then it was back to work. From the People's Park we were
bussed to a People's Commune where a very different spirit
prevailed. Now we became a delegation being lectured on
production methods, education, health care, the arts and what
not, in a suburban food factory. We inspected the duck yards
where Peking duck is on the hoof by the thousands. We were in
and out of greenhouses, warm and lush with tomatoes, cucum-
bers, squash, in all stages of growth. I was impressed with the
quantity of vegetables being grown this first week in April in the
latitude of Philadelphia. We visited houses — "go into any house
you choose" says Mr. Chien. The dwellings are small and quite
neat, and they are obviously on display regularly, but not to the
point of denying some of the realities of life, like pigs and chickens
very near the door.

From home to school was a natural progression, and the neighborhood kindergarten did what it was supposed to do, charmed
us with beautiful children doing their songs and games for our benefit. We commented on the individuality of dress among these
little folks, so entirely in contrast to the uniformity of their parents on the farm. The commune also has a hospital, and we
visited that, walking up and down the halls with complete freedom. The halls were not models of cleanliness, but in general it
seemed an adequate sort of health care center for local everyday
medical problems. The serious illnesses we were told were treated
in the city.

In our walking about we saw a lot of gardener-farmer types.
They did not seem to us very energetic workers, but what they
were producing was impressive. We had tea with the managers
of the commune, and our questions tended to center on the unproductive individual or the creative genius in this communal situation. The answer seemed to be that people who contribute the

most are best cared for, but with definite upper limits to the re-
wards. We were shown works of art by local people, a demonstration of what we all know, that rice and vegetables are not enough
to sustain human aspirations.

What an evening we had. It was the night of the Peking Duck
Dinner, the social pinnacle of our Peking visit. It coincided with
two birthdays in our group, and our Chinese hosts rose to the occasion with birthday cakes after an immense dinner. There were
toasts to enduring friendship between the American and Chinese
peoples. A very memorable banquet.

APRIL 4.

This was Palm Sunday. It fulfilled one of my primary objec-
tives in going to China. My ultimate goal on this trip was to visit
the tomb of Father Matteo Ricci who was really the founder of
modern Chinese missions in China, serving there from 1583 until
his death in 1610. So great was his influence even with the emperor, that Ricci was given a tomb to be buried in just outside the
city of Peking. Every day since my arrival here I had been asking
guides, checking guidebooks, seeking wherever possible for information on the location of Ricci's grave. No one knew anything
about Ricci, it seemed, which says something about the slight current influence of Christianity in China. But the Christian church
is alive and functioning as was demonstrated this Palm Sunday
when we were taken to a Roman Catholic Church where a worship service was taking place—a Chinese priest saying Mass in
Latin. It is an early twentieth century church, and it was not
filled, but there was a respectable congregation. Outside people
chatted in the sunshine in normal Sunday morning fashion.
Someone in our group got into conversation with a Chinese Christian lady—a nun possibly—who knew about Father Ricci, and
soon I was in the conversation. Ricci's tomb was elsewhere, and
required a special government permission to visit, but she said we
were standing on the site of his church. For me that was good
enough—to have spent a little bit of Palm Sunday on the home
ground of my Jesuit heroes, to have sat in worship there was a
meaningful link with that "Generation of Giants" who served
there, beginning four hundred years ago.

The Forbidden City had a similar effect. The magnitude and

opulence of it are overwhelming. Its name is sinister. It was indeed forbidden to all but the ruling few. But through it all to me came the personage of Matteo Ricci, going about the courtyards and rooms repairing clocks and other mechanical gadgets for the emperor. What a victory he must have felt in these surroundings, at the pinnacle of power in this rich and populous country. Did he know that his colleagues in North America were struggling to survive in barren deserts, or beginning to pitch tents in the forests of eastern Canada?

It came time to leave Peking. Nearly every flight bag had a little twig protruding as we trooped into the airport. These were our "palms" from Father Ricci's churchyard. We said goodbye to Mr. Chien. He choked up a bit when he made his little farewell speech, and some of us did too. We applauded spontaneously his wish for friendship between our countries. We had not always appreciated his propaganda, but his spirit was magnificent. He had insisted we learn to count to ten in Chinese, and every morning we had a review. Our efforts were rewarded with his flights into English-American jargon: "Are we bright eyed and bushy-tailed this morning?"

We flew to Xian and arrived in the dark. From our bus we saw little gatherings of people in the streets, sitting around small fires playing checkers or just talking. We came to our hotel — new and sort of flashy, but lacking in some of the amenities, like chests of drawers, and sometimes the elevators and toilets didn't work. But never a more courteous reception.

APRIL 5.

Xian is a sprawling metropolis in farm country — the Chinese midwest. Some two and a half million of us are here in this former and intermittent capital of China, serving in that capacity off and on from the 11th century B.C. to the 10th century A.D. This was once the terminal point of the trans-Asian silk road, and in the 9th century it was the biggest city in the world with some eight million people. Now it is acquiring new fame, a rich archaeological find, the Qin Shi Huang Tomb. This is the mausoleum of the first Qin emperor. He ruled from 221 to 206 B.C. In 1971 it was discovered that a hill outside of Xian contained a vast retinue of terra cotta figures: soldiers, officials, horses, etc., life-sized and life-like, possibly 9,000 of them. The excavation is now in progress, revealing row upon row of these figures, their uniforms stylized according to function and rank, but their faces are very human indeed. Eleven of them have been taken out and placed in a museum on the grounds. Their humanness drew me to them and it was difficult to leave the room. I went back again and again, feeling that if I stayed long enough they would speak to me and I to them. Here is a place to reflect upon all that life has been in China and elsewhere, for these are not only Chinese standing there larger than life. They are all of us in all time: wise, dour, happy, determined, wistful. One becomes humble in their presence, weak might be a better word, insignificant for my brief span of years, yet gratified and almost joyous that their lives and mine had come together.

Another outstanding archaeological dig in Xian is the Banpo site, an excavation revealing a people and their civilization of some 6,000 years ago. Details of housing, cooking implements, community life, and agriculture are impressive. But what is really impressive currently is the modern Chinese state for which such historical work has a fairly high priority. Do we understand their mentality, the need for the past as an accompaniment to the present with its drastic changes?

In the evening we went to the opera, a traditional art form which was magnificent in its color and flamboyance, even if the story line was not always apparent. It was a very impressive day.

APRIL 6.

A good day in the country mostly. Every mile is a revelation, every human being along the way a cause for reflection. How much individualism remains in the individual who is part of a collective? How much was there before the collective was organized? Do they ever think about it? They have not heard of the Magna Carta or the Declaration of Independence. What is their view of us? Two hours of such thoughts from a bus took us to the Quian tomb area, and past dozens of little decorated mounds of earth in the fields — small tombs for the tillers of those fields who have recently died. The giant tomb and the surrounding statues are eloquent Chinese expressions of royal death. Mao's mausoleum is making more sense day by day. But from these hilltop tombs is to be seen a more eloquent expression of the earth and its relation to life. Magnificent terraces grace the steep hillside hundreds of feet down into the valley. Here the land is made to grow the food to sustain these hundreds of millions of people. And both coming and going this day we traveled through countryside that has been cultivated for some 5,000 years, and still is one of China's most productive areas.

The future and the past live together easily on the land: tractors in some fields, oxen in others. On the roads large sturdy trucks haul produce, but not alone. Horse carts, bicycles, hand-drawn carts compete for space too. A delightful impromptu stop at a country crossroad put us in the middle of a farmers' market where grain and cotton were the market staples, but there were pastries, and fowl and cloth goods as well. An immense good humor prevailed among us all as we exchanged money, goods, smiles, and inquiries. We were on display as much as were the Chinese farmers. I wonder how long they will remember it, and what it means to them.

Back in town we visited a mosque. The Moslems came here and began building in 742, about the same time they spread through Spain into France. Such was its expansion in the first century after the life of Mohammed. There are bits of Arabic script here and there in the mosque, but the place is thoroughly Chinese. The Chinese must simply have absorbed the movement and made it Chinese.

To and from the mosque took us on foot through narrow streets and alleys that enabled us to get the feel of very crowded living conditions. There were food vendors along the way, small shops, and children playing in the streets, one of them with a kite far up in the air, an achievement beyond my understanding in so crowded a place.

APRIL 7.

Time is flying. Our trip is more than half over and my head spins with things to think about. Change in flight plans (a common occurrence in China) gives us an extra half-day in Xian and it was a great one. A historical museum presented us with examples of very early pottery and other artifacts, and most interestingly, the "forest of stelae," a group of fine stone tablets six or seven feet tall, arranged around a room in impressive display. These are from the 700–900 A.D. period and contain important historical and religious texts, some of them pertaining to Nestorian Christians who were in Xian at that time. This was the place to which ancient scholars must return to assure the exactness of the texts they were studying, for these texts were copied and re-copied for study elsewhere. Now rubbings are being made of some of them, especially those of artistic interest. We watched a museum worker copying a magnificient peacock design, and listening was almost as good as watching. He patted his inking pad on the paper which had been moistened to hold it to the stone. It was a soft sound — pat-pat-pat-pat. And then he would go back to the inking board for more ink, and a stronger sound was heard — PAT-PAT-PAT-PAT. As the sequence was repeated again and again without interruption, a beautiful rhythmic pattern sounded throughout the room.

In the afternoon we visited the Wild Goose Pagoda, a tower 240 feet high which in earlier times was the place where important Buddhist texts were kept. Here again the scholars of that religion must return to verify the accuracy of the texts which circulated among them. These places are the evidence of Xian's earlier pre-eminence as the intellectual as well as the political capital of China. What a picture it presents: scholars, aged, bearded, in robes and caps according to their station, convening here at Xian as they might now at the British Museum, studying, talking, exchanging news and ideas here at the end of the silk route which pointed westward beyond the knowledge of any of them into lands of conjecture from which merchants and traders brought in what was known.

And what is of the past continues in other ways. The art of cloisonné was shown to us in a small factory. Young women sat at long workbenches placing tiny pieces of copper on the smooth surface of bowls and other objects, filling in the figures with a colored substance in exquisite detail, an art form that came over the silk route from Persia. These young women do not wear glasses. I asked why. There were giggles, and then the explanation: glasses would spoil their appearance. And why no young men at the workbenches? I was told men had no patience for such work. But nearby stood an old man reproducing ancient scrolls. I stood with him for awhile. Standing very straight with one foot forward, his brush almost perpendicular, he bent slightly at the waist and made his marks with great dignity and care. What a noble stance, this orator, making words with a brush.

And then Xian fell below us and out of sight in the dusk as we set our course for the world's largest city, Shanghai.

APRIL 8.

One day only in the world's largest city. Not enough, certainly, but this one day in Shanghai, even one hour of it, provided sights and feelings unique to my experience. The world is full of harbors, arteries of life to any commercial nation, full of the heartbeat of business. But to stand before Shanghai's harbor is to feel the pulse of the middle of the world — and in the middle of time. Great ships, new and old, tugs, junks, ferries, anything that can stay afloat is here. Didn't I see this picture fifty years ago in a geography book or an encyclopedia? And the movement in the harbor is matched by the activity on the sidewalks and streets. Eleven and a half million people are hauling, carrying, walking, biking up and down the famous "Bund," hauling carpets, wood, vegetables, carcasses of butchered animals, people on the way to work, soldiers. And in the midst of it all in a small clearing four older men silently do their morning exercises in perfect unity, contrasting their artistic movement and harmony with the jumble of activity around them. A small child imitates their motions, absorbed in their mood — as if making a choice between harmony and its alternative.

From this bustling, muscular harbor we go to a Buddhist temple, by way of busy but orderly streets. There is a bit of New York or Paris in this atmosphere. But the big city sophistication is dampened this sunny morning with laundry hanging out from almost every building. The Buddhists are having a religious festival, an Easter of sorts, perhaps. The mood is at once festive and worshipful. Tables are piled high with fruit for the priests. Worshippers stand in front of one Buddha or another in prayerful attitudes. Some stand before pictures of deceased family members, in prayer. This is the China we remember from things we read many years ago. It was embarrassing to intrude upon these people, but even among the worshippers there was a festive mood, a holiday time. Most of the devout ones seemed to be middle aged or older. Perhaps it will continue that way, as the younger ones become middle aged or older.

The afternoon took us to a magnificent museum: three floors of bronzes, pottery, and painting from the most ancient times to about 1700. There is a breath-taking beauty in the forms of the early bronze and pottery. It is possible to accept the calm confidence of these people in their future when it is seen as an extension of such an impressive and far-reaching past. The effect of any one piece perfectly preserved was powerful in its ability to diminish the present into a moment of insignificance. And yet the significance of the present is not lost in such places as the industrial exhibition which we visited, a vast display of Chinese manufactures of all kinds — paint, glass, television sets, bicycles, pollution monitoring equipment, cloth — the stuff of modern society.

The evening entertainment was the famed acrobatic performance, an incredible display of great skill and dexterity. We stopped at a tired old night-club, a hangover from the days of French control of this part of Shanghai earlier in this century. We pack late at night for an early departure. Our one day in Shanghai is ended. What a small sample of this vast city. But what impressions it has made. I cannot sleep for feeling the excitement of being where I am.

APRIL 9.

Flying to Kweilin has more excitement about it than most flights. We know what to look for: mountains. Those distinct, once-in-the-world mountains that have brought artists here for centuries. And they are the primary reason we are on our way to Kweilin today. The clouds part, and we slip down through them. There are the mountains, fingerlike, jagged, reaching up from the rice fields to capture us. Of course they succeed. On the ground a photographer-type squints at them and remarks, "they are out of focus." Indeed they are hard to bring into the realm of reality. From my hotel window I look across the river to a mountain with a great hole through it, perhaps three hundred feet above the ground. There is a gentle beauty about this quiet yet busy town. It is Lucerne or Como — a place to meditate, possibly in a small pagoda at the very top of a mountain.

But this is not just a place to think. Kweilin is a busy town, full of enterprising people selling things along the riverfront by our hotel. We are quite far south and the people are of smaller stature, friendly and enterprising. The open-air shops are full of a vast array of goods—jewelry, porcelain, scrolls, cloth. Some strange animals, fox-like, and salamanders of great size were for sale also, in front of an eating establishment. We bought some local wine and some crunchy, popcorn-like eatables, and gave ourselves a scenic happy hour in the evening.

More than mountains captured our attention. A most memorable sight was a young man between the shafts of a cart loaded with wood on the road from the airport. At a stop light we stopped and he stopped, he put down the shafts of the cart and took from his pocket a transistor radio, leaned against his ancient-type vehicle and held his radio to his ear while waiting for the light to change. No sight better illustrated ancient and modern China's technologies in congenial co-existence.

The afternoon tour took us to an art gallery, a sort of open-air building with interesting displays by modern Chinese artists, some of whom were present and selling their paintings. Some of us had trouble looking at things indoors when the outdoors was so remarkable. And the gallery was along the river where some women were washing clothes, while others were washing vegetables for the market. All very picturesque if a bit unsanitary. We went to a kindergarten, a beautiful show but a bit overdone. The children were talented and were programmed to be crowd-pleasers. There are no better propagandists than kids. But even better for me were the free-enterprising ones who sold whirligigs outside the hotel.

We walked the dark streets after dinner. We shopped, we talked, we felt the soft atmosphere of the river and the mountains. We watched the moon bounce off the water and thought of peace, remembering that this town was destroyed in World War II. I cannot imagine a war here on such a night. There should be no suffering in this town.

APRIL 10, the day of the boat ride.

A boat ride all by itself is an attractive experience usually. People get into boats all over the world to feel the thrill of the element that belonged to us in an earlier stage of our evolution. And there is something special about looking at land — our element — from the unobstructed surface of water. These thoughts always go through my mind when I get into a boat. But at Kweilin it was different. We went aboard at 8:30 in the morning in a haze that was almost a mist until the sun burned its way through. The Li River was our route southward for about six hours, all of it through these limestone mountains that rose up around us in all directions. Except for our river we were surrounded by this moonscape. The inadequacy of words to describe the scene has been apparent for centuries, for this is the laboratory and the temple of Chinese painters. The cameras in our group worked overtime. Without a camera I struggled to get the picture in my mind, a picture of the relationship between river, mountains, people, land. Between mountains the water buffalo and his driver made the land a field, green and bountiful. Where the mountain relented for a moment there was a garden. On the river people moved easily on their small boats, hauling produce; or on rafts — simply five bamboo poles lashed together and turned up slightly at the ends — fishing, hauling, simply getting from place to place. The people of these mountains went about their work: quiet, busy, neat, seemingly industrious in whatever they were doing. The river and the mountains and the land sustain them, and they give life to a moonscape that might otherwise be frightening in its beauty.

The return to Kweilin was by bus, and this too was a rewarding trip, through a valley of wall-to-wall rice paddies. We stopped in the country and drew a large crowd of farmers, while a farmer and his water buffalo drew a large crowd of photographers. Our hosts on that road were pleasant country folk, different in appearance from the country people of Xian, darker skinned, shorter in stature, probably more jovial. Also, the people of this region are more business minded in general. Merchants in the shops are not above a little dealing on the price. We are not far from Canton, where the European merchants were allowed to trade four hundred years ago. It was said trade was possible here because it was a long way from Peking's authorities and tax collectors.

In the evening we went to a concert. Western music was presented by a traveling group from Peking. Their presence had nothing to do with our being there, for they would perform for two weeks or so and then another group would move in. The performers and the stage were plainly but well dressed. There was no Steinway, only an upright piano. The final performers of the evening were a sort of barbershop quartet and they got the same response such performers would get here from a public performance. Apparently the regime here makes an effort to get "culture" into the hinterland. Kweilin gives us the feeling that the system is producing in this area a fairly satisfactory way of life. We leave tomorrow, but Kweilin will follow us.

APRIL 11 — Easter Sunday.

This will be our last full day in China. There were jelly-beans at our places at breakfast — the doings of some thoughtful Minnesotans among us, and much appreciated. What did our hosts think of these venerable Americans screaming in delight over bits of brightly colored candy? Maybe it made as much sense as our normal morning passion for coffee. Our Easter morning parade was a "hike" as our guide called it — but really a climb. Most of us accomplished the 340 steps to the top of one of Kweilin's mountains. We looked down on the town and its river, a dream-like scene, with fishermen standing motionless on their long bamboo rafts, the fisherman, his shadow, the raft making an appropriate Easter cross in the water. Did we not all struggle for a line of poetry, a great thought, something creative to make those moments memorable — but the peace on that mountain was more profound than anything we could say about it.

Another kind of peace was down below. Near a tea house where we rested our legs was a Buddhist grotto, and behind it was a most memorable poor man's mens' club. Old timers sat and talked, played cards or checkers, snoozed in the spring sun with their mouths open, a precious place possibly undetected by our camera people. Across the street an orderly row of people crouched on the sidewalk, selling fruit. This cannot be a bad place to live.

Some free time after lunch took me to the nearby business street of open storefronts for a final shopping spree — the purchase of a Mao jacket, to the considerable delight of some youthful bystanders and two charming clerks armed with mirrors and more persuasion than was necessary. The size was right, the price, $3.79, the experience worth far more. At a nearby art gallery the young lady proprietor asked "can you help me?" I thought she had the clerk-client relationship reversed, but she did indeed want my help—with her English lesson-book. We sat down together for half an hour and had a lesson. "The station is to the right, the cinema is to the left, the restaurant will open at noon." The hardest word for this young lady was "restaurant."

Then down the street to a book store (I had been in several in other cities). Here a sale was going on, crowded with young people. The books, all in Chinese, ranged from poetry to how-to-do-it titles, all being taken very seriously, it seemed, by the clientele. This is indeed a civilized town to get out such a crowd for a book sale.

The afternoon tour took us to a magnificent cave, full of strange rock formations, the outcome of millions of years of water and limestone. Then one more walk, a quiet stroll around a lake, a time for thinking about where we have been and what we have seen. And then the mountains and the river were gone in the dark and the distance and we were in Canton, for a night only, in a modern, noisy hotel, made no more quiet by our own cocktail party in the hall. The jelly-beans at breakfast seemed so far away, and so too the mountains and the peaceful river with its Easter morning crosses.

APRIL 12. Canton to Hong Kong.

Canton was an early morning trip from the hotel to the railway station. Up at five, breakfast at six, to the station shortly thereafter. On the bus our guide through the entire trip, Mrs. Shiu, made her brave little goodbye speech. We all choked up a little, and so did she, for in the two weeks we had been together we had become her family, and she had become one of us. She wanted to sing a few more American songs, like "I've been working on the railroad", and she wanted to pack one more American slang expression into her vocabulary. She spoke of China's situation, its development, its recent progress. She knew the difference between its technology and ours, but there were no apologies. She was a beautiful person, a good teacher and companion.

The train ride to Hong Kong was supposed to be two hours but was four, and in a crowded train. One could avoid the crowd best by looking out the window. The view was quiet rice paddies, with ducks everywhere. Water buffalo and people worked together to do what China must do, feed a billion people every day of the year. We worried together about going through customs as we fingered our receipts for money changed and goods purchased — all recorded in Chinese, of course. But customs was a breeze. We walked through the famous, oft photographed archway that divides Hong Kong from China, and then we stood in the sun with a crowd far too large for the train that was to carry us. The result was inevitable, a real mob scene. In retrospect, we should not have been surprised — a very narrow passage is a customs station and a train between two heavily peopled areas. And maybe the difference in social and economic systems on either side of the passage add to the intensity of the people in the passage. This is one of the fabled bottlenecks of the world.

Two more hours on a most uncomfortable train, now in Her Majesty's colony of Kowloon, and dirty and exhausted we debarked into the most lavish hotel some of us had ever seen. We were back in the West. Outside all was a familiar bustle of cars and street sounds. It was exciting to be back in the hustling world, but how do you compare it with the quiet of a mountaintop, the slow pace of the water buffalo in the orderly patterns of the rice fields. One must rejoice in the variety the earth affords us. In China I found a sense of order and industry at once, a countryside quiet and productive, a people seemingly at peace with each other, looking to a future better and more abundant in basic human physical needs than their past. One may not approve of the sources of that order, or of the methods of organizing the production to meet the needs. But one can be grateful for a place where the future is so visible and the distant past so easily within reach. China's people left me with a strong feeling of affection. I want them to succeed, which does not mean westernizing them. Whatever success is there, it will be Chinese. It is hard to imagine a future there where many people will become rich in goods. There are too many of them. But their past will be rich always.

Old Men, Old Books

An essay written for a book published in 1990
to mark the 60th birthday of Anton Gerits.

INTRODUCTION BY KEN NEBENZAHL

Jack Parker arrived in the endlessly fascinating world of early books, manuscripts and maps a couple of years ahead of me. He came to the field from a different, more logical perspective than I; academia in his case, commerce in mine. We both have had over three decades of pleasure and enrichment from our respective occupations, enjoying mutual good fellowship while serving on "opposite sides of the counter." Jack's curatorial responsibilities include searching for, acquiring and making available to scholars the treasures that comprise the world-renowned Bell Collection. He has, however, made important additional contributions via teaching, sponsoring publications by researchers in the Collection, and by his own writing and editing. Since they were published just twenty-five years ago, Parker's *Books to Build an Empire* along with *Merchants and Scholars*, stand right before Parry, Penrose, Quinn and Rogers in my reference library.

In 1969, Jack and I, together with Tom Adams, then Librarian of the John Carter Brown Library, each read papers to a joint meeting of the Bibliographical Society of America and the Rare Books Section, Association of College and Research Libraries, held at the Historical Society of Pennsylvania. Boies Penrose who was president of the HSP, graciously invited us to a private viewing of his collection of books and manuscripts pertaining to "Travel and Discovery in the Renaissance." Our enthusiasm on seeing these treasures was matched by the gracious exuberance with which they were displayed for us. If "Old Men, Old Books" had included collectors, Jack no doubt would have provided an account of his visit to "Barbados Hill."

Boies Penrose and I had been in correspondence regarding my acquiring the collection, but this did not come about. Later I learned that Penrose, whose prominent Pennsylvania family had come to America from Barbados during the colonial period, had attended Oxford as a young man. He was a lifelong Anglophile who for decades had envisioned the Boies Penrose Sale at Sotheby's. When the sale occurred it was as if he had written a script to be followed by himself and the other players.

An hour before the auction, Mr. Penrose walked around to Sotheby's from his London home at Claridge's, dressed in his chesterfield topcoat. He proceeded to the book room, and shook hands with the customary

gathering of last-minute-viewing-dealers from the UK, the Continent
and the U.S. His greeting seemed to implore, "Now get in there and
fight," which as it turned out is what they proceeded to do, setting
numerous price records. Jack, whom I represented, suggested a flexible
formula enabling us to pass up lots bringing too high a price and to add
additional items desired by the Collection that sold reasonably. In this
way we were able to acquire for the Bell a number of important Penrose
books and manuscripts. Jack's system, and our agency, had produced
similar results at the Streeter sales, later at the Horblitt, and others. But
what a juggling act this required in the fast-moving auctions of London
and New York!

In the following reminiscences Jack writes about his appreciation of
the integrity, scholarship and collegiality he experienced among distinguished European scholarly booksellers encountered early in his career.
It is good to know that such dealers, when they deserve it, are appreciated by scholarly librarians. Some of the people in this section, I
also have had the privilege of knowing. For example, I experienced similar emotions to those Jack describes below when being received by Martinus Nijhoff. I remember in particular, as does Jack, the massive desk of
the gentle giant who headed the distinguished firm founded three centuries earlier by his ancestors. Behind the desk was his personal copy of
Blaeu's great 12-volume atlas in a walnut glass-fronted case into which
"Nijhoff 1666" had been incised. Mr. Nijhoff told me that the atlas had
always lived in that bookcase. As a green rookie bookseller from a much
larger, but much younger town, I was suitably impressed.

Jack describes a Portuguese pamphlet acquired at Nijhoff's on one of
his visits (when he beat me there!). He mentions not having seen another
copy in the three decades since. Miraculously, in Lisbon recently, a copy
of that same rare 1485 account of Portuguese discovery down the African
coast materialized and is now in my care.

Jack's good friend, Dr. Ernst Weil, showed me an unusual object
when I visited him in Hampstead. It was a lodestone suspended from a
ring with brass straps, and two iron posts. It was Dutch, seventeenth
century, and was taken to sea by navigators to keep their compass nee-
dles magnetized. I was so intrigued with this charming instrument that
I began to collect scientific instruments relating to navigation and astronomy. After thirty years of assembling astrolabes, compasses, sun-
dials and hour-glasses, my wife and I placed the collection in the Adler
Planetarium and Astronomical Museum in Chicago. The years of pleasure we had from this pursuit also served to keep me from competing
with my own clients for books, manuscripts and maps. All of this started
by the same elderly gentleman who provided Jack with both important

early rarities for the Bell Collection and an occasional glass of old Madeira.

Hopefully, these preliminary words will convey my affection for Jack, respect for his work, and pleasure in having been fortunate enough to have shared part of his world of rare books.

For young people in any profession there are examples to be followed, models — heroes, perhaps — whose knowledge, technique, and philosophy imprint upon the next generation. In my early years in the rare book profession I was favored with many distinguished mentors to pass along to me something important of themselves, and something of the nobility of traffic in books. In selecting a few of them for this memoire I am reminded of John Ruskin's words from his "Lamp of Memory, No. X" in his *The Seven Lamps of Architecture:*

> Therefore as we build, let us think that we build forever. Let it not be for the present delight, or for present use alone; let it be such work as our descendants will thank us for, and let us think, as we lay stone on stone, that a time is to come when these stones will be held sacred because our hands have touched them, and that men will say as they look upon the labor and wrought substance of them:
> "See! This our fathers did for us."

THE HOUSE OF NIJHOFF

Number nine, Lange Verhout was a formidable address for a young rare-book librarian in 1954, making his first visit to The Hague. The slate-gray exterior, the well-scrubbed doorway, the polished windows displaying bustling workers at their desks all spoke of industry, of the traditional Dutch mercantile energy. It all seemed to conform to the impression made by the Nijhoff catalog which I had seen earlier: massive, with carefully written descriptions inviting no argument. So with the taxi driver left wondering why, I presume, I walked away from the place to which he had delivered me. It was not a retreat, but it seemed one should not arrive a moment early or late at such a well-regulated establishment of the book trade.

Once around the square, slowly, my watch brought me back to the steps at number nine at precisely the appointed hour. It was

Hugo Brant-Corstius who met me and guided me through a tour of all that went on at Nijhoff — new books, serials, Nijhoff publications, a veritable tour of the book distribution industry. But this was mere preface, leading to the office of Mr. Nijhoff himself, the first of many visits which in retrospect all roll up into one. When he rose from behind his massive desk he made it seem a normal size. We shook hands and mine seemed enveloped in his. Impeccably tailored, conservative in gray and blue, shoes brilliantly polished, his presence spoke of affluence and of establishment. There was warmth in the voice speaking English with a slight accent. There was warmth in the eyes behind the shiny glasses. It seemed he looked at me like an approving parent.

The office was spacious, the wood dark, the walls lined with book shelves and it seemed like the books were all folios. In the corner a tower of gold-stamped red morocco rose up from the floor: a twelve-volume Blaeu atlas. Coffee was delivered on request in fine china on a silver tray. The cream for it was thicker than I had seen anywhere else in my travels. Even the sugar cubes seemed oversize. Yet all of this imposing environment did not make me feel diminished. The conversation that went with it, good and serious book talk, rather made me feel like I belonged there. On one visit I was accompanied by my six-year old daughter Jackie. She heard Mr. Nijhoff order the refreshments "twee coffee, een melk," and she knew that she counted as a member of the group.

Mr. Nijhoff did not sell me any books. He rather made me feel that I wanted to buy some from this premiere bookselling establishment, and on some visits I returned to his office at the end of the day, not to enumerate my purchases, but to pay my respects. This is not to say he did not know about books in detail. We corresponded from time to time, and he was a willing participant in determining the completeness or condition of one copy or another of a very rare item.

The rare books were to be found in other rooms in that vast bibliographic empire, and I was never wanting for attention by knowledgeable people, mostly very young people. But these pages are about old bookmen and there was one of these who in contrast to Mr. Nijhoff hardly appeared at all, saying very little. Mr. Kern's jurisdiction seemed to be the vault. A frail man of advanced years, he seems now a shadow moving noiselessly about just within reach of the conversation of his colleagues and their client but never really a part of it. Picking up bits of information from the remarks or selections being made, Mr. Kern would move in and out of the vault — noiselessly — and present for consideration a book he thought appropriate to the discussion, and with it his descriptive notes. One of them stays in my mind, the *Oratio de obedientia ad Innocentium VIII* by Vasco Fernandes de Lucena. In those early days of visiting booksellers my first mission was to establish the James Ford Bell Library as a very serious collector of the very earliest books relating to the history of exploration. My little speech at Nijhoff's that day in 1957 brought Mr. Kern out of the vault with an incunable in a green morocco binding. Now there was no reason why a novice book-buyer should know about Lucena's 1485 oration, a speech delivered by Portugal's ambassador to Pope Innocent VIII in which the ambassador boasted of Portugal's discoveries along the west coast of Africa, by that date near to its southern extremity. No reason except that we had lately acquired it from a dealer in New York. But here it was again in a different edition! We would have both printings of the earliest book of the Age of Discovery. Mr. Kern seemed somewhat surprised that I should be so excited about a rather poorly printed pamphlet in a late binding. No doubt in his long life he had seen other, and better copies. In three decades since I have not seen another copy of either edition.

The train ride back to Amsterdam was always a joy in those days. Both for the pastoral scenes along the way, and for the good feeling that I had spent a day at the top of the mountain, at Nijhoff.

HEINRICH ROSENTHAL

On November 5, 1953, just a week after the dedication of the James Ford Bell Library, and two months after my arrival at the University of Minnesota, I wrote to Heinrich Rosenthal in Lucerne: "Would you please send us on approval item 94 from your Catalogue 12, if it is still available." I knew little about the book, Johannes de Sacro Bosco's *Introductorium compendosium in tractatum sphere*, edited by Johannes Glogoviensis, Cracow, 1506. I knew nothing at all of Heinrich Rosenthal, and would not until the following summer. But for as long as he lived a high point in my annual book-buying trip was the train ride to Lucerne, a walk across the covered bridge and along the lake to the shop of Heinrich Rosenthal, on the Haldenstrasse.

Seated across from each other at an ancient table, we could not have been a greater contrast. Mr. Rosenthal, by then perhaps seventy years of age, with a finely trimmed beard, thinning hair combed straight across his head, his face full of the calm that is born of experience, gentle, inquiring, assuring. I was nervous, naive, and seemed to myself very young to be buying books like the Glogoviensis Sacro Bosco. Yet he showed a certain confidence in me even on that first visit, offering a volume that has remained a favorite throughout my career — the first German edition of Sir John Mandeville's *Travels*, the first illustrated edition of that work, published at Augsburg by Anton Sorg in 1481.

In subsequent visits there were always a few books to look at, never very many, some to be purchased. But what was special to me each time was Mr. Rosenthal's request of me: "tell me what books you have seen this trip." He did not want an exhaustive list. My reporting was to be like his shelves, just a few very special items. So I would begin, and sometimes he would comment, "I once had that," or "I only know the Latin edition." Or he would smile and shake his head in some wonder at my discoveries, saying "I have never seen that book." When my report of great finds had established my success he might say, "Now let us speak a while in German." With the best bookstore German I could produce I would continue and he would comment, urging me along, even complimenting me on my German.

There came a time after a few visits when Mr. Rosenthal announced that he was retiring from business and that the premises would be turned over to others. "Will the shop retain your name?" I asked. He smiled that calm and confident smile of a contented and successful person. "No, the name is never for sale."

He retired to a beautiful house on a hill overlooking the lake. With no thought of seeing books I climbed that hill for a final visit. Again he asked what books I had seen, and we talked German for awhile. My last letter from him has the Haldenstrasse address crossed out, the new one typed in. He thanks me for a little book I had sent him, a publication of our Library. He writes in German, concluding "Mit den besten Grüssen."

ERNST WEIL

There was a special quality in the life of the household at 28 Litchfield Way, London. There was nothing about the exterior of the residence of Dr. and Mrs. Ernst Weil that announced it as a bookstore save for a small ABAA decal in the window of Dr. Weil's study. Yet there he sat at his spacious desk, surrounded by a selection of the finest books in the history of science to be found anywhere in the rare book trade. A portly man, quite bald, peering into his treasures through wire-rimmed glasses, Dr. Weil had the appearance of a scholar, comfortable among books, and surely he was the most intellectual of the booksellers I met in my early travels. And his was an intellect used not merely as a tool for his business. It was an intellect that searched the world broadly, an instrument for making it a better, more just place.

Litchfield Way is a street in the Hampstead Garden Suburb, an early twentieth-century experiment in integrating the social classes in London. And that is why Dr. and Mrs. Weil lived there. Emigrants from Germany where they had been educated, they were passionate advocates of social democracy in its most idealized form.

My first visit to 28 Litchfield Way was in the spring of 1955 after an exchange of correspondence with Dr. Weil concerning a world map he had offered, and also a manuscript catalog of the public sale of three Venetian galleys sold in 1484. This was the first of many visits, more than to any other bookseller because in the summers of 1960 and 1964 my family and I leased a house a ten minute walk from the Weils. These visits were extraordinary in that the business of buying books had to be worked into the general conversation about the state of the book trade in general, a stroll through the back garden for a look at the roses, a glass or two of the most ancient Madeira I have ever tasted, coffee served by Rosina, the faithful maid, and a lively discussion with Mrs. Weil about social injustices in Great Britain and elsewhere. During the summers we lived in London most of the visits included all of the above, except buying books, and often adding a long leisurely stroll on Hampstead Heath. Sometimes my wife Pat accompanied us, often she remained behind with Mrs. Weil. It was a fascinating place for our daughter Jackie who always found a dish of strawberries tempting her, and Dr. Weil assisting her to find the biggest one—and he might take the next in size. Sometimes we were invited for dinner, Scottish salmon or leg of lamb, a dinner as beautiful as the prints and paintings on the walls, or the roses in the garden.

For me it was a marvelous introduction into the life of a bookseller working out of his home, and into the genteel life of the classically educated continental intellectual. Here was no thought of quantities of books, only a very choice few, and each one a special challenge to the mind. A student of science and an early appreciator and bibliographer of Einstein, Dr. Weil roamed easily through Renaissance mathematics and astronomy. When these led to geography he had books for us. Never a lot of them. They came one at a time, often on approval, sometimes they were returned, but always the good will between us increased. One volume more than any other in the James Ford Bell Library exemplifies Dr. Weil and his books: the second edition of Strabo's *Geographia*, Venice, Vindelus de Spira, 1472. A folio of splendid typography in its original boards, a product of Venice's first printing press, it is a noble transmitter of a great classical text into the Renaissance, a work of great authority in the fifteenth century, translated from the Greek by Guarino of Verona under commission from Pope Nicholas V.

On one of those summer visits to 28 Litchfield Way I brought Dr. Weil a book of his own making, his translation of the Columbus Letter into German, published in 1922 in a limited edition of 1300 copies. This was number 308. Dr. Weil inscribed it: "Seen after many years again when Mr. John Parker showed it to me on August 14, 1965 and now initialed E.W."

HEINRICH EISEMANN

I went book-buying to London for the first time in the late summer of 1954. Richard Davis, director of the Minneapolis Institute of Arts had given me a letter of introduction to Heinrich Eisemann, a dealer he esteemed highly. Calling repeatedly from my hotel, I had no response from Mr. Eisemann. Confiding my problem to another London bookseller, I was told there would be no one at Eisemann's phone until after the religious holidays. This was my first real confrontation with Jewish orthodoxy.

So Mr. Eisemann came to see me. It is an unforgettable image:

his bowler hat in hand, a black coat with a velvet collar, black gloves; he bowed at the door as he entered, the iron gray hair parted in the middle fell briefly over his forehead and was quickly back in place; he responded to my greeting with a broad smile, his face a soft tan, his beard short and well-trimmed. I felt that I was in the presence of an Old Testament prophet. Yes, he knew that I was in London. He knew that I had called. Now he was in Minneapolis to see Mr. Davis, of course, but primarily to see his son Benjamin, a rabbi in our city. And he wanted to visit the James Ford Bell Library.

Thus began a relationship that taught me something about orthodoxy in all things — including the book trade. There was a correct way to deal with colleagues and clients. That was demonstrated when a manuscript of Sir John Mandeville's *Travels* we had purchased from Mr. Eisemann turned out to have been the property of a library in East Germany. The building had been partly destroyed and some of the contents apparently removed. All identifying marks had been completely erased and the manuscript had passed through the hands of two booksellers and a public auction where Mr. Eisemann had bought it. A research scholar made the connection between the auction catalog entry and the manuscript missing from the East German library, and he alerted the librarian there. It was a troublesome situation for us and for Mr. Eisemann, and he was particularly troubled that the German librarian had written to him in "a very rude and offensive way." There was a correct way, an orthodox way, to handle such things, and with impeccable manners and a clear sense of what was just in such situations as well as what was legal he guided the negotiation so as to get the manuscript returned to the German library with full repayment to us. This from a man whose life and profession as a bookseller had begun in Germany and had been interrupted by forced flight in the 1930s to save his family.

Mr. Eisemann and I had a good correspondence over this matter, and it dragged on for most of two years. In that time he was our agent at several Sotheby auctions in London — never a successful bid, unfortunately, but always with punctuality and correctness on his part, and vigorous attempts to follow the unsuccessful bids with approaches to the buyers if they were booksellers. Mr. Eisemann, I think, liked auctions. He told me once of going to London from Frankfurt as a very young man to attend a sale, having gathered up commissions from various acquaintances, and of finding arrayed against him in the bidding the most powerful people in the book trade. More an agent than a bookseller, he did not have much stock to show when I called on him from time to time at 102 Clive Court, Maida Vale in London. I recall a long hallway leading into the apartment. It was lined with books, floor to ceiling. This was his reference library of which he was most proud. I asked him once how he became interested in selling books (he also sold works of art). It all began, he recalled with receiving at his bar mitzvah the gift of a book, the *Travels* of Benjamin ben Jonah of Tudela, a twelfth-century rabbi who traveled widely visiting Jewish communities in Europe, Africa, and Asia. He promised that if he ever found the first edition of that book, published by Plantin in 1575, we would have it for the Library. He did not live long enough to complete that mission, but someone else did it for him, and I think of it still as a little monument to Mr. Eisemann's life, a life full of traditional values of religion, family, and honor among associates.

MICHEL SINELNIKOFF

Good fortune — luck — plays a large part in one's success in buying rare books. Being at the right place at the right time cannot always be planned. We remember times when it happens. On my second book-buying trip to London, in the summer of 1955, I planned to call on Orion Bookseller Ltd., a firm probably not much remembered any more. The quality of the only Orion catalogue I ever saw had convinced me that this could be a helpful source. Phone calls had proven fruitless and I was running out of time, so for some reason I decided to go to the address in person, Carlton Lodge, 26 Brondesbury Park, possibly to leave a message.

As my cab arrived at the gate another one did also. Michel Sinelnikoff, proprietor of Orion Booksellers, was awaiting it. We met at the gate and I introduced myself. He asked me who I had seen in London, and I named a few of them: Maggs, Quaritch, Sawyer, Stevens, Robinson. Mr. Sinelnikoff was in haste, on his way to Sotheby's. But he had heard enough there at the gate to guess something important was happening in the book trade so he wrote down quickly the address of his bank in Pall Mall. He said "Meet me there tomorrow morning at ten o'clock and I will show you some things."

Our meeting at the gate had taken less than five minutes, but we met again at the bank the next morning. I was leaving London in the afternoon, so again time was short, but in that brief visit to his bank vault I saw more truly unbelievable things than I had seen in all the rest of London's rare book shops. Here was a brilliantly illuminated *roteiro* of the Red Sea by João de Castro, a large collection of sixteenth century maps by Giacomo Gastaldi, an original manuscript letter of Olivier van Noort, all of which we acquired upon my return to Minneapolis. From that time on Mr. Sinelnikoff became a frequent source of the unusual book or map or manuscript. Indeed there was nothing "usual" about him. As we became better acquainted he talked a lot about himself, but I never got over the feeling that mystery went with him. An emigré from Russia following the Revolution he told of reaching North America via Vladivostok. His family had been close to those of the musicians Jascha Heifetz and Vladimir Horowitz who remained his good friends. He did not seem to be truly a part of the book trade, but he spoke with great familiarity of many noble families on the Continent, indicating that he was their outlet for the sale of precious objects in times of financial stress. But more than an agent, he seemed to be one of them. Books and manuscripts were among many types of objects in which he traded. On discovering that James Ford Bell was a collector of silver as well as books, he showed me two of the largest silver objects I had ever seen — wine cisterns, I believe they were called. Later he sent photographs of them for Mr. Bell's inspection. There were, as I recall, rare musical instruments in his house, paintings and drawings of course, heraldic manuscripts, and coins.

The coins I remember especially because he brought some of them to our home in Minneapolis. He visited North America with some frequency because he had a son in Canada. What were Pat and I to do with this Russian aristocrat in our modest little house? He had said he was bringing some coins to the United States for appraisal, and we happened to have a friend, just as flamboyant as Mr. Sinelnikoff but lacking the pedigree, who collected rare coins. So there we sat at our dining room table, Pat and I with

Roy Ritchey and Michel Sinelnikoff exchanging views on thousands of dollars worth of gold coins — gold coins only — over a glass of the best wine we could afford, and some candied almonds Mr. Sinelnikoff had brought, neatly arranged in a small pitcher as a gift to the hostess.

The next day Mr. Sinelnikoff and I met with Mr. Bell to talk about a manuscript, Giles Fletcher's account of his embassy to Russia in the 1580s. Mr. Bell was rather tough about manuscripts. He insisted upon clear provenance which Mr. Sinelnikoff was quick to supply: a Scottish noble family. This led to some talk about quail shooting in Scotland which Mr. Bell had enjoyed, and a promise by Mr. Sinelnikoff to arrange a quail shoot on the estate of the owner of the Fletcher manuscript.

Buying from Mr. Sinelnikoff I was led to the edge of that aristocratic element in European society in which I would never be able to participate more fully. It would always be a part of the mystery I felt surrounded its representative to the book trade. Mr. Sinelnikoff disappeared one day in Switzerland, drowned it was believed. There was no public sale of his collections. A mystery man to the end.

Book Collecting as a Way of Life

INTRODUCTION BY BILL LAIRD

"Book Collecting as a Way of Life" is only one of many scholarly works authored by Jack Parker, but it tells me more about him as a man, than as a scholar.

My first memory of Jack dates from one fall evening in about 1958 at the home of Professor Ernst Abbe, near the University of Minnesota's St. Paul Campus. Jack was attending one of his first meetings as a member of the Twin Cities Manuscript Society. T.C.M.S. is a small group of about twenty good friends who enjoy discussing manuscripts, history, books and collecting as much as the fellowship. Some members probably there were Roy Ritchey, Harold Lensing, Al Witt, Stan Nelson, Phil Jordan, Bill Morgan, Ned Stanford, Kirker Bixby, Harold Kittleson, and Floyd Risvold. "The Manuscript Society" grew out of T.C.M.S., founded by Allyn Ford in Minneapolis, although the connection no longer exists today. Some T.C.M.S. members also were part of "The Boys in the Back Room" at Stan Nelson's or Leland Lien's bookshop, as you will read later in this story. And in 1974 Jack helped T.C.M.S. host the annual meeting of "The Manuscript Society" held in Minneapolis that year.

Many of us know how much Jack has helped many individuals and organizations with his sure but gentle leadership. For the past five years he has given many hours to the Minneapolis Athenaeum to help chart its course into the twenty-first century. Not in the least, he has long maintained a leadership role in his church.

The James Ford Bell Library has come to be recognized internationally under the direction of Jack Parker and Carol Urness. And Jack set the compass course for the Associates of the James Ford Bell Library which has become the premier model in North America for structuring a successful library "friends" group.

As a collector, some of Jack's strongest interests are in travel literature of the last hundred years—especially travel by automobile, the Antarctic, and early North Dakota history, so he understands well the needs of collectors as they interface with library curators or dealers.

Most importantly, "Book Collecting as a Way of Life" is a story about finding the real treasures of book collecting. Jack is an exemplary citizen in all respects, and the Twin Cities are indeed fortunate that he chose to come here almost forty years ago. He gives generously of himself as a family man and as an educator. He seeks no accolades. He deeply understands the social fabric. He is a setter of standards. He is a role model of tremendous proportions. He is the real treasure. I am glad he is my friend.

Foreword to the speech as published by the University of Michigan Library School:

John Parker, Distinguished Alumnus

Historian in spite of himself, his distinction almost unlooked for, John Parker has with his own excellence made his position famous, kept his collection treasured.

Perhaps his dissertation was a prediction. From *Books to Build an Empire* he has gone on to build a kingdom of learning. His own knowledge—expert, extensive, interdisciplinary—has augmented and polished a single excellent collection until it ranks as one of the nation's jewels. All his activity has strengthened it.

He has not been selfish. No specialist immured within his walls, he has been active in his area. Sharing of time and thought, he has been an inspiration to those who work with him; generous with experience, he makes his necessary travels an education to those who accompany him.

To John Parker, bookman, scholar, teacher, the School of Library Science is pleased to present its Distinguished Alumnus Award.

April 8, 1983

I am honored at being invited back to my *alma mater* to be a part of this Library School again, and honored further in being asked to speak to you this evening. I am aware that it is Friday night, and in my time at this University it was most common for gatherings of students and others at this time of week to take place at the Pretzel Bell. We wondered in those conversations about whether microfilm would replace books (we had not yet heard about computers in libraries); we worried about which job to take, for the placement bulletin board in the spring of 1953 cried out to us it seemed from every library in the country. We debated, should we become library administrators, or should we keep our virtue and stay close to books. Indeed, we did talk of books on those Fridays, and we shall do so now.

In those times, thirty years ago, there was a small, hard-core band of evangelists who went about the profession preaching that librarians should be people in love with books. Their high priest was Lawrence Clark Powell. But they did not invent their message. When I told a colleague about this occasion and my part in it she sent me a quotation from a speech given in 1925 by Frank Walter, then Librarian at the University of Minnesota. It went like this: "We are often prone to crowd our working and our leisure hours with projects . . . and forget that our duty as public servants does not keep us from a personal obligation to live our own lives in a way that may promote the good of our own souls. . . . " He went on to talk about librarians and books. Some of us still hit the evangelist trail every chance we get to preach the same message, and that is what I feel called to do tonight. I know that an occasion of this type should be lighthearted, and I shall try to make it so, but we evangelists take our message rather seriously. And I beg your indulgence for the autobiographical tone of what I am about to say. I much prefer to talk about books I know from experience.

I had intended to title this talk "Red canaries and black tulips," but I did not want to have to explain that to your dean. Instead, I shall try to explain it now. In my small village in North Dakota there was a lady — the mother of my best friend — who delighted me. She raised canaries. Adelaide Johnson began with one bird, a singer. Then somewhere she borrowed a female and presently there was a nest and three young ones. Then there were ten, twenty, forty, sixty, then seventy-five. This covered a period of some twenty years. There were shipping cases with birds going and coming in the mail. There were journals and books, announcements of canary shows, and trophies. There was a great variety of song, to say nothing of color. It was color that challenged Mrs. Johnson. She told us that the objective in canary breeding was to get a red one — which was genetically impossible. But you could get a wonderfully deep orange, and in the process, she said, "you will see so many beautiful birds."

So Mrs. Johnson understood me when I told her about tulip growers I had visited in Holland whose objective was to get a black one — again, I believe, genetically impossible. But what beautiful gardens to walk in while trying! What company to keep!

Now what in the world is all of this about? I think it is about quality. Maybe it is about ultimates — things probably beyond reach, and the fun you can have reaching.

As individuals we are always reaching back while we are, or think we are, going forward. We try to recover the records of ancestors, we collect family memorabilia, we treasure fragments of our earlier lives — favorite toys and dolls, remember books, a report card, a baseball glove. We seek continuity with the past of ourselves, knowing we cannot get it all. The social implementation of this desire to remember is called history, and any culture will have some regard for explaining the beginnings and development of itself. Intuitively we know Carl Sandburg was right in saying, "when a society or civilization perishes, one condition may always be found: they forgot where they came from." We build libraries and museums, we support historical societies and history departments in our colleges and universities to supply this basic human need — to remember where we came from.

Now there is a qualitative aspect to remembering, and we must be as exact as we can in our remembering if we are to keep faith with the past and the future. We are the link that joins them. There are paintings and sculpture and artifacts that preserve some of the memory. But when it comes to the memory of what people said, thought, feared, argued about, and loved, there is in my judgement no substitute for words. To put thoughts down in letters which become words and sentences, which become paragraphs and pages and books, exhibiting the workings of minds singly or in juxtaposition to one another, this is humanity's great invention. With it we have a chance at the wisdom and foolishness of the entire recorded past. We can listen to Herodotus retailing a bit of history he found hard to believe, namely, that some southbound sailors along Africa's shore discovered one day that the shadows they cast fell on the other side of the ship. A great mind here, struggling with a simple fact not yet fully understood. We can listen in on the first civil rights debate that related to the New World: Bishop Bartolomé de las Casas and the lawyer Juan Ginés de Sepulveda, trying to establish what the American Indians were, in terms of humanity and God's creation. Nothing but books will give you the true memory of what was said, and only the first editions will give it to you as it was said and read in the 1550s. We can hear Hugo Grotius, the father of international law, formulate his earliest ideas about peace. The resources of the earth, he wrote in *Mare liberum*, are so distributed that each region has need of another's goods, and in this mutual need will come an interdependence to bind distant peoples together, creating the unity that God intended for humanity.

I do not suggest that we can all collect first editions of this magnitude. But there have been a lot of books by the successors of Grotius and Las Casas and Sepulveda. The territory from *Uncle Tom's Cabin* to *Bury my Heart at Wounded Knee* is richly planted with books. And every generation produces a Herodotus, more or less. You do not have to be among the red canaries to see some very fine birds. And they are not easy to capture, those deep orange ones. Just try to put together first editions of the best known American historian of my lifetime, Samuel Eliot Morison. It can be done, I am sure, and I am trying. But I found only one last year. It is a matter of waiting, looking, and eventually of paying, and in the process one develops a sort of peripheral vision that will bring into view other things that are interesting, possibly interesting enough so that we can let Morison wait while we follow another lead. A book collector must not be unduly single-minded or purposeful about any one book, or group of books. That way lies frustration. It is like going about the country looking for corn fritters or gooseberry pie. You just might starve before you get fed.

James Ford Bell, the founder of our Library, made a mistake about 1950. He passed up a book he should have bought. One of my early assignments with him was to try to find another copy for sale. The book was Pierre Biard's *Relation de la Nouvelle France* (Lyon, 1616). So I went about Paris and London and New York, very young and very green, looking for a Biard. All I got was bemused smiles. Wanting to at least see what I was looking for I went to the Bibliothèque Nationale in Paris. They had one. They had two. Now the Bibliothèque Nationale was not selling duplicates to anyone who came in off the street. But the duplicate allowed us to dream, and we told a bookseller in Milan, Signora Carla Marzoli, and she found an approach. The Bibliothèque Nationale had some red canaries on their desiderata list too, and she knew where some of them were. Those libraries were looking for black tulips in other peoples' gardens, and so on. A bibliographical domino situation was constructed, and slowly, steadily, it began to move. Seventeen years later in Paris, Signora Marzoli reached in her purse. Voila! Mr. Bell had died long since, but the Library was living, and that is what the book was for. And in those seventeen years came almost every other French Canadiana item we could hope for. So many beautiful birds.

It has happened again and again. This past February there came in the mail a book we had been searching for since 1953. Jan Huygen van Linschoten's *Itinerario* (Amsterdam, 1595–96) is in my opinion the most important single sixteenth century book for our Library. It described at the end of that century the commercial opportunities and navigational problems of both Asia and the Americas. It has been for us a red canary, an *untrouvable* in the language of booksellers. So we gathered up Latin, German, French, English, and later Dutch editions, all great books in themselves, but all, after all, proceeding from that first edition. If the memory is to be as good as it can be, the Linschoten must be there in the first edition. And now it is. I do not cite this as any personal achievement. It came to us because we were looking, and because we were acquiring all of the other books that belonged with it. It was a keystone whose absence was obvious to the bookseller, Nico Israel. When he found one he wanted it to go where it would do the most good. But if we had never gotten it we would still have had thirty good years of hunting.

I would not try *alma mater's* hospitality longer with an old timer's stories about buying the great books that are beyond nearly everyone's financial reach, but only to say that those professional collecting experiences have convinced me that such is the good life on weekends and holidays as well as eight to five Monday through Friday.

Weekends, for example, there is in Minneapolis an institution known in the vernacular as the Boys in the Back Room. Not as sexist as it sounds, this is an unorganized assemblage of people who gather in Lien's Bookstore on Saturday afternoons. Four or five, sometimes more, bookish people sit around coffee and donuts and tell tales of collecting books, manuscripts, maps, stamps. Like other old men we retell the same stories sometimes, but it's all right. We aren't as quick as we were, and it doesn't hurt to go over a yarn two or three times to get all that is in it. In this little gathering I have encountered people of incredibly detailed knowledge about a wide range of subjects: Civil War, Minnesota history and authors, fur trade, the American Revolution, Indians, General Custer, the Philippine Rebellion, William Faulkner, the Beat Generation, to name a few. It is always serious conversation, with innumerable questions about where the information comes from. It is book talk. Meanwhile the customers are rummaging around, some of them staying close enough to listen in. I love to watch the younger ones sneaking up on our conversation. I don't blame them. I would rather be there on a Saturday afternoon than any place in town, and frequently I am.

One day at Lien's, having picked up a later edition of Willard Glazier's *Down the Great River*, I was asked how come I was interested in Glazier. Everyone there seemed to know something about Glazier. It was a perfect invitation to tell a yarn, so I did. It was expected of me. And I will tell it again, in more brief form.

There was a day back in 1966 when a campus bookseller, known to all present of course, was going out of business. Terms of the close-out sale were these: all you could carry out in your arms for a dollar, or ten cents per volume. A librarian colleague who collected bookplates viewed this mercantile catastrophe as a major opportunity. Would I go along and carry out an armful for him at lunchtime? I went along. He found almost no bookplates, but I found Glazier's *Down the Great River* (Philadelphia, 1887) in the original blue pictorial cloth. I bought it for a dime (my only purchase) and discovered I had the only copy of that first edition in the Twin Cities. In checking I found many later editions in local libraries, and noted that they contained appendices of increasing size with the later printings. Making the rounds of local bookstores over the next two to three years I picked up most of the later editions for three to five dollars each. Then one day I sat down to compare them and, alas, to read them. What unfolded was the story of a man who claimed to have discovered, in 1881, a new headwaters for the Mississippi River, and the appendices were the writings of his admirers and supporters — editors, politicians, preachers, scientists, and most important, textbook publishers. Now if the schools' textbooks and atlases, and the libraries' reference books, do not agree on so basic a detail as where this country's greatest river begins, then you have the makings of a textbook war, nation-wide, and that is exactly what Captain Glazier's book started. The war went on for about a dozen years, and it was a very instructive war in the way it showed how information — or misinformation — gets into books, how it stays there, and who cares and who does something about it. The Boys in the Back Room liked that story, especially when I got to the part about the Donnelly Bill which passed in the Minnesota legislature, proscribing from use in the public schools any text or atlas that put Glazier's name on the map. Then someone in our group picked up on books that Ignatius Donnelly had written, and who had them and how much they were worth, and how scarce they were. The narrative passed on and I became part of the audience. A typical Saturday performance in the Back Room.

My little collection of editions of *Down the Great River* and its sequel *The Headwaters of the Mississippi* would not bring $150 in a sale, but they have been worth a great deal to me as a source of enjoyment and broadened horizons about publishing text and reference books. Minnesotans make a pilgrimage to the headwaters of the Mississippi River every so often, a sort of cultural ritual. It is a very special trip for me now, thanks to a ten-cent book.

It is usually that way. If you are buying books, you get more than you pay for. You walk into the bookstore with ten dollars, and you spend three hours picking over vast realms of literature and history and art. It hasn't cost you a cent to meet these distinguished authors, not a cent. But the hospitality of the place says you should buy something, and you see a volume of Robert Louis Stevenson, *In the South Seas.* You remember a book you had, *A Child's Garden of Verses,* and you remember the inscription: Happy Birthday, Jack, from Lillian, 1934. And for half of your ten dollars you sail off with Stevenson to the South Seas and ponder with him a people who had never heard of Shakespeare. You discover this is one volume of twenty-seven, the Thistle Edition.

With luck you could have all of them for about forty cents a day for a year. You go back looking for more, but you don't have that kind of luck. Still, you have the dream, and you are always looking, and maybe one day, there they will be, all red and gold on the shelf you will build for them. In the meantime you meet Lafcadio Hearn on his way to Japan about 1890 to teach English literature at the University of Tokyo. And you discover there is more, much more: books of travels to many places, magazine articles in great number, and three volumes of published correspondence. Now while we are waiting for the Stevenson set maybe we can pick up those Hearn letters. Again, the dreams may not come true, but they have been good dreams, worth more than the price of the book. Dreams have no prices, only values.

Other kinds of undiscovered treasures lie between those covers, often unnoticed by the world, and by catalogers of books. A collection of missionaries' instructions for setting up in North America in 1704 will contain a "brief prayer" with which to start the school day. This just may be the first prescribed prayer of our schools, the starting point for a topic of some current importance. More than we paid for. Indeed, in our time a book with any religious designation will turn off most readers. But not the curious ones. One of the major benefits that comes from having been a cataloger for thirty years is the understanding that no book ever gets adequately catalogued. RLIN and OCLC have not enhanced our ability to get onto a catalog card all of the good stuff we find in the nooks and crannies of books. We cannot make the card say that this book contains the earliest prescribed prayer for schools in North America, or that another one shows the earliest picture of people smoking tobacco in the New World. But such things are there, waiting to be revealed. Look into that Quaker travel book,

newly published to be sure, but from Francis Tuckett's manuscript of 1837. Where, ask my friends in the Back Room, did he
travel? Charleston, Florida, New Orleans (anti-slavery material
all the way, for the Civil War types). On up the river he went to
St. Louis, gateway to the West, center of the fur trade. And on
to the Falls of St. Anthony. Do you mean a Minnesota travel book
from 1837? Exactly. That, says everyone in the room, is worth
having. Where did you get it? From a Quaker bookseller who just
thought it was a good Quaker travel item.

Or you may too easily pass by a Methodist preacher living
among the Cree Indians near Hudson Bay. Making sermons to be
sure, but also telling about a colleague who printed books up
there. The earliest printing in the Cree language was a prayer
book printed from types made by melting the lead in the lining
of tea chests. The history of printing is perhaps the most collected
field in all of bibliophilia, and this little cranny of printing history
is tucked away without a chapter heading or any hope of a subject
entry in any library in the world, in the Reverend Edgerton
Young's book *By Canoe and Dog Train among the Cree and
Salteaux Indians* (Montreal, 1890). But more than that. "By canoe and dog train" means just that, and Reverend Young gives the
best account of the care and management of sled dogs that I know
of. Anyone interested in the history of transportation in North
America will surely want to have a copy of this book. You nearly
always get more than you pay for. You get ideas about what to
look for next. Something to look forward to, we are told, is one
of the ingredients of a happy life.

You may fear overdosing on the trivia that you turn up in the
nooks and crannies. Have no fear. Some of it you will forget. You
alone will decide which side roads are to become main roads you
will follow. Following any one of them for a lot of trips to the
bookstore, or through a few hundred booksellers' catalogs, will
make you a historian or a literary critic. You will know more
about some things than anyone you meet. A whole academic career and a larger view of life are available for a small financial investment. Also, you are insured for life against boredom. This
does not mean you won't bore other people, but you must trust
that such people will take care of themselves when you are
around.

You need not go to the nooks and crannies to find things of interest to collect if you are impatient. There are whole fields of literature that are relatively unknown, and that is where the fun is. Anyone with enough money can put together a collection of the Grabhorn Press, or the Limited Editions Club. We know what these books are. But I would commend to you territories unknown, fields not yet plowed up by the previous generations. For example, we are just now beginning to look into the history of automotive travel as a serious field for collectors. We have no idea what is out there. Is it great literature? It could be. Important authors traveled and wrote about it. Edith Wharton, for example, wrote of her travels through France in *A Motor-Flight through France* (New York, 1908). These are the books that will tell us how our age of mobility began, and nothing has had a greater impact on our culture than this boundless mobility provided by the automobile. What was the state of mind of the people who first experienced it? Listen to the horseless age being born. "It is difficult for any automobile owner to define the mental workings that brought him within that class: the fever is insidious, its culmination in ownership so sudden, the justifications for the purchase given are often so far from the fact, that one might as well admit in the first instance that he was obsessed, and that the purchase was made without any clear conception of the responsibility that ownership involved." That in 1911 from *Abroad in a Runabout* by A.J. and F.H. Hand. Our very language began to take on new symbols of mobility. Speed jargon emerges as we describe our travels. And we catch a new sense of freedom to explore away from the well-beaten paths. We see the machine steadily taking hold of us, remaking our world in this century. It produced many books, I am sure. We don't know how many, or where they are.

If the automobile turned us loose upon the world, electronics brought the world to us. Does anyone collect the books that cry alarm or seek to soothe us over what television is doing to our habits, our children, our peace of mind? One day someone will, for this is obviously a major turning point in the history of human communications. Wouldn't it be nice to have a collection of reactions to the printing press from the incunabular age? I treasure a few lines of poetry from Sebastian Brant who in 1494 reacted to the new mobility just bursting in upon Europe in the wake of Columbus's voyage:

> He who by foreign travel tries
> To establish himself as wise
> Should rather explore and examine himself
> (Though traveling is fine, it's not enough)
> Since he who puts his mind to roam
> May not serve his God alone.

One day collectors will make the Vietnam war as popular a subject as the Battle of the Little Big Horn has become. The Great Depression could rival the Civil War. Martin Luther King might surpass *Uncle Tom's Cabin.*

Time will sort out the literary giants who fetch the big prices from the writers who are merely interesting to you. But you alone can sort out what you like, and the game is the same, regardless of price. You are looking for the red canaries, the black tulips of your own interest. There will always be something beyond what you can find or afford. But in searching for them you will surely see a lot of beautiful birds. I could not wish you a better career, or a better pastime.

Red Canaries and a Cage too Small

INTRODUCTION BY TOM SHAUGHNESSY

Jack Parker's speech, "Red Canaries and a Cage too Small," was delivered to the 31st preconference of the Rare Books and Manuscripts Section of the Association of College and Research Libraries on June 21, 1990. I, along with all of those in attendance, felt fortunate for the opportunity to hear Dr. Parker. His remarks focused on some themes that need to be recalled and the principles which should guide all library bibliographers and selectors: a preoccupation with quality, the ability to distinguish between material which is of enduring value versus that which is ephemeral, to conserve and interpret the resources entrusted to our care.

The seriousness of this message is underscored by the limited financial resources available to libraries and the space required to collect and preserve their collections. These are questions and issues that all librarians

need to be concerned about. Few of us, however, could present them as
clearly and as effectively as Jack Parker.

You honor us in coming to Minnesota on your way to Chicago.
If my geography is correct, it is out of the way for most of you.
We hope you are being well entertained here in the land of Lake
Wobegon and Main Street. By this time you will have had at least
one meal with wild rice. You will have heard an ethnic joke about
Swedes, Norwegians, or Iowans. You will know that we have two
seasons here: winter and road repair. So this first day of summer
means little to us. We are well into road repair. Cherish it
nevertheless. Winter is just around the corner.

You will be forgiving, I hope, of my title for this effort to say
something about rare and special books and manuscripts in our
time. It is rooted in some autobiography which I hope will also
be forgiven. We are all the outcomes of where we have been. And
when we have been (wherever) long enough we are tempted to
look back and find the roads that have led to the here and now.
The autobiography I will defend as the one part of my talk which
I am quite sure I know something about.

In my childhood in a North Dakota village there was a lady
who raised canaries—Adelaide Johnson, the mother of my best
friend. She raised canaries, which in the beginning I thought
were kept for their singing. And sing they did. But more: They
had great variety in their coloring, which to breeders of canaries
like Mrs. Johnson was even more important. I remember she
started with one male bird, and borrowed a female from a friend.
Soon there were some little ones. And as I grew toward, and into
my teens, the numbers of birds multiplied. They came and went
in the mails to contests and conventions and shows. Journals on
canary breeding piled up in the back porch. The early bright yel-
lows were gradually replaced by deeper colors—orange. The object, Adelaide told us, was to get a red one. And then she explained that genetically that was impossible. I remember her
saying to me, "But I tell you, Jack, in trying for the red one you
will see many, many beautiful birds." So many indeed. Her little
flock grew because she loved them all. Her house was full of
birds—a giant bird cage full of bird cages. But in the end it was
too small. She gave up birds eventually, I think, because she
could not weed her growing collection. She loved it too much.

There is in all of us, I suppose, the conflict between the desire to do it to perfection, and the vision of doing it all. In the spring we order more seeds than we have room to plant — or energy to care for. In summer we contend with abundance. But we have our best moments picking the perfect tomato, the just right head of cabbage. We go to the flower shows and to the county and state fairs to see the finest of what is grown or made. How do we know what is finest? Something out of the past tells us — the long accumulation of human experience in any endeavor recognizes quality and degrees of it — the nearly red canary, the nearly black tulip.

So let us think about quality — a subject that is often offending because there is a certain air of elitism associated with it. And to those of us who are democratic in spirit — all of us, I presume — there is a dilemma to deal with, and it seems to me that this is where we find ourselves at this time in our profession — democratic republicans contemplating the veneration of aristocrats, or embracing the masses.

Many of us have lived through, and participated in a great democratic revolution in the past fifty years: the enhancement of civil rights for minorities, the recognition of justice due to women, the movement toward acceptance of the right of sexual preference, the decline of old-established authoritarianism in all aspects of our society. These changes have brought to our attention a range of literature and subjects we had not thought much about before 1940. And in broadening our curatorial vision we have inevitably swept into it much that is commonplace — and that is not to denigrate it — . We have given our love to some yellow canaries.

In academe it has been said often over these years of revolution that we have democratized our grading system so that we are less scrupulous in weeding out the deficient student, and that we give less attention to those who are truly superior. Surely with students we have come to recognize potential for achievement, and we have nurtured it, polished those diamonds in the rough, possibly to the detriment of the obvious high achiever. And we are not sorry.

Similarly in our quest for social history, for our collective roots, we have gone searching for the lives of nameless people, of their interests and their influences. History is no longer a chronicle of the rich and powerful. Like the supermarket (itself a part of the democratic revolution) our history is a basket filled from every shelf. All of these shelves of humanity have a literature (by and about) and all are important to an understanding of our history and culture, and its place in the larger history and culture of Western Civilization, and the world. So as we examine our collective past we ask our ancestors what they read, for books—all kinds of books—are the surest road back to where we came from. The answer, of course, is that like ourselves they read a lot of rather mediocre stuff—or worse—from the standpoint of the old literary standards of quality. And it was produced in vast amounts by an industry that fattened on the emerging mass literacy. Our work—our opportunity—for the future is to deal with the evaluation of this literature of our roots. It is not going to be easy.

Two centuries ago a collector of what was important to the development of the reading public would almost certainly have concentrated on the great classical underpinnings of western intellectual life: books mostly in Latin or Greek, the great histories, cosmographies, poets, religious works in their earliest printed editions. In quality, and in influence in shaping the public mind there was no doubt about them. They were worthy of being collected, revered, preserved.

A century later—a century ago now—a great new field was coming into vogue—Americana. New World history was to some degree separate from that of Europe. It was the experience of an emerging nation obviously destined for wealth and power, and enormously conscious of its own emerging. It valued the documentation of that experience, and collections of Americana were built, in private hands. And private collecting became a way for new wealth in this country to express itself in a socially acceptable way.

Conscious of our history, we also became conscious of our emerging literature, distinct now from English literature, but not so distinct as to forget its ancestry. So great authors from both sides of the Atlantic were collected. And the passing of time was trusted to define greatness, quality. You are in Minneapolis today, and this was the home of Herschel V. Jones, whose collections of English and American literature, and of Americana, in a representative way defined the scope of rare book collecting in the United States during the first four decades of this century. And these well-identified rarities became steadily more rare as they were competed for by an ever increasing element of our population — the new industrial wealth of the New World.

The new wealth dispersing into new hands after midcentury created new collectors, and the traditional fields could not accommodate them. The old standards of what was rare, and what was *important* gave ground to admit authors of more recent vintage and events of more recent history. What was more American than the Civil War, the movement across the trans-Mississippi West, cowboys, railroads. What was more important world-wide than science? Collectors began reaching beyond the obvious big names, looking for substance in hitherto unnoticed pamphlets. I recall an article in *AB* by Ed Wolfe lamenting that no one was paying attention to pamphlets of the American Revolution. I think he cured that situation as we began scurrying among them while the prices rose. About twenty-five years ago Kenneth Nebenzahl, the Chicago bookseller, went bold with a catalog of strictly eighteenth century stuff, not spectacular, but quickly in demand. Authors of the late nineteenth and early twentieth century pointed us toward the "modern firsts" which now crowd the market. The term "modern first" was not used thirty years ago — and probably much more recently than that. And something — possibly a greater understanding of childhood — sent collectors out to hunt for those books that formed the foundation of their bookish interests.

Now most of these post-war collectors got old, and since book collecting is not a genetically inherited condition, there was a concern for what to do with them. The tax laws made it convenient for both parties, collector and curator, to give them to libraries. Many of the books in these new collections were not of themselves very rare, but they were collected, and the collection had an identity as surely as any one book of the traditional rare type had. So the collections began pouring in, gobbling up vast linear feet of shelf space, and bringing distinction to libraries which were brazenly acquisitive. It was in the 1950s, I think, when the term "special collections" came into use as the cage for these canaries of many hues, all of them good to have, hard to turn down. They came to be housed among or near the rare book collections of old because they were special, often in fine condition, and they did not circulate. Frequently the same titles and editions were on the shelves in the circulating section, duplicates of text, but not duplicates of condition.

And so books less than a century old, titles that may have had no particular notoriety when published, or ever, became treasures because they were part of an important subject collection, the result of the creativity of a collector who knew the subject, and the importance of each piece in the collection. And new subjects around which to collect spawned and grew.

I recall an incident during my early days here at Minnesota — 1953–54. There was a group of books on a shelf for consideration as discards — weedings — and I believe they were about to be dumped. They were a not very attractive lot of American temperance pamphlets. Obviously not objects of great literary value, or of long-range historical influence, it seemed, considering the nation's continuing taste for booze. I volunteered to take them home rather than see them go into the dump, for that seemed to be their fate. There was no department of Special Collections here then, and such matters fell to the attention of the Associate Director. I believe my interest in them *as a collection* had something to do with Mr. Russell's decision to keep them. They went from the edge of oblivion into "special collections".

I would not imply that our Special Collections Department, or yours is an assemblage of ugly ducklings (or colorless canaries, to continue the metaphor), but I would emphasize the collectedness of any subject-oriented group of books as a criterion that came to get serious consideration by those of us who were building libraries in those years. I recall coming upon a collection back about 1960, of books gathered by a young Englishman during his two years on the "Grand Tour" in the late eighteenth century. They were in a huge wooden box, probably unopened since the young Mr. Home returned from his travels. The books looked unopened too, except for his recording the place and price of the purchase. All in the original blue or gray wrappers. Were they great books? Probably not. Were they influential in the life of the young man? There is no evidence of it. I don't think we asked those questions. They were a *collection* reflecting the taste of a young gentleman on the grand tour. The same books offered one or two at a time over a decade might never have attracted any attention. But I hasten to assure you that they are beautiful and I am still glad I told the acquisitions librarian about them. Yet they do take up space in the cage.

And of course some collections take up more space than others. There is the author, conscious of art above all else, who labors slowly, producing half a dozen good books in a lifetime. Possibly they are better than good as literature. There is the formula writer, or simply a prolific producer who develops a following and has a publisher yapping at his elbows to crank out a book a year. We are interested in social impact of authors. Which of these has the greater impact, justifying a complete collection of first editions? If we cannot have it all, if the cage is too small for both, which will we choose, good writing or social acceptance?

In the field of collecting I know something about, travel literature, the early great names produced one or two books: Herodotus, Marco Polo, Sir John Mandeville, Columbus, Vespucci, Pigafetta. The book was the result of travels. By the late nineteenth century the book became the *reason* to travel. And so shelves of Stevenson, Mark Twain, Harriet Martineau, Mrs. Trollope, Willard Glazier and numerous others. The modern collector of travel literature therefore must give serious thought as to region, author, mode of travel, time period, and true significance to have a manageable collection. It is time, I believe, to emphasize quality. Yes, at the expense of numbers. The red canaries in a limited field.

I realize this goes against one of the cornerstones of our cultural assumptions: — more is better, quantity, growth. But if there is something special about special collections it ought to be their quality — literary, historical, bibliographical. In our fast food, supermarket culture we must be within the library community the bastions of what is good and enduring, not merely what was popular. And let us remember that the mere passing of time will make some books on the open shelves eligible for inclusion in Special Collections, calling for the same judgement about quality.

We need to consider these things in the coming years with one eye on the economic and political scene of which we are a part. Cultural facilities like libraries tend to reflect the economy surrounding them. Let's look back forty years — to 1950. The American economy was clearly dominant in the world. There was money for books — quite a lot of it. Places like Kansas and Texas, and UCLA and Minnesota, not previously known for rare books, got into collection-building in a big way. We built new libraries in a lot of places, and special collections was one of the reasons for doing so. The availability of funds was encouragement for further expansion of collections. By the seventies we were in for some belt-tightening as the decline in the dollar gave us less money to play with in the international market, which is where the book trade is. The 1980s have seen our supporting economy decline with respect to its global position, and the decline in federal support for social programs has put great pressure on the local economies and legislative budgets. In Minnesota last year we spent $2.19 per capita for books in public libraries. Better than most states I believe, but no one is suggesting it is enough. Or that it is likely to be increased in the near future. It is not easy to demonstrate a competitive need for public funds for rare books in these times. Or for places to house them or for people to care for them. We are in a mental climate of "no new taxes" and when we emerge from it the causes will be drug control, homeless families, crime, poverty, and education (which will mean computers in classrooms, etc.).

The 1990s, I believe, is a time when selectivity is called for to a degree we have not experienced heretofore in buying or even accepting gift collections. It is a time for seeking quality people who will be able to deal with collections of materials, or individual books, in an intelligent fashion which relates the materials to educational programs and demonstrates their cultural significance. These people are out there (out here). I see them each summer at Rare Book School at Columbia University. What I hear from most of them is the struggle with problems of space and staff. And the shortages in those aspects of our work reflect our past gathering of canaries of all colors. And we are under siege from book thieves who know we have items of monetary value. And under pressure from our administrations often to raise funds to continue the whole operation, to organize and administer friends groups, to live off the land you might say, as we pursue our vocations.

So what is our vocation? It may be well to ask ourselves that at this conference. Our calling is to collect, to protect, to conserve, and to interpret what is good and lasting in our culture, as it is expressed in books and manuscripts. And we must not be negligent in making those judgements about good and lasting. If this sounds like a retreat from where we have been and where we think we are going, then I suggest it might be well at this time to pause, even to retreat, until we have a sense of where we are. Unlike other elements of our society we cannot borrow to buy the illusion of expansion. We need time to digest what we have taken in during the first generation of special collections librarianship, to ponder what is the educational and cultural value of what we have; to consider ways in which we can make our collections and ourselves more active participants in education within our communities.

Here are some excerpts from the application of a librarian who wants to attend this year's introductory course at Columbia's Rare Book School. It is not special. It is representative of many (ca. 75%) we receive and I think captures much of what I am trying to say. "My University was the recipient of a rare book collection forty years ago. After the organization, cataloging, and housing of this collection it has been essentially ignored and inaccessible. A donor has recently provided us with funding to perform necessary conservation, to publicize the existence and availability of the collection. . . . I hope to acquire the knowledge necessary to effectively direct an assessment of preservation needs, provide or perform necessary conservation, describe the scope of the collection in a published guide, and make the existence and availability of the collection widely known."

Most of us, I believe, can identify with this librarian's needs. We are keepers of materials that are in need of repair, conservation, physical rehabilitation. We need to ask ourselves if 40,000 volumes falling apart is better than 20,000 in good condition. Acquisition is the big excitement, I know, but are we doing our institutions a favor by increasing our holdings of materials whose condition is a mortgage upon the future? Or whose condition will decline in our care? When are we going to get even in the conservation game? The Folger Library recently indicated that ten percent of its materials need conservation at any given time. It is unlikely that many of our libraries are in that good condition. When will we be able to show an entire collection without making apologies for any item? Most of us justify our existence by growth figures — holdings and use. I would suggest that in addition to conservation we give some of our energy and money to quality interpretation of holdings which should magnify the number of users, and the quality of use. By this I mean getting closer to the user and the books, being the mediator who brings them together.

This morning I spoke to an honors class: eight high school seniors. Each needs to see and report on five books. Living by statistics is not pleasant, but if we must, then I believe this is the way to build circulation: meeting the needs of students through direct contact with them.

I am not suggesting we give up acquisitions. That must go on, but if the 1990s are no different from the previous four decades we will merely be postponing and enlarging the problems we have inherited or created. Perhaps our greatest challenge will not be in changing our emphasis. We know what the problems are, that the cage is too small. It may be more difficult to convince our administrators, boards of trustees, and Friends that the cage is too small, that we need to change directions, that we should have a high level of convertibility between our acquisitions, our conservation, and our publications budgets. We need this in the name of the quality and usefulness of what we do. We are the keepers of the Library's treasure house. We need to treat our holdings as treasures. We are the ultimate resort of our highest quality scholars. We need to meet them with quality assistance, quality service, quality understanding, quality materials. And we need to be up front about it. It is not elitist to be about what is best and most important. It is no betrayal of our democratic passions to admit to an aristocracy among books. It will be good for our culture if we do so. And by the way it will be good for us as librarians too. Frank Walter, a great early librarian here at the University of Minnesota, wrote in 1925 that we as librarians should "live our own lives in a way that may promote the good of our own souls." What is better for the soul than living among the great authors, caring for their books, listening to their voices, and making it possible for others to hear them. I wish that for all of you in your vocation in the 1990s and beyond.

SELECTED PUBLICATIONS BY JOHN PARKER

BOOKS:

Van Meteren's Virginia, 1607–1612. Minneapolis: University of Minnesota Press, 1961.

Books to Build an Empire. Amsterdam: N. Israel, 1965.

Merchants and Scholars: Essays on the History of Exploration and Travel, edited by John Parker. Minneapolis: University of Minnesota Press, 1965.

Discovery: Developing Views of the Earth from Ancient Times to the Voyages of Captain Cook. New York: Scribner's, 1972.

With Carol Urness. *The American Revolution: A Heritage of Change.* Minneapolis: Associates of the James Ford Bell Library, 1975.

The Journals of Jonathan Carver and Related Documents, 1766–1770. St. Paul: Minnesota Historical Society, 1976.

The World for a Marketplace. Minneapolis: Associates of the James Ford Bell Library, 1978.

ARTICLES, ESSAYS.

"The rare book library and the public," in *Rare book collections,* H. Richard Archer, ed., ACRL Monograph no. 27. Chicago: ALA, 1965.

"Sir John Mandeville," and "Travel literature," in *New Catholic Encyclopedia.*

"The Great Rivers and the Great Lakes: Jonathan Carver's dream of empire," *Burton Lecture.* Lansing: Historical Society of Michigan, 1965.

"A fragment of a fifteenth-century planisphere." In *Imago Mundi,* XIX, 1965.

"Jonathan Carver's map of his travels," in *Homage to a Bookman,* Hellmut Lehmann-Haupt, ed. Berlin: Gebr. Mann Verlag, 1967.

"Jonathan Carver's Travels: The life of a book," in *MnU Bulletin,* May 1970.

"Manuscripts and books, a natural partnership," in *Manuscripts,* XXVI (Spring, 1974).

"Autographs and manuscripts of exploration and travel," in *Autographs and Manuscripts: A Collector's Manual,* Edmund J. Berkeley, Jr., ed. New York: Scribner's, 1978.

"Willard Glazier and the Mississippi Headwaters controversy," in *Terrae Incognitae,* VII, 1976.

"Religion and the Virginia Colony," in *The Westward Enterprise,* K.R. Andrews, N.P. Canny, and P.E.H. Hair, eds. Liverpool: Liverpool University Press, 1978.

"Materials on French Overseas Expansion before 1800 in the James Ford Bell Library, University of Minnesota," in *French Colonial Studies,* number 2, 1978.

Windows into China: The Jesuits and their Books, 1580–1730. The Bromsen Lecture. Boston: Boston Public Library, 1978.

"Original Sources and Weighty Authorities: Some Thoughts on Revisionism and the Historiography of Discovery," in *Terrae Incognitae,* XIII, 1981.

"Book Collecting as a Way of Life," in *The Fourteenth and Fifteenth Alumni-in-Residence Program*, School of Library Science, University of Michigan, 1983.

"The Columbus Landfall Problem: A Historical Perspective," in *Terrae Incognitae*, XV, 1983. This article is included in Louis De Vorsey and John Parker, eds. *In the Wake of Columbus, Islands and Controversy*. Detroit: Wayne State University Press, 1985.

A Long Chain of Words. Minneapolis: Library Council, Minneapolis Institute of Arts, 1986.

"New Light on Jonathan Carver," in *The American Magazine and Historical Chronicle*, 2:1. Ann Arbor: William L. Clements Library, 1986.

Part III. THE LETTERS

The Secret

On 12 March 1990 the following letter was sent:

SECRET SECRET SECRET

Dear Friends,

Many of you already know that John (Jack) Parker will be retiring from his position as Curator of the James Ford Bell Library at the University of Minnesota in May 1991. Even though that is more than a year in the future, the present we have in mind for him—a book, naturally—takes time to prepare. We plan to surprise Jack with the book at the Associates' lecture in May, 1991. You are invited to join us then—and now.

The first part of the book consists of short essays about Jack. Some of his writings on subjects as diverse as his journal of a trip to China to an essay on beekeeping, with introductions, are in the second part. There will also be a few speeches, previously unpublished, dating from 1958 to the present. The third part of the book, if feasible, will consist of extracts of letters from friends. We want you to contribute.

Please write a letter, a poem, an anecdote—whatever, for Jack. It helps, we think, (having just gone through this) to try to write about specific experiences. Do you remember a special occasion—good or bad—that you shared? How do you know Jack—University, the Library, the Society for the History of Discoveries? If you write "Enjoy your retirement, Jack. You are a great guy," we will agree but it will not be very exciting reading. A description of a special occasion would be more fun. Also,

149

please identify your relationship to Jack for us. Please, then, write for Jack. Remember, as we try to, that this is the celebration of a career, not the end of one. Jack will be as active as ever after May of 1991!

From the outset we must make it clear that we will be selective in what is printed from the letters. We'll do our best, but there are several "unknowns" in this project, including cost. Like the philosophers with the camel (or was it an elephant) we can only see part of the creature at the moment. Once we have the letters in hand we will be a lot happier. Therefore, your letters must be received no later than June 1, and May 1 would be a lot nicer. In fact, as soon as possible would be perfect. All the original letters will be given to Jack.

We look forward to your letters. Please keep the secret. Write to either of us at the addresses below. We thank you in advance for your help!

Irv Kreidberg   Carol Urness
2237 Rogers Court   1026 N.E. 23rd Avenue
Mendota Heights, MN 55120 Minneapolis, MN 55418

For the Directors of the Associates of the James Ford Bell Library:
Rutherford Aris, Judy Fennema, Charles Hann, Maynard B. Hasselquist, Irving B. Kreidberg, William P. Laird, Melva Lind, Robert O. Mathson, Bernadette Pyter Muck, Curtis L. Roy, Mrs. Thomas C. Savage, Mrs. Robert J. Schweitzer, Jr., William A. Urseth

The above letter helps to explain the form of salutation and the content of the letters that were written for this book. It may also explain why some of Jack's friends (bless them!) were moved to poetry. As the letters started coming in it was soon clear that editing them would be a mistake. They appear in print as written, each with the special sound of its composer. When a place is not given with the name, assume that the writer is from the Twin Cities or suburbs. Professional titles were cited only if they helped to explain the content of the letters.

Expressing special feelings about Jack and the contributions he has made to our lives is difficult, as everyone discovered. A number of people said they simply couldn't do it. Those who did labor with the pen (or the computer) found the effort worthwhile. The readers of this book will be most grateful. Thank you for the special words and thoughts.

ABBASS, Kathy, Newport, Rhode Island.

Dear Carol:

This is the hardest thing I have had to write in a long time! And
it still doesn't say what I want it to tell Jack. Also, with apologies
to his wife — she shouldn't get the wrong idea . . .

FOR JACK

How do you write a love letter
To someone who listened
    When you hated your job
    When your father died
    When you thought through risks.

How do you write a love letter
To someone who would share
    The wisdom of his past
    The comfort of his soul
    The courage of his life.

How do you write a love letter
When it can only say
    Thank you for making time
    Thank you for giving care
    Thank you for being there.

Hope the volume finds its way to success. Jack deserves it more
than anyone I know.

            Fondly, Kathy Abbass   22 May 1990

ANDERSON, Leland I., Denver, Colorado.

My Fond Recollections of Jack Parker

    I first met Jack about 30 years ago at one of the regular meet-
ings of the Twin Cities Chapter of the Manuscript Society. Meetings were and still are held monthly except during the summer,
rotating locations in the members' homes or institutional settings
of the member's association. The chapter members include manuscript collectors, philatelists, bibliophiles and booksellers, and

librarians and archivists — an encompassing cross section of those interested in the written and printed lines of history.

Once a year, at a fall meeting, Jack would tell us of his annual junkets to European antiquarian booksellers in search of select items for the Bell Library collection — such booksellers as Francis Edwards and Dr. E. Weil in London, Martinus Nijhoff in The Hague, and Ludwig Rohrscheid in Bonn. They would have signs "By Appointment Only" on their doors. Not having carte blanche sponsorship, although finely endowed, Jack was rather cagey ("slick operator" might be the better term!) in extracting some of the exquisitely unique items from the seller's shelves without being forced to pay an arm and a leg for them.

Jack would tell of such charming moves as spotting a particular prize and then adding several other lesser titles to disguise the real object of his prey. The game of the skilled seller, observing every nuance of the visitor in his shop, and shrewd buyer had just begun because the items are not priced — and it would seem to be at the whim of the seller, who may have gotten out of the wrong side of the bed that day, what the price would be. Suppressing eagerness and feigning indifference by leaving a title behind, the deal is closed. Can a hand of a large-pot poker be more exciting than this?

Because of Jack's indefatigable efforts, the annual publication of *The Merchant Explorer* has resulted in a prize among collectors for the entire set. Although the citation line has carried the words "occasional paper" all these years, that recognizable blue-grey cover with muse has been appearing regularly for the past 29 years. Jack has left us with many memories and admiration of his accomplishments.

Leland Anderson   30 April 1990

ANONYMOUS.

Once upon a time there was a very young English bookseller. And very green. Just how young and green he was you can tell from the fact that he thought he could visit all his U.S. customers (from New England to Florida to the Midwest to California) in 30 days; by Amtrack; on 900 pounds.

After Bloomington, Indiana the next stop was Minneapolis (sorry, that's after Ann Arbor?) starting roughly N.E. and finishing S.W. So he was about 70 % through his trip. But more than 70 % through his time and his money. So he had taken to travelling by night and sleeping on the trains. That saved both. For reasons of timetable, that would not work out on the journey to Minneapolis, but there was a train which arrived about 5 o'clock in the afternoon. Makes a nice change from 5 o'clock in the morning he thought. He was rewarded beyond expectation. A most glorious journey up the valley of the great river, the countryside dappled and stippled with its autumnal colours; countryside on a sheer scale previously unimagined. Alone in glass observation car, smoking a cheap cigar (that may have been why) enthralled by his surroundings. With the time (at Amtrack's pace) to inspect the changing beauty of every passing tree reflected in the waters.

His arrival at Minneapolis was unpropitious. It was rather cold whereas Bloomington had been hot, and he was dressed accordingly. And it was drizzling and all the hotels seemed full — there was a Legionnaires' convention, and lunch in Bloomington (yesterday) was a long time off and there was a night train out, wasn't there? But he had an appointment the next morning with Dr. John Parker, the head of the James Ford Bell, who had shown an interest in his first catalogue. So he had to be there. He could not 'phone, by now they would be well closed.

A taxi man saved him. He told the driver the problem and how much he had to spend for the night. The man was doubtful. Then he said that, well, there was one place, it had been ok once but it was rather run down now, but it was cheap and it was not far. That decided it. But he need not have worried. Because the man said that rather than his fare he would like to have some English coins to take back to his boy. And that was his introduction to the people of Minneapolis. And the opinion of them he then formed he has never had reason to change.

In the vast crumbling reception area of the hotel he and the man behind the desk were alone. It seemed that they were alone in the hotel, too. Until he got to the lift. It and the lift boy must have been installed together, in the ancient days of glory of the American railway hotel. They were both now very, very old and both creaked upward in sympathetic unison.

The room was completely familiar. He had seen it before at least once, at the cinema. The brown stains, the peeling paper, cigarette burns and long faded colours. That's it, "Death of a Salesman." He attempted, unsuccessfully, to banish the unreassuring thought. Once the light was off it became swiftly apparent that he was not alone. There were many occupants already. Small, well not that small and apparently able to jump *and* fly. He had not met them before and did not know whether they bit. So he went hunting. But they seemed capable of instantaneous reproduction, and at length, exhausted by his exertions against overwhelming odds, he fell asleep.

In the morning he got directions, he had not seen anywhere to get a map. And he found a bus stop, and a bus driver who said he went near. And though, in his anxiety not to be late he got off a stop early, he soon found his way to the landmark of the James Ford Bell Museum.

But no, Dr. Parker was not here. Try the university library. So he did. It was now raining very hard. But no this is not the James Ford Bell. Back across that bridge. Wet and late. Try the Wilson Library, so he did. That infernal bridge again. Wetter, and later and out of breath. It is a long run with a heavy brief case. Yes, upstairs, at last. Dr. John Parker.

The warmest of welcomes. No, they had not met before. But a fellow bibliophile, therefore an old friend. Can I take your coat and dry it out? Let's see your list. Come and look at some of our treasures. These are our interests, what are yours? All so unexpected, such quiet enthusiasm for the Book, for England, such friendliness for a young green bookseller, no longer in a hurry, and certainly not to go. A leisurely and delicious lunch (the first since a long time and triply welcome) and conversation to match on Books and Bookmen, as if between equals but with the wisdom and experience all on one side. Back to the library, a Sale! Undeserved and probably not really that much wanted. Made above all to encourage, but unpatronizingly. Even the sun shone. Literally as well as metaphorically. We have really enjoyed your visit, you must keep in regular touch. So much time, an incredible amount of time and imperceptible effort to make the tyro feel at home, and he did. Unsparing, unmerited goodwill and generosity of spirit and of learning. He is grateful still.

And if one day a very grand old English bookseller dealing in nothing less than complete De Brys (extra illustrated) shall be, he will still think with affection of his reception at the James Ford Bell and above all of Jack Parker, that day in ages past. And live happily ever after.

15 May 1990

ARCHABAL, Nina. Director, Minnesota Historical Society.

Dear Jack:

News of your retirement as Curator of the James Ford Bell Library has reminded us at the Minnesota Historical Society of all that you have contributed to our organization — and how much we continue to benefit from your presence. You have been a long-time friend of history and honored colleague in our work to collect, preserve, and tell the Minnesota story.

You have contributed significantly to historical scholarship. Your books on early Minnesota history including *The Journals of Jonathan Carver*, which the Society was privileged to publish, have enlightened our understanding of the past. Your leadership in planning the bicentennial commemoration of the Northwest Ordinance and U.S. Constitution was invaluable. With your guidance as a member of the coordinating committee, the excellent and popular exhibit "Liberty's Legacy" was presented.

This letter gives me the opportunity to thank you for your service on the Society's Executive Council for two terms beginning in 1982, and for your leadership on the State Review Board. It is characteristic of you to respond to our call for help — most recently serving as chairman of the State Review Board.

Congratulations on a sterling career at the James Ford Bell Library. You have set a high standard for those who will come after you.

Sincerely, Nina   22 May 1990

ARIS, Rutherford and Claire.

Reflections upon "Keeping Bees" by Jack Parker (Maple Ridge Press, 1984)

> The chief delight of Parker, J.
> Was contemplating bees all day.
> He loved those ten days in July
> When the hive's weight may multiply,
> And busy bees on nectar rounds
> Can store a good one hundred pounds;
> Sipping each drop from flowers' bells,
> Winging it back to clammy cells,
> And passing it with insect kisses
> From mandibles to proboscises.
> Moreover if one finds a field
> Which promises fantastic yield,
> That bee will do a little dance
> To tell its sisters, cousins, aunts
> Just where to go to soon collect a
> Good supply of honey nectar.
> But little honey hath the hive
> Wherein the drones are left alive
> When frosty days of autumn tell
> Each worker to resume her cell
> And feed on honey with the queen
> Throughout the winter cold and keen.
>
> Not only will Jack contemplate
> He can be seen to imitate
> Their industry, with deep devotion,
> Their every task, their very motion.
> For in the hive of James Ford Bell
> He's house bee, field bee — Queen as well;
> His cells are shelves, his nectar, finds,
> Those records rare of eager minds,
> Travels and far-flung explorations,
> And even missioners' Relations
> Which languish in some catalog
> 'Till Jack, antennae all agog,
> Flies (sort of) thither, using the
> Good service of A. T. & T.
> And when the mail supplies his wants

He does a metaphoric dance,
Though none but Carol Urness knows
Whence came those precious folios.
His nectar home, just like the bee,
He must control humidity,
Not quite by fanning of his wings,
But rather to the vault he brings
Each volume to be kept with care.
But that it will not languish there
Unread, unhonored and unsung,
Whate'er the subject or the tongue
He'll read it through and swiftly will,
With sure hand and consummate skill
Condense it for the Manifest —
A task at which he's — simply — BEST.

Now it is true, admittedly,
That Apian Economy
Does not to any great extent
Instruct us on retirement
Yet we are sure that good old Jack
For things to do will never lack.
So do not fear, you'll surely see
He'll be as busy as a bee.

With warmest regards and best wishes for a long and happy
retirement, from Gus and Claire Aris   9 April 1990

ARKWAY, Richard B., New York City.

Dear Jack,

I am pleased that your approaching retirement has given me
the occasion to write a letter expressing how rewarding I've found
our relationship over the years.

The Bell was one of the first libraries I visited when I became
a book dealer in about 1978. As a collector I had read *Books to
Build an Empire* and had been absolutely captivated by the ideas
I found there and impressed by the clarity with which they were
expressed. I met you, Jack, that first visit and I distinctly remem-

ber how you came across. You were just like your writing; honest, clear and concise. It was a great introduction to a new career for me.

Since that first visit, I've been to the Bell many times and each time have come away with a clearer understanding of the books I've come to show you. I'm glad to hear that you're going to remain active within the field as I'd miss both the visits and the writing.

Yours truly, Dick   7 May 1990

ARNEVIK, Lennie.

Dear Jack,

So you too have reached that time in your life when you intend to do things at a more leisurely pace. To me you personify the James Ford Bell Library. You have taken it from conception to one of the premier libraries of its kind in the country, a most remarkable accomplishment. I would like to express my appreciation and thanks for your capable and devoted efforts to bring this library to the status it enjoys today.

As a former employee of the Bell Family, I had the opportunity and the privilege on numerous occasions to work with you and I always found them most enjoyable and rewarding.

May you find your retirement years very satisfying and filled with much happiness.

Warmest personal regards, Lennie   14 May 1990

BAKER, Zachary M., YIVO, New York City.

Dear Carol,

I got your letter of March 12th, and hasten to reply, before I think of an excuse to procrastinate (taxes,my father's impending visit, articles to write, etc.). Strike while the iron is hot. The idea of honoring Jack with a book is wonderful. Will there be a party as well? If so, please keep me informed. I'd like to be on hand, if possible. (I realize that the event won't be taking place for a year, but I like to plan ahead.)

What is there to say about Jack that someone else (who may know him better, or longer than I) won't say better? It is hard. No single encounter or event sticks out in my mind. This much I can say, however; I have always been somewhat in awe of Jack Parker, ever since I was his (and your) student in the disbanded University of Minnesota Library School's Descriptive Bibliography course. He epitomizes what I have always aspired to be, in my own career: the scholar-librarian. That is a model that, in this increasingly technocratic age, is not in such great favor in a profession whose literature more and more emphasizes *modes* of communication (of information), rather than *content*. It is the library equivalent of the conflict (about which much has been written of late) in museums between the role of the curator/scholar and that of the designer/fundraiser/manager. Both roles are necessary, but there needs to be a balance. In this day and age, Jack and the Bell Library stand for the curatorial and content-oriented approach toward the information contained in the Library's collections. Bibliographical control is a tool, a means to an end, not the end in and of itself. I have a friend at the Library of Congress who likes to joke about the catalogers among his colleagues (you might have guessed that he himself works on the public service and collection development side of the street), who point to the bibliographical records that they create with pride, compared to which the actual works cataloged are but a pale reflection. This has never been Jack's approach, and it is not mine.

Most of my fellow librarians have indifferent memories of the professional education that is required in order to take a job as a librarian. Library school is regarded as a burden to be overcome and then forgotten, or at least such was the case among many of my contemporaries. When I attended the U of M Library School back in the mid-1970s, one could scarcely point to the school as a state-of-the-art outfit. There was not one course in computer applications in libraries — this at a time when the bibliographic networks were really getting off the ground. There was an early morning, ill-attended course in reprography, which I avoided like the plague, and feel none the worse for it these many years later. There were the usual introductory courses, required of all students, and of thoroughly mediocre quality. But for all its faults, the U of M Library School was a citadel of excellence, when it came to teaching the basics of traditional librarianship. I have very fond memories indeed, of Raymond Shove's courses on national bibliographies and the history of books and printing. None of what he taught in those courses is truly obsolete. I enjoyed Edward Stanford's course in academic librarianship; for him the topic was hardly "academic." And above all, I feel privileged, truly privileged, to have been Jack's and your student in Descriptive Bibliography.

These days, entire programs at some library schools are built around rare books librarianship; such was not really the case 15 years ago. So what my fellow students and I learned in your course was the rudiments of something we certainly could not study elsewhere in the Library School, perhaps not in many or most library schools of the day. I know that Jack's reputation as a teacher and a librarian has carried far and wide, by virtue of the fact that he has been asked to teach at the Columbia University School of Library Service, during their summer rare books course. (A colleague of mine in New York was fortunate enough to be enrolled as one of Jack's students a year or two ago, and he could not praise him too highly). For me, the Descriptive Bibliography course was one of the most pleasurable formal learning experiences I've ever had. Sitting over the variant editions, reading them for content, learning about the author, performing the requisite bibliographic description — all of these were intensely enjoyable. My "Plan B" paper on five 18th century editions of two works by Jorge Juan and Antonio de Ulloa, about a scientific expedition undertaken to measure the shape and curvature of the earth, still occupies a place of honor on my bookshelves, and every time I open it (less often, as the years go by, regretfully) I think of the Bell Library. I occasionally see one or another of the editions that I described, in an antiquarian bookdealer's catalog. That too turns my thought to Descriptive Bibliography. If the works weren't so expensive I'd buy them!

One of my few vivid classroom memories is of a film that we were shown, about the Plantin-Moretus Museum in Antwerp. The 17th century press of the great Belgian printing dynasty, as the film demonstrated, is still intact and indeed is housed in the same building where, 300 years ago, it produced some of the most important books of its time. The Plantin press, in its technology, closely resembles the press used by Gutenberg, a couple of hundred years earlier — a rare opportunity for us to see a model of that most influential of human inventions. Well, a few years after graduation I found myself in Amsterdam, en route to Paris, and I made a special stop in Antwerp, just to visit the Plantin-Moretus Museum. It is one of the most exciting and inspiring museums I have ever visited, with its displays of the significant editions of the Plantin house (including their great polyglot Bibles). I doubt I would ever have given Antwerp a second thought had it not been for that film we had been shown in Jack's class.

Jack Parker is the only one of my former professors, on both the undergraduate and graduate levels (and I've attended three universities) with whom I am still in regular contact. Whenever I visit Minneapolis I try to schedule a trip to the Bell Library. Jack is always available for a leisurely conversation. We talk about books, work, exhibits, places . . . And whenever I have the opportunity to speak with him I am reminded of a throwaway Hebrew phrase, "Mi-kol melamdai hiskalti" — "I have learned from all of my teachers." Sometimes that phrase is used jocularly, as if to say, I have learned from them and now I know more than they do. That, however, is precisely the opposite of what I want to convey here. From Jack I have learned something about both methods *and* substance. I only wish that I had the chance to learn more. I suspect that all of his former students feel the same way. In his retirement I am sure that Jack will continue to be a beacon for the scholar-librarians who persist in their obstinate loyalty to the humanistic ideals of their chosen profession, who have the ability to look beyond (while not ignoring) title-page, verso, and colophon — for it is only through reading and absorbing the work as a whole that we can be said to have truly learned something from it.

I've gone on quite long enough! Pardon my verbosity. Keep me posted on the Book. Be well. Yours truly, Zack 23 March 1990

BARCKLEY, Gwendolyn. Sun City, Arizona.

June First! June First! June First!
Press the panic button!!!
Carol —

Your idea of the testimonial book for John Parker is great and I hope you receive many fine contributions. Alas, I cannot think of anything special to write except to say that I would not be contributing to the James Ford Bell Library if it were not for him.
        Good luck, Penny Barckley   1 June 1990
                P.S. I have kept the secret.

BARON, Samuel H., University of North Carolina, Chapel Hill.

Unfortunately for me, my personal acquaintance with Jack Parker dates only to 1986. In the fall of that year, I presented a paper, "Herberstein and the English 'Discovery' of Russia," to the annual meeting of the Society for the History of Discoveries. (It was later published in *Terrae Incognitae*, XVIII, 1986). A newcomer to the organization at the time, I was of course interested in meeting persons I knew either by reputation or through professional contact. Jack was prominently on hand and, as I had earlier had some written and telephone communication with him, I was pleased to introduce myself. At the Society's meeting in London the following summer, we were fellow members of a panel devoted to a Hakluyt Society project long in gestation, *The Purchas Handbook*. We were well impressed with each other's paper, a sure basis for the development of friendship, and (together with Carol Urness and my wife) while chatting animatedly we joyfully careened in a taxi from a hotel to the conference banquet and back.

As a historian of Russia, it is not surprising that my awareness of Jack Parker grew out of my interest in the intersection of travel literature and Russia. In 1967 I translated and edited a treatise that appeared as *The Travels of Olearius in Seventeenth Century Russia*. This endeavor marked my transition from a concentration on 19th/20th century Russian history to the Muscovite era (16th-17th centuries). In Muscovite history, I was particularly drawn to studies of merchants and commerce: and because England was then particularly important in Muscovy's commercial relations, I spent a good deal of time poring over the materials in Richard Hakluyt's *Principall Navigations* and in relevant Hakluyt Society publications.

Still, I might never have done anything specifically on travels beyond the work on Olearius but for an invitation tendered me in 1982 by Loren Pennington to contribute a chapter to *The Purchas Handbook*. The invitation came out of the blue, but in an early letter to me Pennington indicated that I had been highly recommended to him by Parker. Moreover, early in my research for the first time I came upon Parker's *Books to Build an Empire*. It was a real eye-opener for me, and I have repeatedly returned to and cited this painstaking and insightful book in other writing I have done. I am indebted to Parker on that score as well as for his recommendation, for my agreement to contribute led me to write not only the chapter for the *Handbook* on "Russia and Central Asia" but also a series of other articles whose genesis lay in my research for the just-named piece.

The most valuable material on Russia in the Purchas materials, so it seems to me, was that relating to an expedition carried out in 1611, and extended for some years thereafter, to the Pechora-Ob region of Muscovy's northern shores. In my view, this material spotlighted a significant but barely noticed episode in the long-term English quest for a northeastern passage. I was impelled to look into the earlier English endeavors as well as into the circumstances and consequences of this last effort. These investigations yielded the substance of a pair of articles I published: "Muscovy and the English Quest for a Northeastern Passage to Cathay (1553–1584)" *Acta Slavica Iaponica*, III (1985) and "Thrust and Parry: Anglo-Russian Relations in the Muscovite North," *Oxford Slavonic Studies*, XXI (1988).

Parker also figured, in at least a small way, in some other papers I have published. When my article "Did the Russians Discover Spitsbergen?" (it appeared in *Forschungen zur osteuropaischen Geschichte*, 38, 1986) was in galleys, I needed urgently to see a work which was to be found nowhere else in the United States but in the James Ford Bell Library. I phoned Parker to explain my problem, and he generously agreed to dispatch the book to me forthwith. Not long after, I applied for a Folger Library grant, hoping there to press forward my research into the influence of Herberstein in sixteenth-century England. In answer to a query I sent to Parker, he assured me that all the sixteenth century publications listed in his appendix to *Books to Build an Empire* could be found in the Folger. I mentioned this in my grant application. I was awarded the grant, and I succeeded in my three months at the Folger in writing two further articles. As often happens, one of the pieces turned out to have only a tangential relation to what I set out to do, and instead drew me into a study in the history of cartography: "William Borough and the Jenkinson Map of Russia (1562)," *Cartographica*, 26, No. 2, 1989.

In sum, although my relations with Jack Parker commenced not long ago, and although they have been neither intense nor sustained, they have been decidedly beneficial to me. Accordingly, I feel much indebted to Jack, whom I think of as the very model of a helpful, gracious, accommodating colleague.

Samuel H. Baron   26 March 1990

BELL, Charles H.

Dear John,

I guess all things, and particularly all good things, must eventually come to an end. It's kind of sad in one way to think that the time for your retirement as Curator of the James Ford Bell Library is to happen within the next year.

Even though that will eventually take place, I'm sure that your interest in the Library will never diminish and that your counsel and advice will always be available.

How fortunate Father was to have made the initial contact with you and then the arrangement for you to take over as Curator of his Library. What a superb job you have done over all these years!

I know how terribly proud and pleased Father was in his relationship with you and the way you were directing and guiding the

Library. If he could be alive today, he would be even more excited, pleased and proud.

So this letter brings to you my thanks and appreciation on behalf of the Bell family for a superb job. I know these have been happy years for you, and I hope the years ahead will be just as fulfilling and give you the contentment and the satisfaction that you deserve.

Best, Charlie   April, 1990

BENTLEY, Jerry H., Editor, *Journal of World History*, University of Hawaii, Honolulu.

Dear Jack:

The word recently arrived here in the antipodes that you plan to retire in May of 1991. Retirement of course means different things to different people. In your case I imagine it bringing a reprieve from administrative routines, but hardly an end to a distinguished career dealing with books — the collection and care of books, the frequent writing about the books of others and even the composition of your own, and the expert and generous help provided to those seeking their own ways into the world of books.

This last point prompts my reflection on our first meeting, back during the winter of 1972, when I wandered into the Bell Library in search of a research project for the following spring quarter. As a first-year graduate student, I had a lot of enthusiasm, but little background or experience doing genuine historical research. With a little help from our friend Carol, we soon identified some materials in the Bell collection that could serve as the basis for a research paper — accounts of travel to Brazil and efforts to establish a French colony there by two sixteenth-century Frenchmen, André Thevet and Jean de Lery. The result was hardly a scholarly masterpiece: this I can say with some confidence, since I still have a copy of the paper and have occasionally looked through it during the course of the past 18 years. But it offered me a first opportunity to grapple with genuine primary source materials — in their original sixteenth century editions — and to develop those skills of analysis and interpretation that professional historians

166 A BOOK FOR JACK

must possess and employ in their work. As a result, that research project brings back good memories, and even now I appreciate your efforts to help an amateur develop some professional qualities.

Thanks again, Jack, and have a great career in retirement!

Cordially, Jerry   21 May 1990

BOSSE, David. The Clements Library, Ann Arbor, Michigan.

David made the map that appears as endpapers of this book. Wonderful!

BOWMAN, Daniel C., Eugene, Oregon.

This is in response to your letter of March 12, concerning Jack Parker's retirement. As an undergraduate at the University in 1965 I enrolled in an Honors class in Travel and Travel Literature, taught by Jack Parker. That course was my first encounter with scholarly research and, as it turned out, one of the most positive ever. It was challenging and fun. I learned as much about myself as about travel literature and the James Ford Bell Room; particularly in terms of having confidence in myself in an academic setting. While my education and my work have taken me in various other directions, I sometimes wonder if I shouldn't have been (or yet be) an historical geographer.

That experience in 1965 had both an immediate and a lasting impact on my life. It definitely helped me decide to pursue an academic career; and a few years ago when I decided I wanted to start contributing to the University, it was clear to me that the James Ford Bell Library was the one right place for me to direct my contributions. I enjoy reading *The Manifest* and occasionally imagine doing research in the Library again some day. It sounds like Jack continues to affect students today as he did me twenty-five years ago. I still read travel literature and I can still put my hands on the paper I wrote for that class in 1965. Jack Parker certainly had a positive, continuing influence on my life. Thank you for the opportunity to reflect on that.

Sincerely yours, Daniel C. Bowman   12 April 1990

BRANIN, Joseph J., Director, Humanities/Social Sciences
Libraries

Dear Jack,

Several years ago Oscar Handlin wrote in *The American Scholar*, "A collection is evidence of a mind at work, making choices in the light of some view of knowledge—past, present, and future. . . . " While you leave the University of Minnesota and the James Ford Bell Library as a worker—a fine librarian, scholar, and teacher—for retirement, you leave behind a collection and program, unique in the world, that will keep your presence with us for generations to come. Your "mind at work" has built and shared a special collection on the history of European expansionism that will influence scholarship for the rest of time. Your teaching and writing also leave a permanent mark on our understanding of world history.

In my five-year association with you and the James Ford Bell Library, I have been most impressed with your unswerving pursuit of quality and genuine knowledge. While much of librarianship these days seems consumed by quantification and data processing, you have remained steady in selecting only the best books, pamphlets, and maps for the James Ford Bell Library and making sure this collection becomes part of knowledge through teaching, research, and writing. Your career has been a model for many of us, although few of us will achieve as much as you. Building great collections, generating and communicating knowledge, not data processing and retrieval, are at the real heart of librarianship. You have shown us the way through work and deed, and we will forever be grateful to you.

Sincerely, Joe   10 July 1990

BRAY, Martha C.

I can't remember how it came about. Memory tends to send its messages from the mountain tops rather than from the plains of experience. This was a mountain top, a watershed. I was in the Chicago airport—although, it having been so long ago, I tend to think of it in a railroad station. It would have been more appropriate. My companion was a scholar and easy and pleasant to talk to about anything that came to mind. Our trip together must have come about quite naturally, as I would have known then. But now I can't remember what had gone before. How did it happen that Jack Parker, Director of the James Ford Bell Library invited, yes urged, me to come with him to a meeting of the Society for the History of Discoveries of which he had been a founder and was then president? What I remember is the sensation of extreme pleasure and relaxation in his company and my feeling of astonishment that this was so.

I had no manuscript in hand, no special project of research. I was only a comparative stranger in the Twin Cities with a degree in Library Science. I was nervous. How had I allowed myself to come on this mad journey to a meeting of scholars where I had nothing to offer?

The answer to this is known to all of you who read this. Jack Parker was born to encourage anyone in whatever walk of life who shows the slightest sign of pursuing an interest beyond the classroom, the necessary job, or any current mode of thought. With his own quiet convictions, he draws from others thoughts and ideas they may never have expressed before. I don't think he and I talked of momentous matters as we sat at dinner, but we talked and I felt at ease and after twenty-five years, I realize more than ever how rare a feeling that is in this increasingly contentious world.

Martha

BROWN, Elizabeth.

John Parker, Curator of the James Ford Bell Library

A distinguished scholarly young man described the new Bell Library at a University Library Staff Meeting in 1953. He was introduced as John Parker.

He came into the Acquisitions Department to order books on early exploration. I worked on the history books. Catalogs from rare book dealers such as Nijhoff in the Netherlands were used for book purchases with Special Bell Funds. An old book about

Marco Polo took months to get. He was always patient and had a great knowledge of the rare book trade.

James Ford Bell came to the Library to discuss the development of the Collection. He inadvertently parked his car on one occasion in a spot the University Police had prohibited. "Jack" was seen diplomatically going about extricating the car from difficulty.

A Christmas party in the beautiful Bell Room was especially lovely. We discussed early South Dakota history by the antique fireplace as we drank punch.

The rapt attention of history students who listened to his lectures on the history of world commerce surrounded by original exhibits of books, maps and manuscripts is most memorable. He broadened their view of history.

Elizabeth Brown   29 April 1990

BUISSERET, David, The Newberry Library, Chicago.

Thanks for your secret letter. As a matter of fact, I do have a strong and persistent image of Jack; it's Jack the Good Captain (of the James Ford Bell Library, naturally). I often had to get in touch with the Library on business concerning either the Newberry or the Society for the History of Discoveries, and over ten years, from 1980 to 1990, I do not think that there was one occasion when Jack was "out to lunch" or "in conference" or any of the other imaginary places that so many of us often are. Nor did I have to go through a barrage of secretaries; you simply dialled 612–624–1528, and the Good Captain replied, at the helm of his Library as ever. What a record for the rest of us!

David   19 March 1990

CATZ, Dr. Rebecca, Beverly Hills, California.

Dear Jack,

I just heard about your (im)pending retirement. I don't know if that's good or bad for you, for Minnesota, or for mankind in general. But before you go on — to bigger and better things of course — I wanted to write you a farewell missive of sorts, since, without the James Ford Bell to bind us, I don't know if our paths will ever cross again.

I wanted this letter to be light, airy, amusing. But how can I poke fun at someone like you who has always been so "correct" in his relations with me? For the life of me, I cannot think of a single misstep, a single imperfection that could make you the butt of my banter. No, Jack, you're no good for roasting.

Ah, nostalgia . . . I'm trying to remember when first we met. It must have been way back in the 70s. I was in Minneapolis attending a medical meeting with my husband. I had brought some work with me which wasn't going too well. Francis Rogers had given me a rare 16th century letter, written by Fernão Mendes Pinto in 1571, which Harvard University had purchased a few years before. He wanted me to publish it in a journal. I thought it was too precious to waste on a journal. I got the brilliant idea of publishing it in a collection of Pinto's other letters and related documents. But where, and how, to begin gathering the material, most of which was scattered in libraries all over the world. Well, there I was — sitting in a hotel room in Minneapolis, ruminating over the matter and reluctant to attend a session on medicine about which I know nothing. I suddenly remembered that in a moment of weakness I had sent a check some time before to the Associates of the James Ford Bell Library, little dreaming of all the benefits that were to ensue. I did not know much about the library at the time, or its holdings, but what could I lose? I called the Library. It was Jack who answered. He knew my name. I was amazed. I had only recently joined the Associates, never really expecting to make use of it or ever to visit it. I told him what I needed. He said, "come right over", and I'm glad I did. (As a matter of fact, most of the material that eventually went into the book came from the James Ford Bell.) I was indeed surprised by the Library's holdings. It was so pleasant working there. I felt special. Jack brought me the material I requested. He xeroxed it for me. He even invited me to lunch. I had never worked in such a warm, relaxed, and amenable atmosphere.

The book was eventually published under the title, *Cartas de Fernão Mendes Pinto e outros documentos*. It made no splash.

Perhaps because it was published in Portugal, in Portuguese; but I did send Jack a copy of the book for the library where to this day I hope it rests. The point of all this is that I felt I had acquired a friend. And the following year I raised my contribution to the Associates, of which I had become a fan, as well as a friend.

I never went back to Minnesota. But over the years, whenever I needed something, you, Jack, were always there. Whether it was material for research, a letter of recommendation, illustrations — as for my recent translation of Mendes Pinto — I got it from you — promptly and efficiently. (Jack, did I thank you for the microfilm of Damião de Gois' Latin work you sent me recently? I don't remember.)

But whatever you do from now on Jack — good luck. And for heaven's sake, *enjoy* whatever it is you do.

> Sincerely, Rebecca Catz   23 April 1990

P.S. Hope to see you at the next SHD meeting in Jamaica.

CHRIST, Tracey.

Dear Jack,

You can't believe how hard it has been to write this. It has been so difficult trying to put my thoughts down into words.

I feel very honored having been able to get the chance to work with you. I have enjoyed working with you, Carol, Mary [Whitehead], Sara [Shannon] and Ellen [Skog] — you have all been like a second family.

I remember when I first started working for the library and I wasn't exactly sure what to expect. I felt very impressed when I learned about the many different things you have done and the places you have traveled. Working with you for the past two years I've had the chance to learn even more about your achievements. You have accomplished so much during your life; I hope that I can lead such a fulfilling life.

I know you will keep on leading a very fulfilling life after your retirement. I'm really glad I got the chance to work with you.

> Love, Tracey Christ

COLE, Maud, Astoria, New York.

Dear John:

Greetings and congratulations on all you have accomplished.

It is good to see you each summer at Columbia Rare Book School lectures — brings back memories of University of Michigan School of Library Science — classes and faculty: Dr. Bishop, Miss Mann, Miss Wead, and Miss Parsons.

A more recent memory: the Rare Book Room at The New York Public Library — visit of Dr. Bell and showing him some of our treasures, *e.g.* Hunt Lenox globe (early 1500s), and other treasures.

More recently — the privilege of visiting the James Ford Bell Library when SHD was held in Minneapolis.

Enjoy your "retirement" but remain professionally active — research, writing, travel + + +

Best wishes always. Sincerely, Maud Cole   25 April 1990

DANIELS, John.

It got started quite a few years ago when I lured you out to see a small sporting book exhibit in my office in the country. You most graciously drove out to inspect that first exhibit and you have continued to come back each summer to see subsequent exhibits. These occasions have been very special events for me because they have provided an opportunity to have long and relaxed discussions about our mutual interest in rare books.

One thing that I remember vividly about one of your visits was the time that I was writing a paper about literary fakes and forgeries. It turned out that you had been an expert witness at the Smithsonian symposium in 1966 when the authenticity of the VINLAND MAP was being so hotly debated. In your modest way you told me about the key role which you had played in suggesting that the controversial document be physically tested to determine its real age. What a remarkably practical suggestion! In retrospect your recommendation was so fundamental and basic that it isn't surprising that the assembled "egg heads" had completely failed to even think of it.

I was fascinated by your store of knowledge about the Vinland Map, and I subsequently used some of the information in my paper about fakes and forgeries. Your expert knowledge and opinions in just this one case are a small sample of the scholarly approach which you have always taken to books and maps and other documents about explorations in general as well as many other subjects. Your balanced, philosophical approach which you bring to these subjects has always been one of your outstanding characteristics.

I hope that you will continue to come out to see me and my little book shows each summer. Martha and I will look forward to your future visits — you are always welcome.

Cordially, John   25 March 1990

DUNN, Oliver, West Lafayette, Indiana.

Dear Jack,

As your retirement approaches I'd like to thank you for the great pleasure that knowing you and knowing something of your work over the past nearly 30 years have given me.

I still have and enjoy re-reading my file of *The Merchant Explorer*, every new issue of which I read avidly. And the Society for the History of Discoveries, which I must have joined within a year or two of its founding, is an organization that not only has provided me with an opportunity to communicate with others interested in geographical discovery, but also has provided lasting friendships, ours in particular. I look forward each year to renewing our association.

I must credit you also, Jack, with the remark that prompted me and others to embark on our close study of Columbus's *Diario*. It was at our 1980 meeting in Florida, at the hotel bar, that you said "it's time to take a new look at Columbus," and so we did. I'm not sure whether this remark preceded or followed your article on "Original Sources and Weighty Authorities" in *Terrae Incognitae* 13, 1981, in which you expressed the same ideas. At any rate, carrying out your plea to study the "original" text of the *Diario*, four years later *In the Wake of Columbus* appeared, and eight years later Jim Kelley's and my edition and translation of the *Diario* were published. And a continuing study of Columbus's first voyage currently engages the attention of a group numbering about 25, which maintains a lively "round robin" of correspondence on Columbus subjects. Quite a "ripple effect!"

Although you may not plan, after your retirement, to spend time in the Bell Library on a daily basis, I'm sure your influence will continue to be felt there and that you will go right on with your studies, perhaps able to take on projects that you could not undertake while in charge. I'll look forward to a string of interesting publications from you, as well as to seeing you regularly at the annual meetings of the Society.

Jane joins me in congratulations to you on work well done, and good wishes for a lively and productive retirement.

Oliver   27 May 1990

ENTERLINE, James, New York City.

Dear Jack Parker:

I first rubbed elbows with you (literally) in 1972 on an SHD panel in Lawrence, Kansas. I quickly discovered that although our specializations were in quite different fields, we shared many fundamental interests, particularly in historiographic method.

Our paths converged more specifically that year when *Imago Mundi* published my article holding some differences with a publication of yours — *Tidings out of Brazil*. We had a disagreement far more radical than that of proponents of any Columbus Landfall or Vinland Location. You believed the voyage went to Brazil and I believed it went to Sumatra! Our ensuing correspondence (I can supply copies) led ultimately to your 1981 article in *Terrae Incognitae*. There you implied that other colleagues might join in and help us break our deadlock.

No one else seems to have been interested, Jack. Perhaps after 1992 more minds will be available for this kind of pursuit. To stir up discussion we might plan a "Jack and Jim Show" at some future SHD meeting, coming together again in a panel. That is the kind of thing that retirement is for.

Most sincerely, Jim   16 April 1990

ERVIN, Jean and John.

Dear Jack,

Where to begin? "Begin at the beginning," said Lewis Carroll's king, very gravely. And so we think back to our arrival in Minnesota in 1957, and to the fact that you and Pat were among the first people we came to know.

Thereafter, together and sometimes also with your girls and our boys, we shared talk, laughter, food. We particularly remember several Thanksgivings when the combined families sat — well, anyway, the grownups sat — and ate, and you remarked that so much of a Thanksgiving, as you recalled from your own childhood, is the endless passing, passing, passing of plates of food.

Sometimes there were visitors, including those who played a role in the work of the James Ford Bell Library and in that of the University of Minnesota Press. One visitor we remember was Francis Rogers of Harvard, a scholar and a catalyst for the scholarship of others. We think back to all of us here at 59 Seymour Avenue and, on another evening during his visit, in the more refined precincts of the Minneapolis Club.

To speak of Fran as a scholarly visitor leads one naturally — since his book *The Obedience of a King of Portugal* is an example — to the many publications that the Bell Library and the University Press brought out together over the years. These books threw light on many areas in world history, including exploration, discovery, commerce, and the complex interaction of Europe with the Americas and other continents.

From among the many roles in your career — as a historian, in librarianship, on the broadcast media, in the life of the University and the state, and in other respects — we want to conclude by speaking of your work as an editor, perhaps because the two of us have spent some years as editors ourselves.

In your editorial role you have developed ideas with others, encouraged them in their research and writing, criticized their work, and orchestrated the enterprise of publication. It seems to us you have seen scholarship as in many ways a collaborative activity, and you have acted on that sense of it, while allowing for the primacy of the individual author's work at its core.

We salute your accomplishments, Jack, as a human being and

as, in the very best sense of the word, a professional. May those accomplishments continue.

Sincerely, Jean   Jack   31 May 1990

FISHER, Raymond H., UCLA, Los Angeles, California.

Dear Jack:

You were my first contact with the Society for the History of Discoveries more than twenty years ago. I had learned of the Society when reading Wilcomb Washburn's article "The Meaning of Discovery in the fifteenth and sixteenth centuries" in the *American Historical Review*. Wondering whether the Society awarded research grants, I wrote you. I found out that it did not and later that it did offer congeniality. I offered a paper for the 1968 meeting at New Bedford. The offer was accepted; I presented it; and I liked what I saw of the Society. It was there that I first met Carol, the first American scholar that I encountered with scholarly interests close to my own. I've been hooked on the Society ever since and so owe you a debt of gratitude as the brain parent and initiator of the Society.

I have not had the opportunity to watch you in operation as Curator of the JFB Library, but I can believe that you direct it with energy, efficiency, and imagination making it a model of its kind. What has most impressed me about your work are the annual issues of *The Merchant Explorer*. You display in them a breadth of knowledge and perspective that I admire. You are adroit in the way in which you use that knowledge to lead up to the recent acquisitions of the Library, giving them significance as a mere listing cannot.

Retirement in the world of scholarship does not have to end activity there. It can bring redirection, and I am sure that that is the road you will choose to follow, with benefit to yourself, your colleagues, and friends.

Sincerely, Ray   26 April 1990

GERITS, Anton, Amsterdam, The Netherlands.

A Merchant's Inspiration

When in 1961 John Parker gave me his book *Van Meteren's Virginia, 1607–1612* as a present I felt flattered. I had just become head of the antiquarian department of Martinus Nijhoff in The Hague, which unfortunately and unnecessarily no longer exists. I had been engaged as a junior clerk with that firm in 1950, when Mr. H.E. Kern was still in command; everybody was still obliged to write with a dip pen and the customary form of address was still the formal Dutch "U" (compare German "Sie", French "Vous").

John Parker too was to me Mr. Parker and "You" (with a capital) and remained so, until after having established my own firm, I visited him in his inner sanctum in Minneapolis a few years ago for the first time.

The fact that in the preface to his book he thanked me for some bibliographical data with which I had provided him, filled me with pride and joy. I was proud because of the recognition I saw in it of what an antiquarian bookseller can mean to a scholarly researcher. I felt joy because this noble-minded gesture of his suddenly made me acutely aware of the extra dimension I would like to add to my career as an antiquarian bookseller.

Once a year Mr. Parker visited us. At first I was only allowed to help prepare the collection of books which Mr. Kern wanted to show him, and from an adjacent room I saw Mr. Parker seated at the big round table, taking one book after another into his hands and inspecting them. After Mr. Kern had retired and I had succeeded him as head of the antiquarian department, I used to act as a host to Mr. Parker, together with Hugo Brandt Corstius, the well-known and popular representative of Martinus Nijhoff's.

It was in those days that *Van Meteren's Virginia* was published and it was in those days that I got to know Mr. Parker better and better and began to appreciate him as an expert buyer of books, who in addition was also an amiable man. In those days he started the annual publication of *The Merchant Explorer*, which always held me enthralled and which reminded me of the unforgettable "library reports" of the Folger Shakespeare Library, which issued from the competent pen of Louis B. Wright from

1948 till late in the sixties and which were more or less compulsory reading at Nijhoff's. In my turn I now recommend *The Merchant Explorer* to my sons and to students at the Tiele Library School (Tiele Academie) whom it is my pleasure to lecture about the trade in old books for a few hours every year. Just imagine the joy I felt when, in his yearly reports, Mr. Parker reviewed books with which I had provided him.

I do not recall Mr. Parker ever questioning the price of a book. He combined a great purchasing urge with a sincere respect for the trader/seller. He inspected, assessed and commented on the contents of texts, sometimes asked my opinion on details and finally he made his choice. Never did he put aside a book on the grounds that it was "too expensive". He may on occasion have thought a book "too expensive" for the means available to him or for the importance he attached to a certain publication, but in those cases he simply put the item in question on the pile of books which did not qualify for purchasing. This respectful attitude towards the seller I have always felt as a recognition of his sincerity and integrity and as evidence of Mr. Parker's trust in them. I have always highly appreciated this attitude, which certainly contributed to the fact that rare books which I found and of which I could presume that they would be suitable for the James Ford Bell Collection, were always offered to Mr. Parker first. And these offers were always promptly reacted to, even if the offer was not accepted, an act of courtesy which is sadly not always a matter of course any more. This scrupulousness in his dealings with antiquarian booksellers marks Mr. Parker not only as a gentleman but also as a bookhunter with psychological insight. No booktrader wants to be kept in the dark too long as to whether or not an offer is accepted. And Mr. Parker's scrupulousness in responding to offers provided the University of Minnesota with one of the rarest items that ever passed through my hands. The fact that it was offered to him first and ended up in the Main Library of Minnesota thanks to him has much to do with the atmosphere of geniality he had managed to create between the two of us.

I had only been with Nijhoff for a short time when Mr. Kern once told me that the rarest series of works that could ever be found on the Dutch market would be formed by the *Resolutiën en Secrete Resolutiën van de Staten van Hollandt en Westvries-*

land. These bulky tomes began to appear in 1524 and kept being published till the days of the Dutch Republic were over in 1796. A complete series comprises 266 volumes, including the 16 volumes in which, between 1653 and 1790, the *Secrete Resolutiën* were published. Very few copies of these *Resolutiën* were printed and they were exclusively intended for the towns which had the vote and a small number of highly placed persons. There were 57 towns which were represented in the States General. The number of copies printed was probably never much larger and the *Secrete Resolutiën* were meant only for the permanent members of the States General. Of these volumes even fewer copies were printed.

"Even if you only find odd volumes, buy them," was Mr. Kern's instruction.

One day, shortly after Mr. Kern had retired (he was almost eighty then) I was called into the sales department of Martinus Nijhoff because there was someone who wanted to sell old books. When I asked the gentleman who greeted me what he wanted to sell, I was told: *De Resolutiën en Secrete Resolutiën van de Staten van Hollandt en Westvriesland*.

"Which volumes?" I asked cautiously.

"The whole series," was the answer.

The gentleman turned out to be a representative of one of the towns which had the vote, where in the course of the years they had received and kept two copies of each volume. Why? Because they lived too far away from The Hague to travel there and back all the time and therefore they had stationed a permanent representative in The Hague. They received one copy of the *Resolutiën* for this representative and one for the town library. They wanted to sell one set now.

When after lengthy negotiations I was allowed to collect the volumes and had finally spread out the whole series on the floor of my room, we found that a great number of volumes, especially those of the earlier years, were still wrapped in 16th century publisher's paper. When we unwrapped one volume a parchment cover appeared which was so perfect, so soft, so cream-coloured that we stood around it in silence, hardly believing our eyes. Each of us wanted to feel the volume for a while. When you opened the volume the printed letters beamed at you, as brightly and clearly as if they had been printed only yesterday.

I phoned Mr. Kern and asked him to take a taxi and come to the firm. He sensed that something sensational was afoot and he loved that! He arrived. He only needed one glance to realize at once what was lying on the floor. He brushed away a tear, took me by the arm — a gesture of intimacy he had never before indulged in — and said: "My boy, this is what I have been looking for all my life!"

Shortly afterwards I attended his deathbed and he talked about another, more personal, childhood dream which had never come true. With great cheer and never-failing energy he had devoted his life to the antiquarian department of Martinus Nijhoff. It is a good thing that he didn't live to see its humiliating decline.

In view of the importance of the *Resolutiën* for the history of trade of not only Holland or Europe, but also of the entire world, especially during the 17th century, it was immediately decided that Mr. Parker should be offered "first refusal." And Mr. Parker saw to it that the series was ultimately bought by the University of Minnesota, albeit not with everyone's approval. One of the trustees was not even allowed to know about the purchase and for years the series lay secretly hidden in the cellars of the university library. When later the coast was clear, the series surfaced. But perhaps Jack will tell that story himself one of these days! For he is certain to remain active for many years to come as it is equally certain that his activities will concern the world of books. And maybe he will one day write his memoirs, which will undoubtedly be a source of inspiration to many bookmerchants, as by means of his attitude and interest he himself has always been able to inspire me and probably everyone who happened to do business with him.

May he continue to do so for many years to come!

Anton Gerits, A. Gerits & Sons   25 April 1990
(Translated from the Dutch by Kees Helsloot and Leo Huisman)

GILLIS, Frank J., Grand Marais.

Dear Jack:

Welcome to the land of retirees! — to plenty of peace and quiet, fewer commitments, a slower pace, more independence, and less pay! You'll love it!

Jack, the years I spent working with you are totally unforgettable. I thoroughly enjoyed becoming familiar with the fascinating subject of travel during the Renaissance period and with manuscripts, maps and early printed works. You taught me much about collecting, administrating a collection, and the role of the librarian-scholar, all of which were very useful to me after I left the James Ford Bell Room in 1964.

The one project which stands out in my mind, among many memorable moments, were the joys and frustrations I felt in preparing the essay for your anthology entitled *Merchants and Scholars*. Remember? Ernst Abbe began the piece but was called out of the country just before the edition was to go to press. Now, what I knew at that time about "Henry Hudson and the Early Exploration and Mapping of Hudson Bay, 1610 to 1631," could easily fit into the proverbial thimble, but you convinced me I could complete the Abbe essay. I approached the project with some trepidation — yet positively, as I remember — and with your good guidance completed the task. On occasionally rereading the essay I feel grateful for having been invited to contribute to the anthology.

I have fond memories, as well, of how appreciative you — and Pat — were of my musical activities, attending many concerts and other events at which I was performing. Truly, it was inspirational to know you were in the audience.

What a joy it was to work with you! And how rewarding it has been to savor our friendship over the twenty-seven years since I left my desk at the James Ford Bell Room. May it continue far into the future.

Stay well, and enjoy your new life in the years ahead.

Cordially, Frank   3 May 1990

GOLDSTEIN, Thomas E., New York City.

Dear Jack:

Helga and I are somewhat stunned by the news of your impending retirement; I don't know why we thought, somewhere in the unconscious recesses of our minds, that you are not subject to the usual aging process. But of course you are—and, of course, your retirement will be as much of a misnomer as it is turning out for me (if not more so!), i.e. a new and most highly productive phase of your highly productive life! We both wish it for you with all our hearts!

This is obviously the occasion when I have to think back at our by now thirty-years-long relationship, letting the images pass before my mind and, without much analytical effort to be sure, savor the quality of our working friendship. That is what I guess it has been and is—and, to say it right off, a completely unique one in both respects at that!

Unique, first of all, because it has been a late-in-life friendship for both of us (although—the lateness—evidently more for me). If I have always been kind of slow from way back in junior high in making friendships, taking my time, it's clearly become still slower with the years: Yes, I have made new friends, some very wonderful and close ones, especially among colleagues at work, but I seem to have been the slower one as a rule until I knew—yes, this is really a friend! I think in our case (because of some similar streaks in our natures, I suspect!) the slowness may well have been on both sides, since we are probably both a little reluctant in opening up to a new friend—just as we both (I believe) are pretty easy in opening (and warming) up in a casual conversation. What I am saying, I think, is that our friendship is all the more solid for that, on both sides.

That it is a *working* friendship, naturally arising from our by now longstanding working relationship has obviously given it its special quality. Let me recapture a few of the highlights, hopefully without being too repetitious of sundry occasions at the SHD: Having Steve Slessarev introduce me to you at the 1960 meeting in Lisbon, and finding—with a start—that we clicked, as we were riding on top of a bus from Lisbon's University City back into town. I believe already on that occasion we found out (for my part, with considerable, only half-suppressed enthusiasm) that we tended naturally to create things together as we talked,—in that instance the outlines of our Society. (I think, as I try to recall it, that it had emerged at least in rough shape before the bus hit the *Avenida da Libertade*).

There was a similar flashpoint somewhere later in the 60's or early 70's, when we were chatting after dinner one night at our house, and the two of us in that same playful manner found ourselves literally founding a new type of College, perfectly tailored to the needs of the time. Again, we did this act of joint mental creation by each of us in an easy give-and-take throwing in one new and appropriate feature after another. (I still think it would have been a fantastic institution!). And I remember that at one point we looked at each other, laughed, and decided this time to let it remain a game. . . .

The *Society for the History of Discoveries* however did not turn out to remain a game. There were early years when we would quietly say to each other at annual meetings that "f.h.b." — which I think is an old German tradition of passing the word that "family holds back" (really "F.h.z." in German) — meaning us two founding fathers, hehem!, should better give the membership as a whole more of a say in the important decisions. Which sounds pretty darn ridiculous now, when an entire new generation of mostly younger scholars has taken over, both in giving the papers and thereby steering us through new waters of scholarship, and deciding about the wheres and whens and hows of coming meetings and the like. The plain fact is that our Society has grown up and developed into a sturdy representative of American scholarship in our field, which gets itself invited by such internationally respected institutions as the British Royal Geographical Society, the British Library, or Yale.

And of course, there was that prophetic moment (how else can I call it), which I am afraid I have cited before, when we were both standing in a corner at some SHD reception sipping our drinks and quietly looking around the room, and you said, equally quietly: "I guess when we shall be old, this will be one of the things we did in our lives we shall be completely proud about!" I feel we are now old enough to confirm that flash insight, without unduly pushing our luck! It has been a source of steady, unambitious, quietly satisfying intellectual pleasure and, as I think all of us know, a great deal more than that: a forum for the exchange of information and ideas in our specialized field which, to me for one, has been — and remains — absolutely invaluable. That, and a source of many lovely personal relationships all around, as we both know and appreciate! . . .

On festive occasions you have sometimes credited me with the original idea (back there on our Lisbon-bound bus!). O.k., who am I to dispute a distinguished historian's recollection of our history? But I know (and so do most of our colleagues) how much of the constant day-by-day work of keeping up contacts, promoting individual scholarly exchanges, encouraging the continued enthusiasm and plain commitment of members, or in short getting us off the ground and keeping us going and growing, has been performed by you. For all that, but most of all for our unique personal friendship, I want to thank you, dear Jack — and wish both of us a long and most pleasant continuation!

Yours, Thom   31 May 1990

GOODMAN, Edward J., Fort Myers, Florida.

Dear Jack:

So you are to enter soon the ranks of retirees! Congratulations and best wishes. If my own experience is any criterion, you will probably wonder in a year or so how you ever found time to work. You will see retirement as I have as a new beginning.

I remember many years ago, when I first learned of the existence of the Society for the History of Discoveries, how I wrote to you (or called you — I'm not sure now) about membership, and you sent me the appropriate information, and were also kind enough to refer me to the then president, Steve Slessarev, a fellow Cincinnatian whom I had never met before. I joined the Society, and attended the meeting in Lawrence, Kansas. I have not missed one since, although I had not planned to attend the meeting in Worcester until you put me on the program as chairman of a session — the last one. Two other incidents come to mind. There was the time when you arrived at the meeting but your baggage did not, and the time we nearly forgot our duties as members of the nominating committee.

So enjoy your new existence, Jack; it has been a great pleasure knowing you all these years, and I look forward to seeing you again in Jamaica.

With all good wishes, Ed   15 May 1990

GOODSELL, James Nelson, Boston, Massachusetts.

Dear Jack:

May I call you that? We've been so formal over the years in our brief, occasional communications that I could continue with "Dear Mr. Parker," but somehow it doesn't seem appropriate. I have long had the feeling that I know you, although we have met only in our correspondence. I certainly regard you as a friend — one whose thoughts on explorations, voyages, history, and life in general have delighted me, made me think, encouraged me to read. Your delicious commentaries in some of the monographs issued by the James Ford Bell Library, together with *The Manifest* and *The Merchant Explorer*, are treasures. These latter two are among the most valued publications arriving in my mail box. The graceful and elegant literary style of *The Merchant Explorer* in particular is a joy to read. Thank you for this labor of love over the years!

I am sure that you will not really be "retiring," for there are new explorations, new voyages, new research challenges ahead — a sort of continuum.

And I hope that this continuum will be shared with those of us who treasure what you have so amply brought to the field. I hope you will continue providing us with a regular stream of writing about the explorations, voyages, and challenges that lie ahead.

My every good wish to you. And thank you for sharing so much of yourself!

> Bon voyage and God-speed. Jim   1 June 1990

GUTHORN, Dr. Peter J., Brielle, New Jersey.

It is a pleasure to participate in a festschrift honoring John Parker. I was first introduced to him in the pages of *The Merchant Explorer*, where his pleasure in writing and compiling the material was evident. After I had met him for the first time, I had a mental image of him seated at a large table piled with reference material from which he was selecting pertinent and interesting facts to be composed into his precise and often amusing and spirited descriptions.

I introduced myself to John sometime later. Our conversation eventually veered toward my research interest. John described some of the accounts with which he had an easy familiarity extending to the authors (who had not been extant for a century or more). He had an unusual sense of appreciating more than bare facts from historical accounts, which he communicated easily.

Among the surprises in *The Merchant Explorer* was tolerance for a wide range of ideas, some of which had always been unpopular somewhere, the quotation from unusual sources (James Reston), and occasional insights which were new to me, in material with which I was very familiar. I look forward to John's continuation in the parts of his work which pleased him for many years.

Sincerely, Peter Guthorn   5 April 1990

HARTWELL, Lucy, (Jr.).

Dear Jack,

Not so many years ago, although it seems like many, my mother sent me on a mission to go to the James Ford Bell Library between classes to see if a book which she had would be of any value to you all at the library. First I met Carol. Then I met you. I was taken by both of you, at that time not so much because of what you were doing because I didn't have a feeling for the library, but because of your warmth and interest in me and my family.

To do calligraphy for the library's exhibits was a thrill. It was a way for me to contribute to my family history, and in college family history started to mean a lot.

I was deeply touched when you and Carol invited me to dinner at Vescios. It was a real thrill to hear about my great-grandfather and the library which he started. Your stories made me wish that I, like you, could have known James Ford Bell; in a way through you and my family I have gotten to know him. One of the great stories I remember is the one about you and a pile of books. Evidently my great-grandfather gave you a pile of books and said, "Take a look at these." After riding the bus home and opening up the package you discovered that the books were worth $30,000!!

Seeing you at Belwin through the years has made a statement to me. You're a giving man, a contributor.

Marbling, visiting, having a tour of the library, hearing you speak in front of a group . . . these are all things I've enjoyed.

Your commitment to the James Ford Bell Library has been truly that, a commitment. Your interest in me has been touching.

I salute you and know that your upcoming years of research will be special, interesting, and happy.

Sincerely, Lucy Hartwell (Jr.)   28 March 1990

HARWOOD, Kathryn C., Coral Gables, Florida.

Dear Jack —

I have just found out that you are retiring as curator of the Bell Library. It is the Library I feel sorry for. I am sure it will mourn your loss. But retire? Personages like you have a habit of getting busier than ever upon so-called retirement. Remember: I warned you! You are due a breather, of course, leisure to stop and smell the roses and I know you'll enjoy it.

Perhaps you heard some reverberations from the celebrations of Marjory Stoneman Douglas' 100th birthday! The state of Florida turned handsprings and newspapers from Los Angeles and New York carried stories and pictures. MSD refused to be impressed. She found it all very silly. Lots of people get to be 100, she says!

My luck comes from being a member of the SHD that has given me friends like you. I miss those breakfasts we used to have. Let's hope we can share another mug of coffee one of these days.

Good luck and happy retirement.

Best, Kitty Harwood   May 1990

HASSELMO, Nils, President, University of Minnesota.

Dear Jack:

Let me join in recognizing your contributions to the University of Minnesota library system and particularly the special library collection within the James Ford Bell Library. You have not only brought academic expertise, but also personal enthusiasm and commitment to this special collection devoted to the development of international commerce. You have been an inspiration to the staff of the University Library and also a motivator of the general public engaging them in the collections within the James Ford Bell Library. The University cannot replace an individual like yourself.

We do hope that you will have many happy years of retirement and that you will use these years to further pursue your interests to the benefit of the University and the scholarly community.

Thank you for your contribution and your commitment to the University and for your contribution to our community.

Cordially, Nils   29 May 1990

HENAU, Brigitte P.F., Brussels, Belgium.

Dear Carol,

Sorry to have waited so long to reply to your letter about John's retirement. I have a paper due June 1st, and lots of things going on (of which one is a Ph.D. thesis and one is a boyfriend — I knew you'd exult about that) that there seems hardly a minute in which to collect my thoughts and go back to the good old pre-everything days.

Much though I'd like to supply you with some marvellously witty anecdote, there is nothing much I can offer you. The way I remember John, is that of a very friendly, helpful, somewhat quiet person, noiselessly but steadily doing his job. In fact, what you might do, is put up a sign over his fish-bowl office: "In case of emergency, break the glass," and he'd be there to save the situation, rescue a panic-stricken student from flunking a paper or having a nervous breakdown. As for my own experience, what I vividly recall is my first appearance at the JFB Library, with a very heavy cold and finding a very warm welcome.

It might be better not to let the world know about the weaker sides of the curator(s?) of the JFBL—I allude to some people's (who shall remain unnamed) partiality for Belgian chocolates. . . .

I did not forget Minnesota and the good times. Neither did I forget you (if most of the above is concerned with John, there is an obvious reason). I'm going back to my paper now. Sorry to be so short. It is good to hear from the Library from time to time.

Take care and good luck with your endeavour.

Brigitte   27 May 1990

HOWE, John.

Dear Jack,

Retirements are certainly bittersweet occasions, but the sweetness comes from reflecting on and finding satisfaction in a distinguished and creative career. Certainly that characterizes this occasion. You've contributed splendidly to the James Ford Bell Library, to the realm of scholarship in maritime, economic, and early modern studies and to the University of Minnesota. I've valued our work together some years ago on the Revolutionary Bicentennial Conference and more recently in the University Libraries. You've given us a legacy of scholarship, librarianship, and citizenship on which we'll all be drawing for years to come. My congratulations!

Most cordially, John   29 May 1990

HOYLE, Karen Nelson.

Dear Jack:

One of my recollections about you took place on a train en route from North Dakota to Minnesota. Up to that time, I'd identified you only as the Curator of the esteemed James Ford Bell Library. You'd made me feel welcome when I joined the Special Collections staff. I'd listened to your wise statements at meetings. I'd heard you lecture on aspects of historical travel books. You always wore your professional suit with tie.

As I wandered through the train looking for something to eat (frequent pastime), I was amazed to recognize you wearing a plaid shirt, talking casually with workmen wearing blue denims. You held them spellbound with your comments as you engaged them in conversation.

It was then that I realized what a remarkable scholar and teacher you are. You share your knowledge and friendship with those you meet, reaching out to all of us over the years. It doesn't matter if we are new library staff, university students on campus or blue collar workers on a train.

Retirement changes your desk, but certainly not your scholarly endeavors, which convert to friendly conversation as well as books and lectures.

Thank you for your friendship and best wishes in your retirement.

Sincerely yours, Karen   1 May 1990

IHRIG, Elizabeth.

Dear Jack,

Congratulations on some time well spent! You are too modest to broadcast it, but you must have some notion of the many, many books and people you've had a good influence on over the years. It was your and Carol's descriptive bibliography course back in 1979 that set this one person on the broad and flowery path that led to working with older and more dignified books. Since then, it's been your example and your unfailing kindness and perfect sense of timing that has inspired, encouraged, and taught me so much of worth both on the job and off. Working life aside, shooting the breeze with you on all kinds of subjects, particularly the subject of growing up in our rural mid-west, is a pleasure from which neither of us shall retire.

With warmest wishes and great affection, Elizabeth May, 1990

JACOBS, Alden, Toms River, New Jersey.

Dear Jack,

Congratulations on your coming retirement which indeed does celebrate a wonderful career and really a beginning. You may well have less free time rather than more but it will probably be time more directly under your control.

All the past is indeed prologue. Your unique participation in leading us to appreciate the significance of how it all began and, yes, how it continues is a real contribution to our knowledge. Generations of explorers, as read about in written word and stories of those as they travelled the globe provide a continuum for those of us who need to know.

There are many exciting, wonderful libraries, but none so dedicated to our quest for knowledge in the cultural, social and economic beginnings as the James Ford Bell Library.

I hope the following says what I want you to know of my reflections on our friendship.

> Three rivers keyed our growth,
> Unleashed knowledge, John's rare instinct . . . books,maps,
> Clear vision of all times!

Enjoy your retirement, Jack, as I have mine by keeping involved in all the challenging areas you like. You will probably explore some new ideas and find them as fascinating as I have.

I hope we will have opportunities to visit in the future and to continue our friendship for years to come.

Warmest regards, Alden   30 March 1990

JENSEN, Vernon.

Dear Jack,

I am happy to have the opportunity to add my voice to the many who no doubt will be expressing congratulations to you as you move into those (relatively) carefree retirement years. What a wonderful contribution you have made to the substance and tone of scholarship here at the University and of course across the nation and around the globe!

I deeply appreciate the sharing of these many decades with you. Living a few blocks from each other, with wives on the faculty at Augsburg, watching our children grow from elementary school to adulthood, our years have indeed been uniquely intertwined. Our many years together in "Gown-in-Town" and our periodic lunches have been very important to me. Few there are with whom I have been able to discuss so freely such a spectrum of subjects—personal, family, professional, political, and religious. Seldom does one have a single person who spans all those categories, and I appreciate the unique role you have played. Ours indeed has been a common journey—common origins, common experiences, common interests and values.

Naturally I expect that many more pleasant years of sharing lie ahead, but this is an obviously opportune moment to look back and be glad. Thanks for what you have done and for what you are. All best wishes for the future! I have recently finished reading a published memoir entitled *Golden Inches*, the title being based on a Chinese saying, "An inch of time is an inch of gold." May you have many more "golden inches" ahead of you!

Cordially, Vern   24 May 1990

JENSON, John R.

Jack:

To quote an old song title, it is "Because of You" that I find myself in the rare book world. Our friendship goes back to the fall of 1961 when I returned from four years in the Navy and back working again at Augsburg College. There my colleague in the library turned out to be your wife Pat. When I learned in 1965 that you were going to offer, for the first time, a course in Descriptive Bibliography, I enrolled. As a member of that first class, and which incidentally I believe you have continued to teach each year since, I still remember the subject of my research—the book by Marc Lescarbot on New France. This course really got my feet wet and my interest in rare books solidified. Of course I had always been a reader, a book collector, and interested in "old books" but this clinched it. So in 1966 when you advised me that

there was an opening at the University of Minnesota for a Rare
Book Librarian in the Special Collections Department, I applied.
And as they say, the rest is history. Because of you, Jack, I have
come to enjoy not only my 23 years of association with you here
at the University but also the whole field of rare books. You, to
me, are the ideal scholar, librarian, and gentleman. I will never
forget the years I was privileged to work with you.

                                    JJ   28 May 1990

JEVNE, Robert.

Dear Jack,

Ave atque vale. I have enjoyed knowing you ever since I first
began work at the library in 1963. A lasting impression I have of
you, along with your unfailing amiability and friendliness, is the
way all your colleagues in assembly meetings turned to you for
calm reason, judgment, and maturity when difficult decisions
had to be made, and how you never let them down.

                                    Bob   25 May 1990

JOHNSON, Carol.

"Looking back and looking ahead is the name of the game
here." (from the *Manifest*, March, 1990).
    Hearty congratulations on what I hope you know will be
remembered as a fine, fine career, and best wishes for the future.
(When's lunch?)

                                    Carol   March, 1990

JOHNSON, Hildegard Binder.

Dear Jack:

The occasion of the hard-to-believe start of your retirement in-
vites reminiscences about the beginning of our friendship and col-

laboration. This letter represents a voice from the past! What led you to say so early that I was a good P-R person for the James Ford Bell Collection? The linear sequence of reasons begins with the Johnsons' subscription to the daily New York Times. Two days after October 30, 1954 I read in the issue of this date that an "Ancient Map of the World" had been bought by the University of Minnesota for the James Ford Bell Collection. The woodcut map with its twelve gores and the name America printed on one of the equatorial islands was reproduced in the New York Times. The text mentioned the Prince of Liechtenstein as former owner and also the sale of a nautical chart of 1424 with the word Antilia written on it, at the same auction. The name of the cartographer, Martin Waldseemüller of St. Dié fascinated me. The article said nothing about the potential difficulties which must arise when the gores of his globular map were to be fitted together for a small globe. Perhaps this explained why only one copy of the map was known to exist – I had to see that map! Without being aware of it, I joined the informal "Who discovered America?" club. Remember how that "club" ballooned when the book about the Vinland map was published by Yale? Did Matti Kaups ever tell you that 114 students enrolled in his new Interim course titled "Who discovered America?" Macalester's small Geography Department was bonded to Columbus even when the Chamber of Commerce guide to the runestone in Alexandria in northern Minnesota suspected the students who came on two busses that "they must be communists" because of their critical questions about Leif Erikson.

In 1954 I needed courage to enter your beautifully furnished reading room. It looked so new – dating from 1953 as I found out later. A young man appeared from the rear and I simply said that I had not come for a book but would like to see the real map which was pictured in the newspaper. You brought out your new treasures and were very gracious. I hope you don't mind my telling you now that I thought you very young for a curator of very old books and other treasures. You agreed readily to my next request – to show the maps to my class in Historical Geography. When I brought the students over from Macalester College they were very impressed and you told us that the auctioneer, when he handed you the Waldseemüller map said "Sir, you have just

bought the birth certificate of America." I felt privileged to have
seen the map twice even if I never learned for how much the map
was insured or had cost. To acquire this important document was
a great deed in my judgement and teachers should know about
the enrichment of the state university's library.

I gave my enthusiastic write-up in the *Bulletin of the Teachers
for the Social Studies* a catchy title: "Amerigo Vespucci, Columbus, or an unknown Portuguese." The report for the Association
of American Geographers in the *Professional Geographer* was
more restrained. The announcement of your acquisition of the
globular map of 1507 came exactly one year after the opening of
the James Ford Bell Room which soon was my favorite place in
the Walter Library. Your continuous search for and acquisition
of new old books may have influenced me to look for and use
sources I had not planned to read or to consult earlier. French
travel reports led to a paper about the development of the French
colonial empire and a publication in the *Canadian Geographer*.
By putting Sebastian Münster's huge tome on film and our mutual
friend, librarian Jim Holly loaning me the projector, I could read
Münster's Cosmos at home over weekends.

By fall 1959 you knew me well enough to ask if I could write
a book about a German guidebook called *Uslegung* which was
written to accompany a Carta Marina drawn by a Dr. Fries for
a publisher in Strasbourg. In retrospect I cannot remember if you
mentioned right away that Fries' map was copied in reduced size
from a Carta Marina of 1516 designed by Waldseemüller. I felt
good about the project. There were not going to be royalties but
I would have an assistant. The University of Minnesota Press was
to publish the book. There was an early 19th century German edition of the twelve sheets of the wall map and you had that folder
of which you made me a present later. Palmer O. Johnson died
suddenly on January 24, 1960 which delayed my starting to work.

The study of the *Uslegung* led to the use of many treasures in
your library. The Waldseemüller Carta Marina of 1516 was
available in an atlas I could study at home. But much other material was not available for loan. With my teaching hours and your
closing time every minute I could spend in the James Ford Bell Library was precious. But there was a way to increase these minutes: On two weekdays I ate my lunch while driving from

Macalester College to the University, arrived at the Walter Library around 11:25 and disappeared into the quarters behind the James Ford Bell Room. While you went out for lunch you locked me in. Several times when I felt particularly good about the whole enterprise I looked at the frequently large-sized books with affection and also with great concern about their monetary value. I knew the feeling that an Amsterdam diamond trader must have when he locks himself up in his secret cabinet to examine his jewels for their true value.

I still remember vividly a fall evening in 1963 when you came unannounced to my house and waited at the door. You were beaming, really, as I never saw you before. You brought over the first copy of the 750 numbered books. The Carta Marina looked beautiful and was flawlessly executed. The illustrations were very attractive—except the reproduction in black and white of the Fries map in a jacket; this one was a little hard to read. Still, it was a very happy hour for me even if I no longer had my late husband to share it with. You had left immediately which I thought was very considerate. The book won an award later for its beautiful appearance. The merit was yours and shared by the University of Minnesota Press. Two or three weeks later you suggested we celebrate this publication with a dinner. I could invite up to twenty persons—you had your own short list. It was to take place in the University Women's Club on Summit Avenue; "very close to Macalester which makes it convenient" you added. This was a gesture of politeness which was not lost on the president and provost and their wives. My younger daughter Karin surprised us with her visit from her college in Iowa in the middle of the semester. Thanks to you I had been challenged to a task and was able to complete it. My small family has not experienced any happier evening together.

Through your assistance I found an unexpected outlet for my humanistic education with much Latin at the Chamisso Realgymnasium and the University of Berlin where I took a seminar in gothic minuscule. My Ph.D. diploma of 1933 is still in Latin. Perhaps it is not too immodest to think that you and the James Ford Bell Room and I getting together was a somewhat mutual good fortune.

I want to thank you for your and Carol's great services in the preparing for my presentation at the UCLA conference titled *First Images of America*. My topic was "New Geographical Horizons and Concepts" and you came to this conference. A figure from Waldseemüller's Carta Marina was reproduced in the subsequent two-volume publication with several colored plates.

Besides the James Ford Bell Room we shared many experiences at the meetings of the Society for the History of Discoveries. You will get many letters from their members I trust. I will mention only a particularly nice drive home in your car after a meeting in Madison, Wisconsin, in the fall of 1982, during which we agreed that even if I was retired now it would be nice to write once more about a source from your collection. You suggested a German broadside published at Leipzig in 1718 which advertised Louisiana as a place for future advantageous settlement by Germans. You had found the source, of course. I translated it and wrote an evaluation of the large German influence in the whole Mississippi basin. It was your idea to publish this with your explanatory notes and to distribute the large sheets of heavy paper as an attractive roll. Then our long friendship was brought around full circle. It was not originally planned, but the roll was ready in time for the celebration of the Tricentennial of the first German immigration to America (1683) by the James Ford Bell Associates.

You prepared an exhibit with the title "Germany and the New World, 1500–1800". A wonderful title! And the original Waldseemüller map of 1507, meant for a little globe, was also in the exhibit. I was glad to see it once more! A folder referred to Ringmann and Waldseemüller as the two scholars who suggested the name America for our continent. It was amusing that the broadside in the roll which was distributed to all who attended the celebration had a small map on which the "rivière Hiens" in the region of Arkansas appears. It is the French name for a foot soldier named Hans in the detachment following De Soto on his exploration around 1542. Was he the first person from Germany on what was to become American ground?! Your folder mentions Ringmann and Waldseemüller as the two German scholars who first used the name America. I learned of the Ringmann claim earlier and was not very excited, let alone upset. For me, you were the very young-looking librarian Dr. Parker in 1954 and are known for a long time now as Jack and as librarian, curator, scholar, archivist, academic teacher and apiarist. For me you are first of all the genius who brought to Minnesota the map you and I treasure — the Birth Certificate of America. It is a sort of logo for the James Ford Bell Room.

With best wishes for your diversified future I remain affectionately and sincerely yours, Hildegard
Hildegard Binder Johnson, Professor of Geography Emerita

JOHNSON, Russ and Winnie, Elk River.

For the last ten years, Jack has been a partner in our beekeeping operation. He has generally found his weekly excursions to the Nowthen area of Anoka County to be a welcome reprieve from the hustle and bustle of his "city life."

One June Saturday several years ago stands out as an exception. We were vacationing, so Jack was inspecting the hives himself. The day was hot, dry, and windy. As Jack filled the smoker with dry grass and lit it, the flames got away from him. The field of dry grass started on fire. He battled the flames until it was obvious he needed help. The nearest farm house was a quarter mile away. He hurried there. Only one person was home, as the rest had gone to watch a local parade. Upon calling the volunteer fire department, Jack found luck on his side. The firemen were already assembled. Having just finished the parade route, the firemen headed to Jack's grass fire five miles away.

Although the neighbor tells us Jack was as white as a ghost, he had saved the hives and the fire had not spread far. It was a close call he would not soon forget.

Russ and Winnie Johnson   30 April 1990

JUDGE, Joseph R., National Geographic Magazine.

Dear Jack:

Turns out I beat you to it, having laid aside the day-to-day operations of the magazine for a year of book writing prior to retirement. In the past month I have noticed a curious thing; I look only forward. I have realized that the most terrible part of employment, even though it runs on schedules and calendars, is its all consuming attention on the present and immediate — today's problem. What working stiff looks forward to summer anymore?

Those occasional backward glances I make are for such benign purposes as this, to help celebrate the newest phase of a distinguished career. I think the first time I became aware of your work was in an issue of *The Merchant Explorer* some years ago, a distinct and distinctive voice that reminded me of that of Glynn Daniel's in the up-front notes to the old *Antiquity*.

But what I really have against you is resurrecting the Columbus landfall question with the reading of Verhoog's paper to the SHD in 1980 or 81, I forget which. It gave me the mistaken notion that the question could thenceforth be examined in a rational way and rules of evidence be observed. Having provided the only solution that the data of the log as it stands on the page yields, a landfall at Samana Cay, and having watched the reaction to this from the presumed scholars of discovery, *I don't blame you for running for the fence.*

I myself am not sanguine that the world can be saved, politics and business made uncorrupt, and education made viable in these hypocritical times distinguished by extremism in the defense of liberty but if there is a small nudge in that direction on any of those fronts it will be because of people who preserve old books, trusted ideas, proven values, who are calm and considerate and thoughtful. An example of the breed is about to retire from the James Ford Bell Library in Minneapolis and he has the good wishes and thanks of this one pilgrim.

Enjoy, Jack — it's a wonderful life out here!

Warm Regards, Joe   16 May 1990

KARON, Bernard L.

Dear Jack,

To paraphrase Red Smith, please remember as you exit the

University "Leaving the Library is no big deal. The least of us as your colleagues will manage that. Living here is the trick!"

Your production in both the varied and interesting ways; your interests that spanned the gamut of the undergrad to the emeritus faculty; and your concern for people with whom you interacted leave a template for all of us to try to emulate.

It's not easy to find someone who will mix "rare book cataloging" with "baseball," and "professional ethics and issues" with the "local horticultural and entomological scene," but I have fond memories of discussing all of the previous topics with you.

Good luck — God speed — and may the decades ahead be filled with only health, happiness, peace, and a continued zest for LIVING with all your many interests and projects.

Bernie 6 April 1990

KELLEY, James E., Jr., Melrose Park, Pennsylvania.

Dear Jack:

You may not remember it — a day in February, 1969, when, with some misgivings, I arrived at your shop in search of portolan charts and related materials. Your warmth and courtesy, your personal touch, really struck me at a time when I had been greeted with bureaucratic disinterest at other research libraries. That readiness to serve — which has held up over the years — has put you and your group at the James Ford Bell at the top of my list.

More important — to me, at least — was your invitation to join SHD. As you wrote the very next day, "May I urge you to give serious consideration to membership in the Society for the History of Discoveries. It has among its members many people like you — practitioners of some other profession who find exploration and the related sciences interesting."

Jack, joining SHD changed my life — literally. I never would have believed a rank amateur would be given a respectful hearing from professionals about his dabblings in the history of discoveries and its technology. I fed on the encouragement you and the membership gave my "revisionist" ideas. It made me work hard,

with the hope that my contributions might make a difference. Indeed, I've tried to pass on that same positive encouragement to
others, most especially when I have doubts about their ideas. Not
only does encouragement help people grow, serious defense of unpopular hypotheses seems to have a way of exposing new facets
of old problems.

I attribute to you my involvement in the search for Guanahani,
initiated with the *Wake of Columbus* conference. Since retiring
it's become my full-time job. It's unbelievable that one of the
products of this effort is a critical edition of a literary work—
Columbus's *Diario*. Heavens, I was the Philistine mathematician,
the butt of good-natured humor among my humanist chums.

Thank you, dear friend, for these and other things you've done
for me over the years. One seldom appreciates the extent of one's
influence. So I want you to know how grateful I am that you came
into my life that winter day so long ago.

Best regards, Jim   10 April 1990

KELLY, Richard J.

For Jack Parker:

I want to add my voice to the chorus raised in praise of Jack
Parker. As a librarian-scholar and a colleague, Jack has been the
standard against which the rest of us have, or should have, measured ourselves. As a friend he has been generous and thoughtful
and loyal and a true Renaissance man with whom it is possible to
discuss, with profit, everything from books to bees to baseball.
May the qualities embodied in our friend and colleague live
forever!

Dick Kelly   7 May 1990

KIEFT, Janis.

Dear Dr. Parker:

As a student, working with you at the James Ford Bell Library in the mid-1970's, I considered my job to be one of the best at the University. I worked in beautiful surroundings with great people and was able to learn a lot in the course of my job. I was an undergraduate studying horticulture which meant many of my classes were on the St. Paul campus. I remember the mad dashes to get from the library on West Bank over to St. Paul in time for class and vice versa.

I have many special memories of my association with you; proofreading galleys of your books; you taking time to talk to me about the historical significance of the books in the library; showing me how to care for the library's special books; and your wife giving me a chance to practice my horticultural skills on a sick plant at your house.

One event stands out in my mind. For months we were busy planning, cataloguing, and sorting items for an auction to support the James Ford Bell Library. One item, a Panamanian mola, had caught my eye when it was first donated. I was impressed by the intricate needlework and colorful designs, and thought how much I would like to have it.

I worked the night of the auction, holding up items as the audience of collectors, historians, and supporters made their bids. It was ironic that the mola was one of the items I got to hold for display. The bidding started at a few dollars and before I knew it, I shouted out my bid for five dollars. I remember my knees were shaking because I was nervous and I didn't know if I was even allowed to bid. It didn't matter because I was soon outbid. I thought I would try one last time and bid fifteen dollars. In addition to being more sophisticated, the crowd was also much richer than I, and the mola eventually went for significantly more than I could afford. Needless to say, I was disappointed.

My disappointment was short-lived, however. When I went into work the next day, you said you had something for me and gave me a beautiful botanical illustration from the auction. It was several years before I could afford to have it framed, but it is a reminder of your kindness, generosity, and thoughtfulness and of my wonderful experiences at the James Ford Bell Library.

Congratulations on your retirement!

Janis Kieft   1 June 1990

KITTLESON, Harold.

I don't remember the exact year I met Jack Parker for the first time but it must have been very soon after the James Ford Bell Library was established and Jack was selected by Mr. Bell to become the first curator of this prestigious and world famous library.

I have enjoyed the privilege of his friendship and standards to follow, as a book collector myself. Jack's contribution to the development of this library is incredible (he would modestly dispute this!). His devotion, scholarship, creativity to a cause created in the mind of Mr. Bell is in every way outstanding.

For those of us who consider ourselves builders of a collection or collections that will preserve the intellectual, historic and scientific records of mankind's growth the past two thousand years we can do nothing less than follow in the footsteps of Jack Parker. There is no doubt in my mind Mr. Bell would be happy and content with what has and is happening to his vision.

I have visited with Jack many times over the past years. He is always unfailingly courteous, interested in one's own thoughts and ventures. He is refreshingly warm, modest and diligent. His wisdom and knowledge of his special fields, yes and more, is an example of how to live, how to grow, how to inspire.

One must never forget or overlook of what major significance the preservation and conservation of learning thru books is to man's development — great private libraries are the foundation on which we, the people, grow and use the past to understand the present and hopefully point to the future.

Jack has accomplished so much and if there is ever a Hall of Fame for scholar librarians and preservationists of "The Book" certainly he should and must be a charter member.

Harold Kittleson   4/11/90

KUKLA, Edward R.

Dear Jack,

One of the local works I have come to know since my arrival

in the Twin Cities in 1987 is Tom Hegg's *A Cup of Christmas Tea*.

How well I learned that work during the Yuletide of 1989.

The Athenaeum had scheduled what was to become its first annual Christmas party for Friday, December 8. Current and past board members were invited. A special display with an accompanying handout of the top ten acquisitions from the years of my tenure was set out in the board room. The table outside the room groaned with dainties. A brace of pourers was engaged. A handful of people appeared, including one current board member named John Parker.

On Monday, December 11, I called you, Nestor. You fed me food for thought. Libraries are not sexy, not visible enough. One needs to do something with show. Booksellers put you on to collectors. Running after money can often be quite disappointing. Basically it is books that make the library; change in personnel is less important.

Then you poured the stimulant that revived my flagging spirits. I returned with you to a Sunday afternoon at a prestigious Midwestern university library during the Yuletide of 1952. Another Christmas party had been planned. The silver had been polished. The lace tablecloth had been laid. It snowed. Nobody came.

Thank you, Jack, for pouring that cup of Christmas tea.

Respectfully yours, Ed   28 May 1990

LAMB, Ursula, Tucson, Arizona.

. . . just add my name to the warmest and heartiest congratulations.

I can't think of a story to tell. Rather Jack has been a man of no surprises but of endless revelations of more of the same humanity, reliability, graciousness over the years: a man of no age and for all seasons.

Ursula   23 April 1990

LARSON, Wendy Pell Wettergren.

Of Marcel Proust and Typewriters

Marcel Proust had his cookie to set off memories. I have my computer keyboard. When people ask me, "How can you type so fast?," my mind goes back almost twenty years to the time I learned to type.

It must have been the summer of 1970, when I worked as a clerk at the James Ford Bell Library. Jack needed a clerk with typing skills and he was acquainted with the librarian for the Twin Cities Opportunity Industrialization Center. So, Jack sent me there to learn to type. I took a bus every day to the near north side and began to learn a new skill.

I remember how patient Jack and Carol were, and how many gallons of correction fluid were used that summer. The correction fluid appeared on the envelopes in the Associates' addresses and all over the IBM Selectric typewriter and all over my hands and clothing. I also remember the hot sun beating down on the city streets, the pungent diesel exhaust and the roar of the bus, the cool air conditioning in the library, and the steady, persistent hum of that typewriter which was flecked with white spots of correction fluid.

In my memory, the James Ford Bell Library was like that typewriter. There was a steady, persistent hum of industry and activity in the place with publishing, teaching, research, the coming and going of people from all over the community and from all over the world. One could not be around Jack without becoming aware of his service to the local community as well as to the worldwide scholarly community. One of many activities was his long commitment to the Cafe Extempore, which was located on the West Bank near the library. The Society for the History of Discoveries, on the other hand, is an example of the far and extended reach of the Library. And no matter how fascinating or challenging any work might be, Jack would meet it with a dry, down-to-earth sense of humor. Two choice examples of Jack's humor that I have really enjoyed are: (1) "Share, dammit, share!" (this is attributed to Mother Parker, whom Jack remembers arranging jars full of shimmering, vibrantly-colored jelly in perfect order on the shelf), and (2) "The road to hell is paved with Swedish documents," which I heard from Jack as he labored for who knows how long over these things.

It's funny how things stay in memory, whether it's the taste of cookies or the learning of typing in that beautiful office. I have managed to steer clear of Swedish documents, but enjoy putting things in order on the shelf, and exhort my children to share! We visit Jack and Carol at Christmas. I meet the new clerks and secretaries. The typewriter is in the same place. I smile and think about these things as I type at my computer. Thanks, Jack!

Wendy   29 April 1990

LESTER, M. Louise and Richard G., M.D., Norfolk, Virginia.

Dear Jack,

Our friendship took root in such abundantly rich soil that it was bound to thrive and endure long after proximity ended.

What an idyllic time and place was our small corner of Minneapolis in the late summer of 1955. In retrospect, quite utopian! And how fortunate we were to find ourselves in that special little enclave just west of the Mississippi and south of the Franklin Bridge, welcomed so warmly by you and Pat, surrounded by such congenial neighbors and colleagues as the Kingsleys and Freemans, Mrs. Jennings and Dr. Peterson.

There as friendships flourished we learned the joys of living in an academic environment. Although our sojourn was all too short its impact on our lives has been profound. Indeed it strongly influenced our adopting the academic way of life as well as some of our volunteer activities over the years. Currently, for example, I serve on the Board of the Friends of Eastern Virginia Medical School Library.

Through "The Manifest" we have avidly followed the progress and development of both the James Ford Bell Library and the Associates with feelings of proprietary pride since our friendship gave us a presence at their creation. As you begin a new chapter, Jack, please know that you and Pat have played a vital role in our lives by your accomplishments, your kindness and by being your very special selves. Our fondest good wishes to you both.

Affectionately, Louise and Dick   27 May 1990

LIND, Melva.

Dear Jack,

My association with the James Ford Bell Library of Rare Books over the past 15 or 20 years has brought me true intellectual and artistic enjoyment as well as new acquaintances whom I value.

A native of Minneapolis, I was a graduate student at the Sorbonne in Paris, who spent her early professional years at Smith and Mt. Holyoke Colleges in New England. A sojourn as Specialist in Higher Education at the national headquarters of the American Association of University Women (AAUW) in Washington, D.C., was followed by a post as Dean of 3,000 undergraduate women students at Miami University in Oxford, Ohio. On returning eventually to my native Minnesota in 1953, I became Dean of Students for some 2,000 undergraduates, both men and women, at Gustavus Adolphus College in St. Peter.

Thanks to membership in your group of Associates and participation in the activities of the society, I have had multiple opportunities to become acquainted with the early French history of our state through documentation available at the library, special events, and programs. Related achievements, exploratory and otherwise, of other ethnic groups have also broadened our horizons. What fun it was in this cycle of years dedicated to intensified re-evaluation of the role played by Columbus, to present a generally unknown Lope de Vega play with costumes, music and dances characteristic of the period. Might this event have been a veritable *première?*

Your duties, cultural and administrative, include editorial supervision of the official publications of the JFB Library, sustained research in regard to the potential availability of tempting manuscripts that might be acquired, and direction of a group of selected young student interns in the field of research.

The Library being an affiliate member of various national and international groups we enjoy, when appropriate, attendance at events featured on the programs of key gatherings at the University of Minnesota.

In your varied activities you are fortunately assisted by members of a professional staff endowed with exemplary high level excellence and dedication. May I cite an example? In the spring of

1989 I attended a regular meeting of the JFB Library's Board of Directors held at the University of Minnesota. When I asked the question "How are we going to celebrate the positive aspects of the French Revolution?," the answer was "We do not happen to have considered this particular possibility." "Well," I observed, "we have a fabulous collection of documents written by French explorers and early missionaries living in Canadian territory. The material contains rare books, maps, charts, drawings and sketches, journals, logs, and diary notations."

Several months later, thanks to the professional competence and artistry of Assistant Curator Carol Urness, a superb exhibit appeared in the display area of JFB Library — FRANCE OVER-SEAS, 1760–1800: A Selection of Books by Explorers, Critics, and Philosophers. Inaugurated July 1, 1989, the display remained intact during the summer months. Created as a tribute to the positive aspects of the French Revolution on the occasion of its 200th anniversary, it featured archival items owned by our own JFB Library.

It was hoped that early leaders of official government expeditions, such as Bougainville and La Perouse, who headed adventures over far-off seas, might be lucky enough to discover potential new routes for trade.

By the Treaty of Paris in 1763, France had relinquished Québec and the Québeçois to the British. Many Frenchmen in Europe agreed with Voltaire who wondered why the French should fight over a few acres of snow in Canada. As for the West Indies, especially with their thriving sugar and coffee plantations worked by blacks from Africa and their mulatto descendants, that was another story. *Vivent la Martinique, Guadaloupe, et St. Domingue!*

The concluding theme of the exhibit dealt with the quest for freedom sought by black slaves and their mulatto descendants, the advent of Toussaint L'Ouverture, and the pursuit of liberty that ended in the explosion of revolutionary violence.

In some respects the exhibit might have seemed to be a miraculously derived blueprint for much that is happening on our planet today. Have events in our world come full circle again?

You have faithfully interpreted the philosophical concepts formulated by the late James Ford Bell, Founding Father of the JFB

Library, concepts approved by his appointee, the late T.R. Anderson, as corporate member of the center. As colleagues and friends, undoubtedly the library has benefited from the joint implementation of policies through the united impact of the three major forces in its existence.

May the JFB Library continue to flourish and may your approaching retirement prove to be a happy one!

It is our hope that divested of multiple professional obligations, you will find it possible to develop from material in our archives, companion pieces to your definitive study of Jonathan Carver.

Sincerely yours, Melva Lind   4 July 1990

Docteur de l'Université de Paris en Sorbonne
Fédération des Alliances Françaises des Etats-Unis, Inc. National
Board of Directors, Member

LUNDSTROM, Linden J., Spring Valley, Wisconsin.

Dear Jack,

How good it was to learn that a "Festschrift" was being prepared for your retirement. No one deserves it more than you do.

I will always remember your help and encouragement when after retirement, I came to the James Ford Bell Library in my search for Henry Hudson.

As I tramped the eastern shore of James Bay, Ronnie Minister, our Cree Indian guide would ask me each time when I returned from a trek in the wilderness, "Have you found Henry yet?" Your kind, gentle and persistent questioning has encouraged and motivated generations of students and scholars in their search.

Some seek and find—others still seek.

Best wishes for a rich retirement.

Respectfully yours, Linden J. Lundstrom   23 April 1990

McCORISON, Marcus A., American Antiquarian Society, Worcester, Massachusetts.

Dear Jack:

I have had a communication from your colleagues informing me that you are planning to retire in May, 1991. I shall not be very far behind you!

I cannot recall where we first met, but I do remember how — Frank Handlin introduced us. It was in 1959 when I was at Iowa for that one year before coming here to the Antiquarian Society. I recall Frank telling me stories about you, Carl Jackson, and himself flying to meetings in Carl's airplane. He (Carl) surely was a dare-devil, wasn't he? And, I regret poor Frank's unfortunate illness and death. He was such a good person, and so capable.

In any case, I am happy that *we* have been friends for all these years and that we have had reunions in Minneapolis, in Worcester, and elsewhere to keep our friendship thriving. Also, I must tell you that I admire greatly what you have done at the James Ford Bell Library during your tenure. Not only have you increased the collections magnificently, you have successfully made the collection a useful and thriving agent for historical scholarship. Congratulations on all your good works.

I imagine that in retirement you will go back to Jamestown or Devil's Lake and once again take up dry farming. That should keep you out of trouble!

All the best.

Sincerely yours, Mark   7 May 1990

McCORKLE, Barbara, Secretary-Treasurer, The Society for the History of Discoveries, Hamden, Connecticut.

Dear Jack:

My life has been significantly livelier — and busier! — since I joined the Society for the History of Discoveries in 1972. Looking back over those years I realize how inextricably you are meshed into many of the memories. As a former, and long-time Secretary of SHD you were my mentor (although that word was not then in my vocabulary) and I used samples of your *Newsletter* as a guide to the first one I ever produced. Tremblingly, I may add. You were a comforting, familiar face when I had to attend my first SHD meeting alone; I have counted on seeing that face every year since. I look forward to your wise counsel and dry humor, and hope to do so for many years to come!

I expect your "retirement" will be only a shifting of gears. May it be long, happy, and productive.

                              Fondly, Barbara   May, 1990

MacDONNELL, Thomas P., Henry Stevens, Son, and Stiles, Williamsburg, Virginia.

Do I remember Jack Parker? I can not forget him. I first met Jack when he became James Ford Bell's right arm. I was on a business trip visiting Jim Kingsley, tl.en the acquisition head of the Walter Library, University of Minnesota. Being a busy traveller I read a lot of non-fiction paper books about World War II. Jim also liked that subject and I would hasten my reading so that I could leave the most recent book with him. Jack came over to the library and Jim introduced me to him for I had a few nice books I knew Mr. Bell would be interested in. We had been selling books to Mr. Bell since 1931. A few years prior to meeting Jack, Mr. Bell had purchased an almost complete set of the Jesuit Relations from us when we had purchased Mr. James C. McCoy's collection from his widow. From this collection Mr. Bell had also purchased some of Mr. McCoy's rarest early Canadian and American travel books. Jack has been adding great books to the Bell collection ever since. At the time of our first meeting I discovered that Jack and I had something in common, we had both served in the military during WW2, Jack in the air force in India and I in the navy, 3 years in the South Pacific. So began a good relationship which has carried on to this day. Jack has had all the characteristics of an outstanding book collector which he has carefully used building on to the great Bell collection over his many years as curator. When Jack teaches a course at the University the Bell collection is his background. He easily does the best job possible. The books, manuscripts, and maps were, in many cases, items he had personally selected to be added to Mr. Bell's collection. This collection is one of the outstanding collections in the field of trade. Jack knew Mr. Bell's ideas and wishes and his commitment to Mr. Bell's direction has never wavered. I do not think Jack has ever purchased a book by mistake, certainly not from me!

In 1963 I was on a trip to Paris with my wife Diana. We had decided to take photographs along the charming left bank rue de l'Echaude, with Polak's bookshop as background. With camera in hand and slowly backing up for focusing, a hand tapped my shoulder — what a pleasant surprise, for it was Jack. As it turned out we were both to be dinner guests, along with Kenneth Nebenzahl, of François Chamonal, a well-known Parisian bookseller. I have always had a feeling that fish was not exactly Jack's favorite preference. Of course we dined at a fish restaurant.

Jack has never procrastinated in making decisions. He always knew what was good, what he wanted and needed for the Bell Library. I think that is one of the reasons the antiquarian booksellers respect him and found him to be a good friend.

Jack, may you discover a way to stop the progress of the Killer bee.

Tom   19 May 1990

McLEAN, Austin J.

ON FIRST LOOKING INTO PARKER'S CARVER
Much have I travell'd in the tomes of old,
And many wondrous plains and forests seen;
On many western rivers have I been
Through books the great Bell Library holds.
Oft of one wide expanse had I been told
That deep-brow'd Carver ruled as his demesne;
Yet did I never breathe its pure serene
Till I heard Parker speak out loud and bold:
Then felt I like some trekker of the skies

When a new quasar swims into his ken;
Or like stout Urness when binocular'd eyed
She star'd silent at a dodo hen —
Amazed in a swamp near Sleepy Eye —
And God looked down in mild surprise.
A.J. McKeats   May 1990

(Editor's note: Keats and I will get you for this, Austin!)

MARZOLI, Carla. Libri Antichi, Milan, Italy.

Dear Jack,

Ursula, (ed. note: Mrs. Marzoli has called me "Ursula" ever since I first met her years ago. I like the name and have considered a change to "Ursula Urness" — CU) as always very kind and friendly, let me know that you will retire from your position as Curator of the James Ford Bell Library at the University of Minnesota, in May 1991.

It is a great event in your life and it seems impossible to me, as I am always thinking of you as a very young man, enthusiastic in your work, always actively researching treasures to add to the fabulous James Ford Bell Library, that you directed for so many years.

I have all the interesting yellow and blue pamphlets of the Merchant Explorer, that you published for so many years, and I see that the way of success is very long.

I always remember the first time you entered in my office asking if I had some important treasures to add to the James Ford Bell Collection.

And, in fact, I had on approval the magnificent map by Albino de Canepa, that, immediately, you purchased.

I was very embarrassed as until that moment my special interest had been manuscripts, but humanistic ones, not cartographic items. I owe to Albino the fact that I became immediately your most devoted friend, enjoying very much working and researching cartographic treasures for your Library.

And a proof of your friendship was given to me when, many years later, you came back to Milano with the great Man who was Dr. J.F.Bell.

You visited me with him, and Dr. Bell invited me to dinner with you both at the Palace Hotel. You will remember: I was very timid in front of him, but after a few moments he became very friendly, talking and talking together. At a certain moment he asked me to get for his Library a precious copy of the famous Biard! It took many years of researches, but finally I succeeded in securing for your Library the duplicate copy that I had discovered existing in the Bibliothèque Nationale of Paris. Do you remember that for this difficult negotiation we also met in Paris? I think that one of your pretty daughters was with you. And, with great difficulties . . . You had also the Biard!! in memory of Dr. Bell.

It followed your invitation to come to Minneapolis, where you organized a reception ceremony for me! My visit to your Library, the kindness of you and your Family, of Ursula, of all the staff of the Library as well as all your friends, will remain in my memory the most beautiful souvenir of one of the best days of my career and life.

Thank you, dear Jack, for all you have done for me, thank you with all my heart!

I hope that in your retirement you will continue to work, and I am sure you will do it: I convey to you my best wishes for your publishing the books you did not have the time to write until now. I will enjoy reading them immensely.

And why not come back to Italy for some holiday?

You had marvelous help in Ursula Urness, that we must thank her for her fidelity and friendship, and enthusiasm in working.

I am getting very old and in 1991 — that is still far from now — should I be in good health, as I am now, it might be possible that I jump on a plane for Minneapolis, to be with you in the great day of your celebration in May 1991.

All my best wishes and . . . un affettuoso abbraccio

Yours, Carla   14 May 1990

MILLER, Mary Emily, Salem, Massachusetts.

Dear Jack:

Many happy days for your retirement and we are all looking forward to the results of the extra time you will have now for research, writing, and lecturing.

My first association with you was through the mail when I joined the Society for the History of Discoveries in the early 1960's. As a young academic and administrator the first meeting I was able to attend was the one in Bloomington, Indiana. I was hooked. Pleasant people, lively conversation, material I could use for classes, and no job hunting. For the many years you were secretary-treasurer and president I looked forward to the annual meetings of SHD to catch up on your many activities. I have lost count of the many gatherings at waterholes around the country with you, Carol Urness, the Dunns, the Goldsteins, the Powers, other SHD members who have left lasting research for future scholars. I can recall the stories of the founding of the Society in Portugal over wine, early discussions on the Drake plate and Drake landings in California. In fact, these are all issues still open and hotly debated. You were always able to keep the topics moving along and the opponents from bashing each other physically. There were special meetings that stand out: the first session at the American Historical Association annual meeting in San Francisco, the wonderful sessions and extra activities at the Drake conference with special activities organized by Bob Power and Norman Thrower, the first meeting in Canada, the 1987 meeting in London organized by Helen Wallis, and many others. Actually each one has been special. The Society's efforts to maintain a journal, first edited so ably by Bruce Solnick, were actively supported by you. This enabled younger scholars, like myself, to get involved in the reviewing of new books. You also supported the monograph series. All this while making the resources of the James Ford Bell Library available to scholars and students through such forms as the essays on a variety of topics in *The World for a Marketplace: Episodes in the History of European Expansion*, 1978. Most especially, I want to thank you for your continued interest and support of my own research on the *H.M.S. Mermaid*.

I wish you a very productive retirement.
With best wishes I am, Sincerely yours,
             Mary Emily Miller   14 July 1990

MOLANDER, Arne, Gaithersburg, Maryland.

My primary association with Jack has been in the landfall
arena. In honor of his stubborn, but fair-minded, treatment of
landfall proponents challenging Morison, I offer the following:
         In disputes of where Christopher landed,
           He's ever with Morison banded,
            But while Jack has a yack
           For each track out of whack,
       To proponents he's always been candid.
Here's hoping that Jack's fresh new start will give him fresh new
insights concerning Guanahani!!
           Warmest regards, Arne   19 March '90
             (D-938 days, and counting!)

NELSON, Dorothy K.

Dear Jack,

We certainly had many discussions over our latest spring (or
fall, or winter, or summer) wardrobes, what birds were seen, and
other important subjects like vacations.

Some of the biggest decisions we have shared have been where
to have lunch, and, of course, Peter's Grill always came out on
top. So if you are not doing anything one of these upcoming
noons, let's have lunch.

Your friendship means a lot to me and I wish for you a very
happy, productive, or unproductive if you prefer, retirement
from your position, and to begin or continue whatever you most
want to do.
           Sincerely, Dorothy   May, 1991

PANKAKE, Marcia J.

Dear Carol,

I first met Jack in the fall of 1962. A tall, quietly elegant man joined the round coffee table in that drab staff lounge in the basement of Walter Library. I knew who he was: John Parker, the Famous Scholar Librarian. I, the mousy new Library Assistant from the Circulation desk, felt awed to sit at the table with a half-dozen of the library staff and when Jack joined us I shrunk in my chair and swallowed deeply twice.

As usual, the talk was of books and everyday life. I remember that it ranged loosely, until Jack asked, "I wonder why people smoke?" I don't remember what all the speculations were; some people gave anecdotes from their experience, some from books. Jack talked about exotic peoples described smoking in some travel account. I dared to enter the conversation saying, "It gives them something to do with their hands." Jack smiled.

That first meeting with Jack typifies many of his characteristics: Civic-minded, sociable, egalitarian, curious, intellectual, exploring, contemplative, tolerant.

When I think of Jack I think of a scholar and a gentleman, a humanist and a mentor, a citizen of the world of ideas, and best of all, a friend. He is a source of inspiration and a role model, a gardener and a traveler, a beekeeper and a writer, and always a teacher. The perfect librarian, he has shown us new possibilities and far horizons in books and in life. These gifts will be diminished among us when he retires, but we will try to keep and emulate some of his qualities, because he worked and socialized with us and because he encouraged, taught, and helped us. I'll miss him terribly and tears come to my eyes now as I write you this note.

Love, Marcia   31 May 1990

PEARSON, M.N., The University of New South Wales, Kensington, NSW, Australia.

I had known of Jack Parker long before I first met him, for his books and the fame of the James Ford Bell Library had penetrated even so far into the Antipodes as Sydney. Unsurprising really, for the Bell of course contains important works relating to early European contacts with Terra Australis.

More substantial contact, and brief personal meetings, came from my involvement in the Rise of Merchant Empires conference in the History Department at UM. In connection with this I visited the university, and the Bell Library, in 1985 and 1987. I well remember Jack showing a very diverse group of foreign scholars around his library; we were as impressed by his urbanity as by the richnesses of the library.

One thing led to another, and I was appointed the first Union Pacific Visiting Professor of Early Modern History at UM for the Spring quarter of 1989. This was an opportunity I jumped at, in large part because it meant I could hope to make an extended investigation of the holdings of the Bell Library. During my tenure of this position I came to know Jack as a scholar, and a friend and helper of other scholars. So often I would ask for a book in the Bell, and Jack would deliver it with a little commentary of his own on its contents and usefulness. My two favourite places to work at are the British Library, and the Bell. Different scales of course, but they both have an atmosphere, a scholarly ambiance, and a handsome environment which make them exceptional. And at the Bell you have the added advantage of personal, and informed, service from Jack and Carol.

I had two projects going on at this time: a study of the Muslim pilgrimage, or *hajj* to Mecca in the early modern period, and of early contacts between Indian and European medicine. I found a host of curious, entertaining, and useful material on the former, but my extended contact with Jack Parker came from the latter.

Jack had the courtesy to invite me to deliver the 27th James Ford Bell Lecture while I was on campus at UM. We decided that the medical topic might be of some general interest, and this was what I presented. It was at this time that I saw another side of Jack Parker, one in which he also excelled. This was, I suppose, to act as an intermediary between the world of scholarship and the outside, between town and gown perhaps. The high profile of the Bell, and its continuing viability, relies very largely on this aspect of Jack Parker's work. At the lecture he was graciousness personified, and predictably introduced me with a witty, urbane and yet scholarly speech. Subsequently he was even so magnanimous as to accept a printed text which goes considerably over the normal limit. For these several kindnesses I am grateful.

Cheers for now, Michael   29 March 1990

PENNINGTON, Loren E., Emporia State University, Emporia, Kansas.

Back in the late 1950's, I was working on my doctoral dissertation in the University of Michigan History Department on the promotional literature of early American colonization. When I was almost finished, my wife, who was a graduate student in the Library School, informed me she had just learned that a student over there by the name of Jack Parker was working on the same topic. Jack's dissertation became his *Books to Build an Empire*. If you want to read mine, you have to get it from University Microfilms.

I never did meet Jack at the University of Michigan, and I first ran into him at the Society for the History of Discoveries meeting in New Bedford in 1968. We joked about doing dissertations on the same topic, and then I mentioned that I was contemplating a book on the Studebaker Corporation. He gave me a strange look and replied, "I did my master's thesis on Packard."

Now we are both working on *The Purchas Handbook*, but if I ever get done with that, I am going to finish the book on Studebaker. As I doubt he will do one on Packard, at that point we will be even.

11 April 1990

PHILLIPS, Carla Rahn.

Dear Jack:

Like so many of your friends in the Twin Cities, I wish you all the best in your retirement, even though I will miss your sage counsel as I continue to explore the treasures of the collection you did so much to create. How could I guess that a small packet of documents about six Spanish galleons, which you acquired for the Bell Library, would occupy my scholarly attention for so long? Much to my surprise, I find myself turning into a maritime historian, thanks to your eclectic interests. I look forward to finding other treasures in the Bell Library as well, reminders of your contributions to the collection.

As you know, I am very much involved in preparations for the Columbian Quincentenary just now, and I want to thank you for helping to inspire and shape my investigations into the fascinating topic of European exploration. Describing your wide experience in talking to business and civic groups also helped me learn how to approach audiences outside the university. As 1992 looms ahead, that knowledge is increasingly important to me.

Talking with you about things Columbian also turned my attention to Martin Behaim's globe as a focal point for discussing the state of knowledge in Columbus's times. I have since learned, as you already knew, that audiences are amazed by that globe, with its island-strewn Atlantic Ocean and the absence of North and South America. Nothing else brings home as vividly the geographical revolution that occurred after Columbus.

I remember standing with you beside a case in the Maritime Museum at Greenwich in 1987. There sat a replica of Behaim's globe, and both of us were struck anew at the power of that visual reminder of a world view that was shattered forever in the wake of Columbus.

Thank you for your perceptions and your scholarship, your experience, and your unfailing kindness. I have benefited from them all.

                              Cordially, Carla   28 May 1990

PONKO, Vincent, Jr., Dominican College, Orangeburg, New York.

I met Jack Parker for the first time at the meeting of the Society for the History of Discoveries held at Minneapolis, I believe in 1969, in association with the University of Minnesota Library. That meeting is remembered by me as being special in the fact that it was the first one I had attended and in the fact that the members of the society, many of pronounced prominence in their field, treated me with kindness as a friend even though I was a relatively unknown historian and had never met them before. Jack Parker, I believe, personified this spirit and went out of his way to make me feel comfortable as a member of the team even though I was not a top seed.

In the years subsequent to that meeting, Jack Parker has continued to treat me as a friend and colleague in the best sense of the term. Recently he recommended me to be a contributor to a multi-volume work under the general editorship of Dr. John Allen of the University of Connecticut, timed for publication in 1992.

All of these favors have come to me from John Parker without the opportunity to reciprocate. His friendship has been and is a jewel whose facets shine with the brilliance of remembrance, unselfishness, and a magnificent desire to do good for others. To and for me he has been unique. I value beyond measure my association with him.

Sincerely, Vince   11 April 1990

PUFFER, Kenneth E., PE, Minneapolis Rotary.

My association with Jack dates back to his joining the Minneapolis Rotary Club about 1980. The evening seminars opened up a whole new appreciation for the Bell Library. The seeing of the ancient manuscripts and being able to page through was a thrill. I came to appreciate the hard work and the necessity of preserving these manuscripts for study.

As a student at the University in 1936 and 1937, I worked as

a runner in the stacks of the Walter Library. The special room
was off-limits for runners. We were curious about it, but no one
offered to show us around.

The other impression from Jack was his discussion of the voyage of Columbus before the Rotary Club. He made history exciting and come-alive before our eyes.

He is a fine person and a dedicated scholar. I wish him an exciting and fruitful retirement. It can be done, I have experienced it.

                    Sincerely, Ken   19 March 1990

QUINN, David B., Liverpool, England.

First Visit to Minneapolis

I can't recall, with my fading memory, when I first met Jack
Parker (I knew him as John for years) but it was in 1957 (or was
it 1959?) that I got an invitation from him to come out to Minneapolis to give a lecture for the then princely sum of $200. I was
a Visiting Fellow at the Folger in Washington at the time and the
letter had evidently been chasing me from place to place so I had
just time to reply saying "yes" when I was due to arrive. I was
provided with a day or so to do so but found that there was only
one plane from Washington which could get there in time. It was
a Northwest flight (now Northwest Orient) and Executive Class
(or whatever they called it then) only and the cost was the greater
part of my $200 fee. However, it was a very fine flight — my first
long-distance one inside the U.S. and we were served with champagne throughout the flight (though nothing more solid). Wishing to get value for my money I drank what was offered and by
the time I got to Minneapolis I was somewhat elated, though not
I think, drunk. However, John and one or two others were at the
foot of the steps to meet me (those were the days before "security"
was thought of) and I think he was a little surprised to find me
somewhat effusive (something of which one could never accuse
Jack). However, I was taken off and given something to eat which
sobered me up. I was then brought to a large lecture room and
introduced to Mr Bell himself, a portly figure who was a little dis-
concerted, I think, by my Anglo-Irish accent — more pronounced

in those days. I had a lecture script with me in Washington and a set of slides. I was speaking about the early explorers and the natural history of America. I thought it went tolerably well and there were no hitches that I remember in the slide projection (always a risk in the U.S. as sizes were not always compatible). I got through it anyhow and answered a few questions and said goodbye to Mr Bell. I rather fancied he found the lecture very dull as he closed his eyes part of the time I was speaking. I then saw, not in its present fine setting, the nucleus of the Collection which amazed me already by its range. I thought Jack was very lucky to be in charge of so many fine books, though it was nothing to what he presides over now. I may say that I was very hospitably treated and conveyed in due course to the airport where a more normal service was provided so that I arrived back in Washington quite sober.

From that day on John (Jack) and I have been close friends and have met each other so many times in England and the U.S. that we have both lost count. But the *Merchant Explorer* and the James Ford Bell Lectures have kept my admiration for his work in amassing so many new works every year alive in the intervals so that he fills a continuing space in my admiration and on my shelves!

David Quinn   20 March 1990

REIERSGORD, Thomas E.

Reflections on the James Ford Bell Library and Jack Parker.

From October 1950 to June 1956 I was there — a student at the University of Minnesota — living in Pioneer Hall, Centennial Hall and in the Dinkytown neighborhood. About midway in that time period, as the Korean War was ending, the James Ford Bell Library was founded at the University and Jack Parker became its curator. I'm sure that I read about it in the Daily at the time, but it did not have much impact on a student who had many other things on his mind. I recall looking in at the reception room which was installed in the Walter Library and being impressed by its elegance. It truly seemed another world.

About a decade after graduation, in the late 1960s, I had the

good fortune to become a member of a group of collectors, and
there I first met Jack Parker, who was also a member. About once
a year the group met at the James Ford Bell Library, in its present
quarters on the west bank, in the evening for conversation and
program. Over the years I became acquainted with Jack and
learned that he did not come from "another world" but from rural North Dakota, not far from the Red River Valley towns where
I grew up.

Another decade later, in 1975, we discovered that we both had
travel plans to Norway that summer, and we booked the same
flight. Jack's itinerary included the rare book dealers in Oslo, and
he invited me to go along when he visited Claes Nyegaard's antiquarian bookshop. Nyegaard brought out some of his treasures in
hopes of further building the collections of the James Ford Bell
Library. While I browsed the lower price end of the bookstore,
Jack did make an acquisition for the library. It was an edition of
the New Testament, printed in Stockholm, in an Indian language, for use in teaching the Indians at the Swedish and Finn
settlement in Delaware, begun in 1638. Later, Nyegaard invited
Jack and me out to his retreat on Oslo Fjord for a memorable afternoon of conversation and refreshments.

I joined the Associates of the James Ford Bell Library which
has given me more opportunity to participate in events sponsored
by the library. Also our group of collectors continues to meet, and
whenever Jack Parker is the host at the library you know that you
are going to have an interesting evening. Once when Jack was ab-
sent from a meeting I later learned that the queen bee in one of
his beehives had died that day and to deal with this emergency
Jack had to secure a replacement queen and take it to the hive,
which was located on a farm some miles out from the city. Such
a tiny passenger. Something like *Driving Miss Daisy*. It shows
that Jack will go the extra miles to do the best job he can.

The focus of the library is the history, prior to 1800, of European expansion by exploration and trade into the rest of the
world. That exploration and the promotion of risky trade ventures in far-off places was not literary work — it was real work,
and real adventure by bold individuals who took risks and often
lost everything in pursuing their dream. I think that Jack Parker
knew people, and lived with people like that, as he grew up on

a North Dakota farm in the 1920s and 1930s. In Jack Parker's work, telling the story by showing and appreciating the perspective of the people who were involved is a key element. Working with original materials and manuscripts helps a writer keep this focus, but it also depends a great deal on where the eyes of the historian have looked in the past.

Now, in the 1990s when Jack is planning to retire, is a good time to reflect on the building of the James Ford Bell Library into the prominent institution which it has become. The publications and other outgoing activities of the library have been major factors in using a collection of rare books and manuscripts as a springboard for education and scholarship, for students at the University, and for many others. Because the collection and the publications of the library so clearly reflect the work of Jack Parker, and because through his leadership the library has become established as a prominent and important collection in its field, I think his work and contributions should be recognized by renaming the library; The Bell & Parker Library.

Thomas E. Reiersgord   18 April 1990

RICHARDSON, Jessie F.

Dear Jack,

Over the many years I have known you as colleague and friend, there are many happy memories of various events or shared interests that I might be writing about. Your significant achievements in so many areas all call for mention and acclaim. But in thinking it over, I decided to write about a common thread that for me runs through many occasions — namely, my deep admiration for your way with words, both spoken and written.

It is a singular pleasure to hear you speak or to read your writings. Not only do you have something to say, but you express it beautifully with the skill of one who has an ear for the beauty of our language. There is no jargon, no hint of the pompous. Rather, you present us with well-organized material which not only conveys your meaning clearly and precisely, but which also delights the ear and the mind with its grace of expression. Whenever I've heard you speak to an audience, or whenever I read something you've written, I'm aware (happily!) of the well-chosen words, the apt comparisons, and how the language flows.

It is my hope that a long and active retirement finds you continuing to share this gift for words with us all. Best wishes!

Sincerely, Jessie   29 May 1990

ROBERTS, Valerie R.

Dear Jack,

REMEMBER:

—When I first began cataloging Bell books in 1976?

Your descriptions helped me learn to navigate the shoals of pre-1800 title pages.

Merci beaucoup!

—When the Bell books accumulated while I and the other Catalogers learned MARC tagging and coding in 1977, and I spent February to June, 1978 getting caught up?

You began copying information which you found in NUC pre-1956, and putting the photocopies in the books with your descriptions. This was a tremendous help, and you have continued doing it. All these years I have been able to get right to work cataloging Bell books without having to search NUC first.

Gelobet sei Gott!

—The 25th anniversary celebration for the Bell Library in 1978? You included me in the slide show, and I was so pleased and proud.

Danke sehr viel!

—Bell parties—the lavish feasts at Christmas, and the cosier back room gatherings for birthdays.

You've always included me, and I've felt like a member of the Bell family

Gemütlichkeit!

—When the cataloging rules changed in 1981 or 1982 and we realized, to our horror, that if we didn't know who "A Lover of His Country" was, I would have to enter his pamphlet under this pseudonymous phrase?

Was this when you proposed that we form SPOT: Society for the Preservation of Obsolete Technology?

Horosho!

—When you were recovering from surgery, and I wrote you a note urging you to take life easy, to enjoy the fall leaves, to listen to the birds, and to watch out for the yellow jackets, which were abundant that year?

You responded with a jar of your marvelous honey—from the experienced bee keeper.

Gracias!

—How we cleaned up the Bell "behindage" in 1988–1990?

And I am so pleased and proud of us!

Sköl!!!

Your cataloger and friend, Valerie

Political P.S.:

Local: Through the storms of university and library politics which have buffeted the library staff, you have been a firm and steadfast friend to all of us. My gratitude goes far beyond words!

National: When we found that you, Carol, and I had all bought the same color cars, your comment summed up the 80s beautifully. "The Reagan years gave us gray cars."

Thank you

Thank you

Thank you

Stay in touch and visit often!

RONAN, Charles E., S.J., Loyola University of Chicago.

Dear Jack,

This letter carries a long-overdue thanks to you for assisting me in selecting a title for my almost-completed biography of the eighteenth-century Chilean Jesuit historian, Juan Ignacio Molina (1740–1829). Choosing titles has always been a heavy task for me; but as I was browsing through some of my favorite books, I came upon your very interesting *Windows into China*. As I read through it, the thought struck me all of a sudden that Jack's title is a solution to my problem; for just as the European Jesuits who

went to China acquainted Europe with that great Empire
through their writings, so also did Molina acquaint Europe with
Chile through his histories of that country. As you recall, Jack,
Molina — together with his Jesuit colleagues — was expelled from
the Spanish Empire in 1767. He lived the rest of his life in Bolo-
gna, Italy, where he encountered vast ignorance about Spanish
America, especially Chile, and spent the rest of his life endeavor-
ing to acquaint Europe with the truth about his fatherland. This
also brought him into the sharp debate that was raging in Europe
at the time over the superiority of the Old World over the New.
So with your kind permission, Jack, I would like to name my book
Juan Ignacio Molina, 1740–1829: Europe's Window into Chile.

Hoping this finds you enjoying the best of everything, I remain,
Cordially yours, Charles E. Ronan, SJ   23 April 1990

SAVAGE, Elizabeth Z.

Dear Jack,

Are we old enough to have met at a dinner party thirty years
ago? In trying to be conversational that long ago evening I mentioned Tom and I had recently been to the Arctic. Instead of answering, "why?" as most of our friends did, you actually seemed
interested in Frobisher Bay, Bathurst Inlet and the Beaufort Sea.
I believe you later went up there yourself to see the tundra wild-
flowers and caribou herds along with the Eskimos and Indians.
That was the start of our continuing friendship; and retirement
for you will be another adventure as fascinating as exploring the
Mackenzie River.

                    Good luck, Elizabeth   28 April 1990

SCHOLBERG, Henry.

Dear Jack,

You have undoubtedly heard the cliché that one is busier following retirement than he was before. I am living proof that that
is true.

So you know what you have to look forward to.

This is a short letter to tell you how much I appreciated your presence in the library during the quarter century I was there with you. Actually, I still appreciate your being there.

You have always been someone I could come to when I needed advice or help. Because we shared a common sphere of interest (European expansion in South Asia), my need to consult you was, and still is, frequent. I have always been confident that I would get the very best professional advice from you, and that you and your able staff would always be willing to help me.

Winston Churchill said when he retired from government service, "My years of greatest service lie ahead." It may be that you can say the same thing as you prepare to explore the vast, uncharted ocean of retirement.

I wish you well.

All the best! Henry   24 April 1990

SCHRODER, Lucille.

> Plant trees you may, and see
>   them shoote
> Up with your children, to be
>   serv'd
> To your cleane boards, and the
>   fair'st fruite
> To be preserv'd.
>
> And learne to use their several
>   gummes;
> 'Tis innocence in the sweet blood
> Of Cherry, Apricocks and Plummes
> To be imbru'd.

An ode, upon occasion of His Majestie's Proclamation in the year 1630 Commanding the Gentry to reside upon their Estates in the Country.

I thought of our many 'garden chats' when I came upon this

verse. I think it very fine counsel and know you'll take it quite
seriously in your retirement.

Wishing you the very best, Jack.

Lucille   1 May 1990

SCHWAPPACH, Kirsten. A graduate student in Library Science
in 1982, who "had fallen in love with rare books and sought Jack's
help in developing a related topic for a major research paper. He's
been a wise and congenial teacher, mentor and friend ever since."

Dear Jack,

I'm so glad I dropped in on you at James Ford Bell back in
1982. The research paper you guided remains one of my proudest
accomplishments and the writing of it wasn't nearly as awful an
experience as the prevailing graduate student wisdom promised
it would be. This is largely due to you — your wisdom, support
and friendship. I'm also glad that you and I have maintained the
friendship since the teacher-student roles ended. I count on it
very much — and not just for moral support as I forge a niche in
this crazy book business.

One afternoon in late January 1990, I paid you one of my impromptu office visits. I was incensed over a new rule at work, re-
quiring me to be on duty until midnight instead of 10 pm in my
job as a college reference librarian. My input had been dis-
regarded, the change was ridiculous and I was fed up. What was
your response? Did you commiserate with me, sympathizing with
my frustration? You did not. Did you remind me that I didn't
want to make reference work a career anyway and assure me that
a better job was waiting in the wings? Again, negative. Did you
have some look-on-the-bright-side wise words, to soften my anger
and help me make the best of a not great situation? Nope.

Your response was not unfriendly, but certainly dispassionate.
Library hours were influenced significantly by dissatisfied patrons, you said. College administrators were sensitive to com-
plaints like insufficient library hours; thus, even a few such patrons, if they were noisy enough, will most likely get what they
want. I wasn't going to change this attitude, you told me, because

if I didn't want to put up with it, there were plenty of others who would. Unarticulated point: Maybe it's time to get out.

You were absolutely right, of course, and once I'd gotten over the feeling of having had a chair pulled out from under me I felt strong and clear-eyed and in control. It wasn't the sympathetic support I'd expected but it was what I needed to hear. Afterwards, I felt glad, lucky and *relieved* to have such a friend as you. And I wasn't angry anymore!

Thank you, Jack — for everything. I know that your life after Bell will be full and rewarding. I hope I can be part of it, somehow.

My best to you always, Kirsten   16 April 1990

SHANNON, Sara.

Dear Jack,

Vaclev Havel has written about what he calls the "memory of being" which is in part the idea that people aren't individual entities in themselves. Instead, Havel believes that the people we have known become part of us and we a part of them. He writes that the personality of an acquaintance or friend is "a dimension or aspect of our own existence. As a certain 'aspect of the world's Being' which we depend upon in our own actions and which thus belongs to our 'particular horizon', he is ultimately . . . a part of that aspect of the world's being which is our own 'I'."

Although I've only known you for a year, in that short time you've touched my life in many ways. As my teacher and friend you've given me guidance and encouragement and you've been a constant source of inspiration. Thank you, Jack, for enriching my "particular horizon".

Sara   7 May 1990

SHEPHERD, Mary.

Dear Jack:

The James Ford Bell Library is a wonderful asset to the University of Minnesota, and how fortunate it was to have had your curatorship, which has strengthened the library's international reputation.

On a personal note I want to thank you for my first/only venture into "scholarly" writing. If you had not encouraged me to submit my article to *The Pennsylvania Magazine of History and Biography*, it would not have experienced printer's ink, nor I a glow of success.

Jerry joins me in recommending retirement and sending our best wishes! My son, Andy Turnbull, remembers with pleasure his days at the Bell Library and sends his kind regards.

Cordially yours, Mary   14 April 1990

SKOG, Ellen.

A Poem for Jack:

> There once was a man named Jack
> Whose mind was always on track
> he attended his bees
> and curated with ease
> but now he'll have time to sit back
>
> As for Jack being my boss
> for words, I'm at a loss
> He's quick to praise
> when I'm having good days
> and he's slow to scold
> when my brain's on hold
> so I guess he never gets cross
>
> As for Jack the person
> he does no cursin'
> he's as polite as a being could be

He'll help you his best
without taking a rest
cause that's what he's been like to me

And the future for Jack
should hold much — not a lack
'cause he's such a well-rounded guy
He'll be so busy with business
that he probably won't even miss us
but for now we must say "good-bye"
                              Ellen   Spring, 1990

SMITH, Merrily A., The Library of Congress, Washington, D.C.

Dear Jack,

If it weren't for you, I definitely would not have had my car stolen three times in the last twelve months, I probably would not have spent my entire career working underground in offices without windows, and I possibly would not have seen (let alone cared about) the rock in Botany Bay from which Captain Cook "conquered" Australia by simply stating that, henceforth it belonged to England. All of which is to say that you are responsible for starting me on the road to the rich and varied life I now lead living in Washington, DC and working as a preservation administrator in the Library of Congress National Preservation Program Office.

By my reckoning it was about twenty-six years ago, when I was a senior in high school, that I first came through the doors of the James Ford Bell Library — only after knocking first, of course. My father, who was at that time on the University's Senate Library Committee, had told me it was a marvelous place that I should see. I looked at the panelling, the Oriental rugs, the old tables and chairs, and decided I'd like to work there. As I recall, I asked you for a job on the spot. You were very nice about it, said you didn't have any openings, and told me to come back in a few months. I did, and got the same response. The third time I showed up, you said ok, and took me on as a student assistant for ten hours a week, in spite of the fact that I failed part of the qualifying test—the part where you had to compare columns of figures to see if there were any errors. Little did I know at the time that I'd be associated in some way with the James Ford Bell Library from that day to this, and probably for the rest of my life.

In any case, for the next eight years (1964–72) you set about the task of expanding my horizons and nudging me along in the search for an interesting and useful career. Mostly, your approach was subtle: you put me to work oiling leather bindings; you assigned me the task of finding out all I could about Marshall's Peristrephic Panorama of the Polar Regions; and you asked me to tackle the translation of one or two texts from German into English. Occasionally, it was a little less subtle: You suggested that I learn how to mend torn pages in books; you sent me to George Baer at the Cuneo Press in Chicago to learn the rudiments of bookbinding and box making, then set me to work making portfolios and slipcases for items in the collection; and when I once inquired where Genoa was you exploded, "Merrily Smith, you have some amazing gaps in your education!"

As I think back on those years and recall some of the programs and projects that you and Carol undertook, many recollections associated with them come to mind. For example, you started the Associates group—the membership fee was $5.00 per year. You wanted every contributor to get an individual typed letter of thanks, and I took great pride in banging them out as fast as possible on the Library's manual typewriter. When we finally got an electric typewriter I refused for weeks to use it. I was sure that I would hate it and could never master it. You finally decreed that I *would* use it, which—with considerable grumbling—I did, with the result that I shortly became addicted to it.

The Library also acquired during that time the manuscript records, bound in multiple oversized volumes, of the trial of Warren Hastings. You decided that the books were dirty and that each page of every volume had to be vacuumed. We dug up a huge canister machine that made an ungodly racket, and I spent *hours* at the task. The reward for that effort was finding an 18th century quill pen at the back of one volume. History lived at that moment, and you added to its magic by explaining to me how the pen was trimmed repeatedly for use and how the wet ink was dried by sprinkling sand on it.

Remember the inventory project you initiated when we were still in Walter Library? It seemed to go on forever. Carol and I checked each card in the shelf list and then searched to make sure the book was in the stacks. They weren't all easy to locate. Sometimes we'd look and look without success, then get a little panicky because we thought it might be lost (and you have always been a stickler for security). Finally, we would ask you about it. You'd look at the card, then say, Oh yes, this one is bound in red leather. Then you'd get up from your chair, march into the vault, and two minutes later come back with it. I'll bet you can still do the same thing.

Another thing I'll never forget is the marbled paper caper. You pointed out the gold in the Dutch papers, showed me the French ones, and talked about how they differed from the Spanish. Then you said, "Why don't you try making some?" and before long we had the inks and the pans and I was spending just about all my time in the Library's only work room, spreading wet marbled papers — some of them in the most outrageous color combinations — all over the floor and desks.

You are a natural teacher and mentor, Jack, and the more time that passes the more I realize the value of all I experienced and learned while I was working with you. You encouraged and focused my love for books; you helped me find a professional niche in the library world that is important, exciting, and rewarding; and through example, you taught me values and principles that have served as guidelines for both my professional and personal life. Thank you for these gifts, and thank you for answering my knock on the door of the James Ford Bell Library.

Sincerely yours, Merrily 24 May 1990

STANFORD, Edward B.

Dear Jack,

Your forthcoming retirement prompts me to recall the day nearly forty years ago when our paths first came together. You had come to Minneapolis to be interviewed for the newly created post of Curator of the James Ford Bell Collection.

It all began with a visit from Mr. Bell to my office in the old Walter Library when I was fairly new to the Directorship of the University of Minnesota Libraries. He came to ask my help in finding a Curator for the rare collection on the History of Trade he was about to present to the University. In addition to the gift of the books themselves he intended to provide a suitably appointed James Ford Bell Room to house them, and initial funding both for the collection's growth and for a curatorship to assure the implementation of his vision for its future.

Our search soon presented us with the choice of wooing an established antiquarian bookperson away from another research library or offering the post to a less experienced candidate to whom the chance to build up an entirely new library would present an unusual yet potentially very rewarding challenge. Your visit made our decision very easy. Even then when the project was only in a formative stage your view of it as an exciting opportunity for developing and interpreting such a unique resource made it evident that you shared our belief in the undertaking. Thus it all began.

Your long career at Minnesota has more than fulfilled the hopes we had, back in 1953, for what is now the James Ford Bell Library, a resource that under your leadership has attracted scholars from far and near academic centers who have produced scholarly monographs of distinction based on many of the holdings you personally have located and acquired for the collection. Your own writings and lectures, as well as those you have arranged for visiting authors have produced a body of collection-based publications that bring credit to the University throughout the world.

As you retire I want to tell you directly what I have often said to others, that helping to recruit you may have been one of the most notable actions I took during the years of my tenure with the University.

Thanks for what you have done here AND for your friendship.

    Edward B. Stanford (Ned, to you)   Spring, 1991

TANENBAUM, Charles J., New York City.

Dear Jack:

I remember meeting you when the Grolier Club visited your Library nearly twenty years ago, and you inspired my membership in the Associates, a pleasure ever since.

I will be always grateful to you for the gracious credit you gave me in the preface to your *Journal of Jonathan Carver*. It was a first for me and has encouraged me to think of ways to aid scholars in the course of enjoying the pleasures of collecting.

I always look forward to your visits to New York and hope they will be more frequent in your future activities.

Yours sincerely, Charles   9 May 1990

TELLES DA SYLVA, José António, Lisbon, Portugal.

My good Friend John Parker,

It must have been in 1964 that I had the pleasure of meeting you by the kindness of our mutual and much missed friend George Duff. Soon after that we began our agreeable interchange of letters, with my offering you books and manuscripts, which were rarely refused.

Later I went into the business, and had the honour of being invited to become one of the Associates of the James Ford Bell Library.

Perhaps I may add at this point that in fact this institution, which you have directed so admirably, may have been my first important American client.

So it happened for me that things developed, and the business grew, and after 1971 and 1972 when I published my first catalogues, I soon received a most encouraging letter from you, praising " . . . beautiful publication. The *Manuscritos & Livros Valiosos* is outstanding."

We continued our collaboration, and I read everything that your natural propensity for the history of the Discoveries caused you to publish, and from these works I have learnt enormously.

So we come to March 1990, when I received a letter from someone of that Institute, whom we are both very fond of, announcing
to me that you are about to retire; that letter had a manuscript
note: "I know Jack would be pleased if you wrote a letter. So
would I! Carol."

However, everyday our races finish and start again, everyday
we know little and also that far less we know, everyday we ponder that tomorrow is early or late, but indeed, in this dawn of
1990, that is 498 years later, we refound a portentous America,
and with this, I mean that the New World and the Old World are
more and more in need of John Parkers, for they, in possession of
such culture, wisdom and knowledge will be the Bartolomeu Di-
ases, the Columbuses, the Gamas, the Cabrals, of the eternal
worlds to come.

Your "favourite Portuguese bookseller."

   J.A. Telles da Sylva, Lisbon   20 April 1990

TERRELL, Burnham and Julie.

For Jack Parker and all his friends on the occasion of his retirement as Curator of the James Ford Bell Library in May, 1991:

Julie and I came to know Jack Parker best as a scholar, when
we attended a program of lectures he presented on early explorations. They were, of course, models of clear and economical expo-
sition of a substantial body of information. The cartographical illustrations, from the James Ford Bell Library's collection, were
fascinating. It was a memorable experience. Julie and I prize the
copious notes she took.

My own favorite recollection of Jack in the Library has to do
with an occasion on which I was there with a small group of CLA
honors students interested in medieval philosophy and culture.
They had seen the fine audio-visual program that Gus Aris had
produced a few years before in his Honors Seminar on "The History of Handwriting." Now they were enjoying a selection from
the James Ford Bell Collection. One of the students joined the
group a little late and casually settled herself against a corner of
the library table where Jack had laid out his display. I do not re-

call exactly what Jack said, very gently, for he is a gentle man. I do recall vividly the student's startled exclamation as she leaped up: "Oh! Is it real?!"

Jack is as real, and as irreplaceable, as the collection of works that grace the Library. Lately, with no thought of Jack Parker, I happened to be looking into an old volume in our own library, *Biographical Sketches and Anecdotes of Members of the Religious Society of Friends*. To my surprise, one John Parker was among them! Jack is a long-time member of the Minneapolis Friends Church, known also as the York Avenue Meeting. I have no idea whether he is a descendant of Friend John Parker, 1748–1829, celebrated in that 1871 book. Yet how appropriate was what I learned about the John Parker in the book: "He was distinguished by genuine, plain hospitality, and his friends were ever wont to be received at his house with a cordiality that made them feel that they were welcome."

Let us say that Jack's house is on the Fourth Floor of Wilson Library and that his friends are the many scholars of all ages and ranks who have received from him an always warm and cordial, a knowledgeable and nurturing welcome. If it is not true that John Parker was our Jack's great and a few more greats grandfather, it's plain enough that he ought to have been. This makes it what Hugh Kenner calls an Irish Fact. It is no Irish Fact that our Jack Parker is loved and appreciated. It ought to be so and in truth it really is so.

Burnham Terrell   Julie Terrell   May, 1990

THROWER, Norman J.W., UCLA, Los Angeles, California.

When I gave the banquet address at the Society for the History of Discoveries meeting at Athens, Georgia, Jack Parker introduced me. As a preliminary to my talk I suggested that we had had such a good meal that someone should have said "grace." Jack replied that he had given thanks silently for all of us. I thought this characteristic of Jack's concern and of his manner.

Sincerely, Norman   29 March 1990

TORODASH, Martin, Lenox, Massachusetts.

Some people have said that John Parker is a "Renaissance Man." They are wrong! He is, beyond peradventure or doubt, a Twentieth Century man. No renaissance man had the opportunity to master the corpus of literature being produced at the time. And no renaissance man appreciated and, yes, relished the physical product of the printing press as John Parker has. Not one of them combined in a single individual the aptitudes, esthetic sense, and training which are uniquely blended in John Parker.

Thus, let us acknowledge and celebrate our — and the century's — good fortune to have had the privilege of associating with John Parker: bookman, scholar, author, administrator, librarian, connoisseur, and, most important of all, friend.

Cordially, Martin   27 March 1990

TRACY, James D.

Parker Din

When late in life the hearth fires burn,
and mem'ries glow from Gopher youth,
of faroff worlds that made us yearn
to wind our thoughts down wells of truth —

Now gather round as we recall that classic frown,
Jack stern of mien, his motto, "Don't be daffy,
we're students all, so buckle down,
we'll sound the depths of hist'ry's cart-o-graphy."

We'd say 'twixt piles of books and manuscripts,
"There's no way out, we're Parkered in."
And so we'd swot, deciph'ring scripts
all enigmatic, yea druidical, and thin.

Ah, then 'twas Din, yes Parker Din,
You hooked us all, you made us chase

that treasure here yet gone, that Lascar's grin,
that beckons e'er to Adam's race.

We'll miss you Din, yes Parker Din,
who taught us true, through countless hours,
with maps awry, and folios by the bin,
the quest was theirs, but now it's ours.

Jim Tracy   16 April 1990

TRAISTER, Daniel, University of Pennsylvania, Philadelphia.

Dear Carol,

Thank you for writing about your planned tribute to Jack Parker. I'm honored to be asked to contribute.

Your note suggests that I write about the early, unairconditioned days at the summer Rare Book School sessions offered by Columbia University's School of Library Service. It's in those sessions that Jack and I met; there the two of us have taught together since Rare Book School opened in 1983. We are now impresario Terry Belanger's longest running vaudeville duo, the only folk who have repeated their course, their *singspiels*, their jokes, Jack's knowledge, and my chatter, summer after summer after summer after summer, every summer that the School has run.

But this story cannot begin with the lack of air conditioning. Maybe you have to come from New York to know the grim lack of humor presented by Fun City in full summer fig *sans* air. That rarity in nature, a native New Yorker, all I have to say is: the less said the better. You don't want to hear it; I don't want to remember it. Power failures are just about as amusing, and in just about the same warm and wonderful ways: if you don't ever have to, then I strongly advise that you *don't* climb sixteen stories with Jack, the elevators having gone off in the high rise dormitory in which you are both staying. This was years before he had his heart surgery; I too still gave off an illusory whiff of rosy-cheeked health. Nonetheless, it was a toss-up which of us was going to hit the repair shops first when (or, worse, *before*) we made the final landing. Memories are *not* made of this.

You seem to ask for the anecdotal, the warmly (or the wryly) humorous, maybe even the richly funny. That's not how I think of Jack or of our work together. In any case, when I recall our early days of teaching, or more recent ones, it isn't the physical amenities or their want that spring to mind.

What mattered then is what still matters now: it is rather the instant intellectual comfort I found in working, in and out of a classroom for five days of what was (and remains) astonishingly intense and constant conversation with astonishingly intense and constant students, paired with a teaching partner whom I had never met.

Oh, sure, we'd said hello at the New York Book Fair during the spring before our course; we must also have seen each other at one rare book conference or another. But that was literally it. I knew what Jack looked like; he knew what I looked like. Otherwise, we began with remarkably little else—and backgrounds *so* diverse that Terry's febrile imagination in pairing us derived either from a perfectly perfervid state or he already intuited something that neither Jack nor I had had any reason (yet) to grasp.

Jack had been working in the field since I was in junior high school; when we began our stint, I'd been in it slightly more than five years. Were our students nervous facing us in this intense and overheated classroom? Beats me; but I remember noticing that *I* was, sure as shootin'.

And I had good reasons. What did I know that this guy didn't? He'd done it all: after beginning as a private collector's librarian, he'd moved with the collection to a large research university's research library, made it an integral part of that institution's "research ecology," overseen its growth, fostered its use, put up exhibitions, brought in visiting firepersons, written catalogues, published keepsakes, written amazingly readable annual reports, put out the odd monograph. . . . Oh, it was a very depressing time, let me tell you.

And then a funny thing happened. Jack and I found that we could play off one another. I could be the chatty, gabby, and maddeningly ignorant voice of the computer age run amuck in the special collections library. Jack could counter as the sage voice of the one-on-one relationship between book and curator, curator and reader, typical of the rare book collection. Calm, focused, and learned vs. hyperactive, diffuse, and a champion of on-the-job, earn-while-you-learn, education, the two of us offered our students the charm — if that is *le mot juste* — of contrast. We managed to reinforce what must clearly be genuinely serious whenever the two of us agreed — and, as it happens, that was more often than not.

Like Plunkitt of Tammany Hall, I seen my opportunities and I took 'em. This class was — and does it ever remain! — an opportunity for me as much as for our students. Year in, year out, I sit there and talk talk talk; year in, year out, I sit there and listen listen listen. I have no doubt which is the more profitable. I have come to know many of Jack's stories, among them The Day the Car Burned Up in the Street; Searching for the Source of the Mississippi; Custer Collectors I Have Known; and Louis L'Amour of Jamestown, ND. I can tell you why special collections are not the same thing as rare book collections, why exhibitions should be graced by short catalogue entries, why you need to be patient with a growing Friends of the Library group — and so much more that, whatever our students have done with it, *I've* tried to use when I got back from our course to my job here at Penn.

Is it cheating to take so much from the person you're supposed to be teaching with, not learning from? I hope not; it's a pleasure I'd be loath to part with. So, I think, would our students. What makes the class work so well is that it's clear to all of us that there's someone there who knows a thing or two and is willing to share it. It's just as clear that there isn't a person there — including the other "instructor" — who isn't packing it away quick like a squirrel in the fall.

There was a time when I thought my reaction was idiosyncratic. I no longer think so. Over the years, too many people have told me that my reaction is standard: a colleague at The Pierpont Morgan Library in New York continues to value her experience studying with Jack in Minnesota; a reader — here today, as I write — has worked with Jack at Minnesota and tells me, at lunch this afternoon, how much of a mentor he is to all who work in the Minnesota library. These and the others who tell me the same things come as no surprise. I've seen the man teach.

Most of those who write to you about Jack on this occasion must remember him as a book collector, a librarian, a person who kept a great collection a-building and healthy. There must be others beside me who know him, however, *not* as a librarian but instead as a great *teacher*. I've lived my life with great teachers; I don't toss the term around loosely. Jack is a great teacher. He gives in the way great teachers give, from a practically inexhaustible well of knowledge and experience, and with enthusiasm for and love of subject — *and* student. He starts talking with them in the humid cool of the morning as they head from their dormitory to breakfast at Mamma's on Amsterdam Avenue; he continues through class and break, through steamy lunch at the Hunan Garden, more class, more break, through rainy dinner at The Green Tree, through the evening lecture, and finally back in the dorm. I called it "intense" earlier in this letter; intense is what it is. Friday afternoons, he looks as if trucks had been rolling over him on Broadway for several hours.

I don't think there's anything that's really "anecdotal" in any of this; I just think it's wonderful. You who got to work with him year in and year out must know how special he is; you'd not be putting together such a tribute as this if you didn't. And all I really have to say is: you're absolutely right.

Yours cordially, Dan   2 April 1990

TURNER, Patricia.

Brief Words

I first met John Parker in the late 1960s when I was an instructor in the Graduate Library School of the University of Minnesota. He was an adjunct professor of the Library School who taught courses in Descriptive Bibliography.

Students need to know of all the career options and the many kinds of librarianship, so I made it a practice for the students in bibliography courses I taught to have one session with Dr. Parker for an introduction to special and rare book librarianship.

They were given an introduction to the James Ford Bell Collection, its history and development, acquisition of rare materials, and the care and preservation of rare materials. They were told about the work of the librarian-curator of such a collection.

After this introduction and his responses to the students' questions, he always gave them a gift — some advice — which made a lasting impression on me — the instructor.

His gift and advice to them was that they would learn as librarians that their work was so involved with the research and information needs of others, that they should seek and find their own research — to have outside of their daily work — their own "quiet corner" for personal growth and satisfaction.

As I recall this gift and advice of John Parker to Graduate Library School students of the late 1960s, I hope that many were challenged by and accepted this gift. I hope they have found a "quiet corner" for their own research.

Patricia Turner   1990

WAKEFIELD, Ray.

Dearest Jack, greatest of resident netherlandophiles, I wish I could dub you a Knight of Orange or some other equally exalted and well deserved title. You have done more for Dutch Studies in Minnesota than any other individual, and you have done it with a grace that would be admired in even the most snobbish clubs of 's-Gravenhagen, a city full of exquisite snobs. I want to recall now one fairly typical visit to the James Ford Bell Library. I had a visiting Dutch dignitary in tow and knew I could count on you for something impressive. In this case, it was the Consul General from Chicago, at that time Simon van Nispin on his first visit to the Twin Cities. When you began sharing your Dutch treasures with him, his eyes almost popped out of his head. Later on, he began talking about an event to make more people aware of the Dutch holdings. Various groups collaborated, a stunning exhibition was set up, a buffet supper was served and several important people sang the praises of Dutch Studies at the University of Minnesota. I have colleagues who still remind me that I've never been able to top that event for quality and elegance. (Believe me, I've tried.) And this is just one of many warm memories, some going back to the very beginning of Dutch at the University nearly 20 years ago.

Hartstikke bedankt! Ray Wakefield   21 March 1990

WASHBURN, Wilcomb E., Director, Office of American Studies, Smithsonian Institution.

Dear Jack:

As a fellow participant in the creation and organization of the Society for the History of Discoveries, may I send my profound thanks for your contribution to the renaissance of this field of study on the occasion of what I am told is your retirement.

I'm not sure whether starting on a voyage is more satisfying than arriving at one's destination. I am not sure we knew exactly where we were going when we formed the Society. Perhaps we don't know exactly where we have been. In that regard our "history" may be something like the Bell Library's 1424 map with those "problematic" islands of Antillia and the like. We still have not solved the mystery of the Vinland Map or the landfall of Columbus.

But the trip has been exciting and I know I share with you many similar experiences, sometimes in company with you and sometimes not. I recall our late lamented mutual friend, Steve Slessarev, and his sympathy when my son's camera was "pinched" in the Piazza San Marco after I had examined some maps in one of Venice's libraries. I am sure you have similar memories of the 60's and 70's of the companionship of Steve, Tom Goldstein, or others who helped put discoveries back into the scholarly and popular mind. I am sorry that geographical separation kept us apart more than I would have liked, and I hope that I will see more of you now that you are freed from administrative burdens.

Sincerely yours, Wid   24 May 1990

WELLS, Judy.

I have known John as a friend and colleague since 1969 when I first started to work in the University Libraries.

JOHN

One morning over coffee
as we talked of cats we loved
And lectures we had given

I looked at you and knew
We would be great friends.
And so we are.

You helped me make the best of
Puzzles and people at work
And taught me to make candles
To light against the dark.
You comforted me when I thought
There was no comfort in life
And gave me freely the treasure
Of your rarest book.

You are the sun in winter
A force that can melt ice
And waken green shoots.
You are a gentle man
Who would mourn the loss of just one bee
Unable to return to the hive
Frozen in the winter air.

No one person can tell the story
Of a life so rich as yours,
But I am honored and delighted
To know some of the parts:
The poet, the teacher, the traveler,
The North Dakota farmer,
The Renaissance man,
The Jack of Hearts,
The leader of the band.

                                   27 April 1990

WHITEHEAD, Mary A.

Dear Jack,

   During the three years that I've worked at the James Ford Bell
Library you have given me many gifts. In the summer and fall

you have given me jars of your homemade honey, and vegetables from your garden. For Christmas you have given me your hand-dipped candles. While I appreciate each of these things, Jack, even more tangible and precious to me are your other gifts. When I'm down, you offer encouragement. When I lose faith in my abilities, you show that you believe in me. When I need someone to listen, you're all ears. And when I want to laugh, you're there with a smile.

Thank you for your gift of friendship.

Mary   31 May 1990

WULLING, Emerson, La Crosse, Wisconsin.

Dear Jack:

So you are taking the leap. To What? We're told that you will be as active as ever, and I wonder what your choices are. I'd like to see you at one end of the auctioneer's hammer, now and then. Your mounting of the Associates' auctions was cool. With a succinct and pointed catalog on the table before you, a thousand eyes to spot the varied bidding, a firm decision as to priority of contested bids, and a sly remark unexpectedly, these made a lively ballet. You seemed to enjoy the role.

But so much else to choose from, you will enjoy the agony of decision (I hope.)

Press on!   Emerson   10 April 1990

ZOBEL, Vicki.

Dear Jack,

As I sit here composing this letter, I'm thinking back over the last 16 years. Yes—it's been that long since I walked into the Library for a job interview!

I have so many good memories of working with you and Carol. I *so* appreciated being treated as an equal part of the J.F. Bell

team. You gave me confidence in myself back then and those experiences can give me a boost even today.

Thanks for the non-judgmental advice during one of my "identity crises." I always enjoyed the "food-related" parts of the job —
evening Associates' meetings, Friday afternoon Twinkie parties,
lunches at the Middlebrook cafeteria, etc. You may not remember this, but thanks for *not* yelling at me when I forgot to pick up
your Gown-in-Town dinner party invitations from the printer
(much less send them out!). You were so *nice* about my BIG
goof-up!

It was a privilege to go through the entire *World for a Marketplace* process with you. I still get tears in my eyes when I read "A
Latin Essay at Cambridge, 1785." E.B. White's *Charlotte's Web*
ends this way: "It is not often that someone comes along who is
a true friend and a good writer. Charlotte was both." And so are
you, Jack!

I suspect my experiences as your co-worker and friend will continue to influence me as I think about further schooling, etc.

Jack, I wish you a happy, busy, and healthy retirement. You
deserve it!

      Love, thanks and best wishes   Vicki   May 1990

Part IV: ASSOCIATES OF THE
JAMES FORD BELL LIBRARY

A History of the Associates

BY Mary Whitehead

During the early years of the Bell collection in the 1950s and early 1960s, library friends' organizations were in vogue. This was an aspect of the growing emphasis among American libraries in collections of rare books and other specialized research materials. Not all of the friends' groups that were established at that time, and subsequently, have survived. Often there was an imbalance between ambition, finances and energy. The James Ford Bell Library Associates seem to have found the proper balance. The Associates have been responsible for numerous publications as well as diverse programs including a bicentennial conference, several Columbus-related activities, an annual winter seminar, and twelve benefit auctions.

In establishing the Library, Mr. Bell's goals were to bring it to the attention of the world, and to demonstrate the collection's usefulness to scholars and to the general public. He knew that this formidable task could best be accomplished through a supporting group, and it was his wish that after his death a significant book-oriented organization would be started for the purpose of enhancing the Library's visibility. Not surprisingly then, shortly after Mr. Bell's death in May of 1961, a few of his friends began a series of conversations which marked the beginning of the Associates, and their commitment to continuing the work begun by this Library's founder. Among the earliest of these friends were Mrs. John S. Dalrymple, J. Cameron Thomson, Wheelock Whitney, and Lyman Wakefield.

253

By December of 1963 the groundwork had been laid, and the group's articles of incorporation were officially registered with Minnesota's secretary of state. This document was signed by three "incorporators," T.R. Anderson, Maynard Hasselquist, and John Parker.

The articles state that the group's purpose is to operate:

> exclusively for literary, educational, and scientific purposes for the benefit of the University of Minnesota, in order to preserve, promote, and make additions to the collection of rare books, maps, manuscripts and other material on the history of trade which have been assembled together at the General Library of the University of Minnesota under the name of the Bell Collection.

Mr. Bell hoped that one of the group's major aims would be the sponsorship of publications highlighting the collection. The annually published *Merchant Explorer*, and the *James Ford Bell Lecture*, as well as the thrice-yearly newsletter *The Manifest*, offer three approaches to informing people of the Library's acquisitions and activities.

It was Mr. Bell's belief that old books and current events are related. The vehicle he proposed for doing so was *The Merchant Explorer*. With this idea in mind, in the first issue published in 1961, John Parker wrote:

> As these pages are written, our newspapers are carrying stories of dollar crises, of embargoes, of commercial development in the less advanced countries. Newspapers around the world carry the same type of story, and their publishers know that international alliances and conflicts, the rise and decline of nations are tied to these stories. We find little that is new in these news items. We find their prototypes in books from the fifteenth to the end of the eighteenth century, for our purpose is to gather the literature that grew up with the expansion of Europe's commerce, recording the events of that expansion, the means to expansion, and the contemporary reactions to it.

Mr. Bell was so caught up in the publication of the first issue of *The Merchant Explorer* that although he was in the hospital when it came back from the printer, he asked Dr. Parker to bring a copy to his bedside. In *The World for a Marketplace*, published in 1978 to mark the Library's 25th anniversary, Dr. Parker wrote about Mr. Bell's reaction to this new publication. "He liked it and the idea it represented, of continuity between today's news and events of the more distant past." Unfortunately this was the last visit between the Library's founder and its curator for Mr. Bell died a few days later.

A legacy had been left and it was now up to the Associates and its Board of Directors to sustain *The Merchant Explorer* and to brainstorm ideas for future publications. In 1963 a lecture series was created with the intention of combining the Library's holdings with distinguished scholarship.

The first lecture was held on a cold night in February of 1963 at the Bell Museum of Natural History. It was there that R.A. Skelton, then superintendent of the Map Room in the British Museum, delivered a lecture titled *The European Image and Mapping of America A.D. 1000–1600*. Associates who wished to attend the dinner preceding the lecture were asked to pay $3.50! About 50 people were in the audience and the James Ford Bell Lecture series was born.

Today the price of dinner has changed, but the purpose of the lecture has not. Throughout its 27 years this program has boasted an impressive array of scholars from both near and far, and a wide range of subjects. In 1969, one of the most respected rare book dealers, the late H.P. Kraus of New York City, delivered the lecture, *On Book Collecting: The Story of My Drake Library*. In 1974 the topic was *The Economy and Society of Colonial Brazil: A Brief Overview* when long-time friend of the Library, Professor Stuart Schwartz of the University of Minnesota's History Department, spoke. We were treated to a scientific discussion by Professor A. Hunter Dupree, of Brown University, who in 1984 spoke on *Sir Joseph Banks and the Origins of Science Policy*. In 1989 we had a far-away visitor, Professor Michael Pearson of the University of New South Wales, who also elaborated on a scientific theme, *Towards Superiority: European and Indian Medicine 1500–1700*. These few examples demonstrate the diversity of the speakers and their topics.

With the *James Ford Bell Lecture* and *The Merchant Explorer* established, in 1965 *The Manifest* was started because there was a need for a "chatty" format which would update Associates and other people interested in the Library. Why a newsletter? *The Manifest's* first issue in February of 1965 explains:

> The newsletter has long been associated with mercantile and publishing traditions, and it is our hope that in your association with a library devoted to the history of mercantile affairs you will enjoy sharing in this tradition by receiving regularly some news of happenings in the James Ford Bell Collection.

A brief perusal of *The Manifest's* 77 issues reveals the types of subjects it has covered over the years. Acquisitions have always been a popular topic, but books have no value if people don't appreciate them. Thus *The Manifest* provides a format for recognizing the contributions of a diverse group of individuals who nurture this Library and therefore are responsible for its success. A few examples follow:

Students have been the focus of several issues including the last *Manifest* which featured interviews with several young researchers who discussed their topics and their experiences working with the collection.

Research conducted by scholars such as Richard and Sally Price of the Anthropology Department of The Johns Hopkins University helps to establish the collection's importance in the academic community. Associates were introduced to the Prices in the September, 1984 *Manifest* when they were just beginning to edit the John Gabriel Stedman manuscript. In 1988 their hard work culminated in a book titled *Narrative of a Five Years Expedition against the Revolted Negroes of Surinam*. In 1989 Richard Price offered a more condensed analysis of Stedman's writings when he delivered the James Ford Bell Lecture.

In January of 1971 *The Manifest* marked the retirement of book designer Jane McCarthy from the University Press. This issue commemorated her years at the Press, where she designed many award-winning publications for the Library. Fortunately for us, she continued to design our publications until her death in 1979.

In December of 1982 *The Manifest* was devoted to the late T.R. Anderson and his wife LaJean, and their many efforts on behalf of the Library. The Andersons were among the earliest of the collection's supporters and throughout the years remained committed to the Library's success. Mr. Anderson's recent death represents a great loss to this Library. We are pleased, however, that his daughter, Judith Fennema, has recently joined the Associates' Board of Directors.

In addition to people and acquisitions, events sponsored by the Associates have always been newsworthy items for *The Manifest*. In this respect, perhaps the greatest accomplishment to date has been "The James Ford Bell Library Bicentennial Conference," held on the University's West Bank Campus in May of 1973. One of the goals of the conference was to bring together in one place the most respected scholars on the subject of the Revolution. Another aim was to hold the conference before all the commercial hype would take over and cloud the true significance of the Bicentennial. This sounds like a major undertaking, and it was.

The June, 1973 *Manifest* reports on the conference:

> We think it was a success. A total of about 1700 people attended the four sessions. The papers presented were well received and we are hopeful that they will make an interesting publication. The speakers felt that the Associates had provided excellent hospitality. Scholars from such distant points as Washington State, Washington, D.C., and Oklahoma were in the audience. There were also a lot of faculty and students from the University and from other colleges and universities in the area. And there were many school teachers, as well as people from outside of the educational world—housewives, lawyers, accountants, etc. . . . The Associates' generosity and enthusiasm in sponsoring the conference calls for a statement of gratitude on behalf of all who attended.

The crowning achievement of this event was the publication of the proceedings titled, *The American Revolution: A Heritage of Change*, edited by John Parker and Carol Urness, and published by the Associates. This collection of essays received good reviews by critics such as Harvey H. Jackson who in *The North Carolina Historical Review* wrote:

> A unique opportunity to see some of the best American historians at work. In these eleven essays one can find not only examples of how modern historians see their Revolutionary heritage but also clues as to the new directions historical scholarship might well be taking. It is a look into the past and the future.

In the sponsorship of programs to observe the Columbus Quin-centenary, the Associates again have been far ahead of many other organizations. Back in 1982 the Board of Directors voted to inaugurate "The Decade of Columbus" which is a program com-posed of concerts, dramatic productions, exhibits, and lectures during the decade leading to the 1992 Columbus anniversary year.

At a meeting in May of 1983 the president of the Associates' Board of Directors, Elizabeth Savage, proposed that the organi-zation commission Leonardo Lasansky, a distinguished professor of art at Hamline University, to do a new portrait of Christopher Columbus. The minutes of the meeting state that the purpose of the portrait would be "to undertake something significant, educa-tional, and entertaining." This project would be an especially creative endeavor since there is no contemporary portrait of Columbus extant and the portraits of him which do exist are based only on artists' perceptions of his appearance.

In October of 1984 the completed work was unveiled at the Minneapolis Institute of Arts where the Associates donated one of 70 copper-engraved original prints to the Institute's permanent collection.

Soon after the originals were completed, a poster was made of the portrait for wider-scale distribution and subsequent promo-tion of the Library. Like the man himself, the poster has evoked controversy. Although it received praise throughout art circles and was the recipient of the American Society of Museums' Award of Distinction, some people have not appreciated Lasansky's interpretation of Columbus. The Institute's ARTS magazine described it as "one of the most complex" of the Columbus portraits, depicting its subject as a "dark, crabbed and brooding visionary." In sharp contrast, an especially disgruntled viewer who was not at the unveiling ceremony wrote in a letter to the curator, "Were I among you when this monstrosity was un-veiled, I would have been embarrassed to anger and vocal pro-test." Perhaps this varied criticism is proof of the portrait's value for, regardless of one's opinion of it, this work has renewed in-terest in one of our nation's most celebrated and controversial figures who almost five hundred years after his death still pro-vokes discussion.

The portrait was only the first in a series of events to com-
memorate the Quincentenary. At the winter seminar in 1985 the
Associates enjoyed an evening of Renaissance music performed by
musicians from the College of St. Scholastica. The winter of 1986
saw a flurry of Columbus-related activity. The exhibit "A Library
for Christopher Columbus," which highlighted the books he may
have read, was presented in conjunction with a winter seminar
lecture titled "Columbus and the Mediterranean" delivered by
Professor Schwartz. The January, 1986 *Manifest* was published as
a catalog for the exhibit and it has been our most frequently-
requested issue. In addition, later that year Professor Schwartz's
lecture was published by the Associates under the title, "The
Iberian Mediterranean and Atlantic Traditions in the Formation
of Columbus as a Colonizer." Our guest speaker at the winter
seminar in 1987 was Joseph Judge, Senior Editor at the *National
Geographic Magazine*, who elaborated on his study of the 1492
Columbus Landfall.

Future Quincentenary events include an exhibit program in
1992 directed by Professor Carla Rahn Phillips of the University
of Minnesota's History Department. Also in 1992 Associates will
have the opportunity to view a traveling exhibit titled "Maps and
the Columbian Encounter," which has been a collaborative project long in the planning. Featured will be acquisitions from this
Library, the American Geographical Society, located in Milwaukee, the Newberry Library in Chicago, and the William L. Clements Library at the University of Michigan. Each of these institutions will display this exhibition at their respective locations.

In addition to the observance of landmark events, the Associates also have mainstay programs which are less glamorous but no
less significant to the organization's purpose. One of these is the
Winter Seminar, an idea proposed in 1968 by John Tilton when
he was on our Board of Directors. We Minnesotans tend to become isolated during the cold months, and it was thought that an
evening in January or February devoted to an informal lecture
and demonstration on an aspect of the book arts would appeal to
our membership. And why not? The Twin Cities has an array of
local resources to enrich such an evening. Over the years the seminar has offered an eclectic series of discussions on printing, book
design, paper conservation, the interpretation of manuscript

hands, and book indexing, to name just a few of the subjects covered.

The history of the Associates of the James Ford Bell Library is a record of solid accomplishments. All Associates can take pride in the past and look with high expectations to the future.

Chronology of the Associates

Prepared by Vicki Zobel

The Associates were organized in December, 1963.

On Dec. 30, 1963, the group was named the "Sponsors of the Associates of the James Ford Bell Library." The officers were:

Chairman	T. R. Anderson
1st Vice Chairman	Maynard B. Hasselquist
Secretary	John Parker
Treasurer	Lyman E. Wakefield

The first group of Sponsors were:

Mrs. John S. Dalrymple	John E. Tilton
J. Cameron Thomson	W. G. Shepherd

On Nov. 15, 1965 the Bylaws were amended to increase the number of Directors to nine and "Sponsors" was dropped in favor of "Directors." The past and present Directors of the Associates are:

T. R. Anderson	1963–1989
Maynard B. Hasselquist	1963-present
John Parker	1963-present
Lyman E. Wakefield	1963–1974
Mrs. John S. Dalrymple	1963–1968
J. Cameron Thomson	1963–1965
John E. Tilton	1963–1968
W. G. Shepherd	1963–1964

261

Mrs. Walter Hauser	1965–1973
Irving B. Kreidberg	1965-present
Elmer L. Andersen	1965–1972
H. E. Van der Boom	1967–1984
Russell Bennett	1968–1973
Mrs. Robert Schweitzer, Jr.	1968-present
Mrs. Wheelock Whitney, Jr.	1968–1972
Melva Lind	1972-present
Gerhard Weiss˙	1972–1979
William P. Laird	1973-present
Mrs. Thomas C. Savage	1973-present
Bernadette Pyter Muck	1974-present
Paul L. Parker	1975–1978
Erwin Mitch Goldstein	1978–1980
Rutherford Aris	1979-present
Charles Hann	1981-present
Lennie L. Arnevik	1981–1988
William Urseth	1984-present
Curtis L. Roy	1988-present
Robert O. Mathson	1988-present
Judith Fennema	1990-present

WINTER SEMINARS

1964   Predecessor to the Winter Seminar:
A series of Bell Room Seminars was held each year to which small groups (10–15) of Associates were invited. Faculty from the University explained their research, etc.

Sept. 25, 1968	The Directors' Minutes state: "Mr. Tilton's proposal for a winter meeting, a seminar involving a faculty member and graduate student, was discussed and approved."
Winter 1969	The first Winter Seminar was presented by Prof. Stuart Schwartz. He spoke about his research on Brazil.
Feb. 2, 1970	Mr. George Baer, bookbinder, demonstrated techniques and styles of fine binding.
Feb. 3, 1971	Mr. Irving Kreidberg spoke about the art of book production. A film, "The Making of a Renais-

sance Book," was shown, with Mr. Kreidberg providing the commentary. The film was made at the Plantin-Moretus Museum in Antwerp.

Feb. 21, 1972   Miss Jane McCarthy, book designer, spoke about book design and production. Her presentation followed a text from typescript through galleys and proofs.

Feb. 19, 1973   Mr. Thomas MacDonnell, a partner in Henry Stevens, Son and Stiles, spoke about his company, which specializes in Americana, and about the antiquarian bookselling business in general.

Feb. 4, 1974   Mr. Julian G. Plante, Director of the Monastic Manuscript Microfilm Library at St. John's University, was our speaker. He presented a slide show about some of the manuscripts in the Library.

Jan. 30, 1975   Prof. Rutherford Aris, an expert in early manuscript hands, presented a lecture entitled "Of Scribes and Scripts: Latin Manuscripts from the Fifth through the Fifteenth Century."

Feb. 4, 1976   Ms. Merrily Smith, who works in the field of conservation and restoration of rare materials, shared her knowledge in her talk "The Conservation of Books and Papers: Problems and Solutions."

Jan. 10, 1977   The Associates met at North Central Publishing Company in St. Paul. Mr. Al Muellerleile demonstrated hand printing with a 1909 Albion press.

Feb. 27, 1978   Mr. Emerson G. Wulling, proprietor of the Sumac Press, shared his experiences as a private printer with us.

Feb. 8, 1979   Prof. Stuart Schwartz, author of *A Governor and His Image in Colonial Brazil: The Funereal Eulogy of Afonso Furtado de Castro do Rio de Mendonça*, shared his experiences doing research in Portugal and Brazil.

Feb., 1980   Professors John Parker and Carol Urness presented a series of five lectures on French and English exploration of North America to celebrate the Hennepin tricentennial. The first of these lectures was the Winter Seminar.

Feb. 16, 1981   Prof. Arnold G. Fredrickson, in his talk, "The French weren't the first traders in the Mississippi Valley," spoke about early Indian commerce on the Mississippi. The Associates also helped to print the "thank you" publication for next year.

Feb., 1982   Einer Anderson shared with us stories of his life among the Eskimos.

Feb., 1983   Ms. Bernie Muck spoke to us about book indexing.

1984   Prof. Leonardo Lasansky described his methods used in producing the Columbus portrait which was commissioned by the Associates for our Columbus celebration.

Feb. 28, 1985   The Associates enjoyed an evening of Renaissance music performed by a chorus from the College of St. Scholastica.

1986   Prof. Stuart Schwartz presented a lecture on Christopher Columbus.

Feb. 5, 1987   Our guest was Mr. Joseph Judge, a Senior Editor at the National Geographic Magazine. He is also the Director of the recent 1492 Columbus Landfall Study and spoke to us about the findings of the study.

Jan. 14, 1988   The Associates had a joint meeting with the Minnesota chapter of the Manx Society.

Feb. 28, 1989   Ms. Amanda Degener, from the Minnesota Center for Book Arts, gave a demonstration on paper marbling and then helped us as we tried it ourselves.

THE JAMES FORD BELL LECTURES

1. Mr. R. A. Skelton, *The European Image and Mapping of America A.D. 1000–1600*, published in 1964.

The lecture was delivered on February 28, 1963 at the University of Minnesota. Mr. Skelton was the Superintendent of the Map Room in the British Museum.

2. Dr. Melvin H. Jackson, *Salt, Sugar, and Slaves: The Dutch in the Caribbean*, published in 1965.

The lecture was presented on April 6, 1964 at the University of Minnesota. Dr. Jackson was the Associate Curator of Naval History at the Smithsonian Institution.

3. Prof. Herbert Heaton, *The Economics of Empire*, published in 1966.

This lecture was given on April 12, 1965 at the University of Minnesota's Alumni Club. Prof. Heaton was a Professor in the Department of History at the University.

4. Prof. George Kish, *Medicina, Mensura, Mathematica: The Life and Works of Gemma Frisius, 1508–1555*, published in 1967.

The lecture was delivered on May 11, 1966 at the Minneapolis Club. Prof. Kish was Chairman of the Department of Geography at the University of Michigan.

5. Prof. Vincent H. Cassidy, *Saints and Sinners at Sea*, published in 1968.

This lecture was presented at the Minneapolis Club on May 8, 1967. Prof. Cassidy was a professor of History at the University of Southwestern Louisiana.

6. Mr. H. P. Kraus, *On Book Collecting: The Story of My Drake Library*, published in 1969.

Mr. Kraus, who was a bookseller, delivered this lecture on May 6, 1968 at the St. Paul College Club.

7. Dr. Nils William Olsson, *Pehr Kalm and the Image of North America*, published in 1970.

The lecture was presented on May 5, 1969 in the Crystal Room of the Minneapolis Club. Dr. Olsson was the Director of the American Swedish Institute in Minneapolis.

8. Dr. Lewis Hanke, *All the Peoples of the World are Men*, published in 1970.

This lecture was given on May 11, 1970 at the St. Paul College Club. Dr. Hanke was a professor of History at the University of Massachusetts.

9. Mr. Eric W. Morse, *The Exploration of Canada: Some Geographical Considerations*, published in 1971.

The lecture was delivered on April 28, 1971 at the Minneapolis Club. Mr. Morse was the recently retired National Director of the Association of Canadian Clubs.

10. Dr. Paul W. Bamford, *The Barbary Pirates: Victims and the Scourge of Christendom*, published in 1972.

This lecture was presented at the St. Paul Athletic Club on May 1, 1972. Dr. Bamford is a professor of History at the University of Minnesota.

11. Professor Robert J. Poor, *Teapots and Top Hats: Cultural Relations between Asia and the West*, not published.

The lecture was delivered on April 2, 1973 at the Minneapolis Athletic Club. Prof. Poor is an associate professor of Art History at the University of Minnesota and Curator of Asian Art at the Minnesota Museum.

12. Dr. Stuart B. Schwartz, *The Economy and Society of Colonial Brazil: A Brief Overview*, published in 1974.

This lecture was presented on May 8, 1974 at the American Swedish Institute. Dr. Schwartz is a member of the History Department at the University of Minnesota specializing in Colonial Latin America.

13. Prof. Victoria Bomba Coifman, *The European Presence in West Africa before 1800*, published in 1975.

Prof. Coifman delivered this lecture on April 28, 1975 at the American Association of University Women's Club in St. Paul. She is a member of the Afro-American Studies Department at the University of Minnesota.

14. Dr. Alison Stones, *The Minnesota Vincent of Beauvais Manuscript and Cistercian Thirteenth-Century Book Decoration*, published in 1977.

The lecture was presented on May 10, 1976 at the Minneapolis Athletic Club. Dr. Stones was a member of the Department of Art History.

15. Dr. Hildegard Binder Johnson, *The Orderly Landscape: Landscape Tastes and the United States Survey*, published in 1977.

The lecture was delivered on April 25, 1977 at the St. Paul Athletic Club. Dr. Johnson is a Professor Emeritus of Geography at Macalester College.

16. Prof. Ward J. Barrett, *The Efficient Plantation and the Inefficient Hacienda*, published in 1979.

The lecture was given at the University of Minnesota's Alumni Club on April 27, 1978. Prof. Barrett is a member of the Geography Department of the University of Minnesota specializing in the economic geography of the Pacific Ocean, Mexico and the West Indies.

17. Mr. Linden J. Lundstrom, *The Bay Where Hudson did Winter*, published in 1980.

Mr. Lundstrom presented his lecture at the Minneapolis Club of the American Association of University Women on May 2, 1979. Mr. Lundstrom's study of Hudson was his avocation; until his retirement he was a music teacher.

18. Ms. Rhoda Gilman, *Reversing the Telescope: Louis Hennepin and Three Hundred Years of Historical Perspective*, published in 1981.

This lecture was presented on May 5, 1980 at the Parker House in Mendota, Minnesota. Ms. Gilman was then Assistant to the Director for Education and Folklife at the Minnesota Historical Society.

19. Mr. Otto Charles Thieme, *By Inch of Candle: A Sale at East-India-House, 21 September 1675*, published in 1982.

The lecture was delivered on May 7, 1981 at the Hotel Radisson Plaza in St. Paul. Mr. Thieme was a graduate student specializing in the history of cloth, its manufacture and its uses.

20. Prof. Gerhard H. Weiss, *In Search of Silk: Adam Olearius' Mission to Russia and Persia*, published in 1983.

The lecture was given on May 4, 1982 in the Club Rooms of the American Association of University Women. Prof. Weiss is a member of the University of Minnesota's Department of German.

21. Prof. Edward L. Farmer, *Technology Transfer and Cultural Subversion: Tensions in the Early Jesuit Mission to China*, published in 1983.

This lecture was presented at the St. Paul College Club on May 4, 1983. Prof. Farmer is a member of the History Department at the University of Minnesota specializing in the history of China's Ming Dynasty.

22. Prof. A. Hunter Dupree, *Sir Joseph Banks and the Origins of Science Policy*, published in 1984.

The lecture was delivered on May 3, 1984 at the Student Center at Augsburg College. Prof. Dupree is George Littlefield Professor of History Emeritus at Brown University. He was Visiting Professor in the History of Science and Technology at the University of Minnesota during Spring Quarter 1984.

23. Dr. Robert C. Ritchie, *Pirates: Myths and Realities*, published in 1986.

The lecture was given on April 16, 1985 at Cochran Union at Macalester College. Dr. Ritchie is a historian, teaching at the University of California, San Diego.

24. Dr. Carla Rahn Phillips, *Life at Sea in the Sixteenth Century: The Landlubber's Lament of Eugenio de Salazar*, published in 1987.

Dr. Phillips presented her lecture on May 1, 1986 at St. Joseph's Hall at the College of St. Catherine. She is a member of the History Department of the University of Minnesota.

25. Dr. Michael F. Metcalf, *Goods, Ideas, and Values: The East Indies Trade as an Agent of Change in Eighteenth-Century Sweden*, published in 1988.

The lecture was delivered at the Campus Club, University of Minnesota on May 7, 1987. Prof. Metcalf is associate professor of Scandinavian History at the University of Minnesota.

26. Prof. Richard Price, *Representations of Slavery: John Gabriel Stedman's "Minnesota" Manuscripts*, published in 1989.

The lecture was presented at the Student Center of Hamline University on May 26, 1988. Prof. Price and his wife, Prof. Sally Price, are authors of a landmark edition of John Gabriel Stedman's account of his experiences in Surinam in the eighteenth century.

27. Prof. Michael Pearson, *Towards Superiority: European and Indian Medicine 1500–1700*, published in 1989.

The lecture was given on May 3, 1989 at the American Association of University Women's Club. Prof. Pearson was a Visiting Professor in the History Department of the University of Minnesota. He is a specialist in the history of Indian Ocean commerce at the University of New South Wales.

28. Prof. Philip D. Curtin, *Disease and Imperialism before the Nineteenth Century*, published in 1990.

The lecture was given on April 16, 1990, at the College of St. Catherine in St. Paul. Professor Curtin, of The Johns Hopkins University, is noted for his studies of early trade as well as disease.

ANNUAL MEETINGS OF THE ASSOCIATES
OF THE JAMES FORD BELL LIBRARY

Dec. 30, 1963   The first meeting of the incorporators and the first Board of Directors for the "Associates of the James Ford Bell Collection" was held on this date at 9200 Wayzata Boulevard, Minneapolis, Minnesota.

Nov. 15, 1965   The first annual meeting was held at the Minneapolis Club. Prof. Charles E. Nowell, author of *A Letter to Ferdinand and Isabella*, was the speaker. Miss Jane McCarthy, the book designer, was introduced. Mr. Douglas Campbell presented a reading of the *Columbus Letter*.

Nov. 9, 1966   The Ptashne Trio provided 16th century Italian music at this dinner meeting held at the Minneapolis Club. Donald Stolz, Director of the Old Log Theater, read from a modern translation of *Mundus Novus* by Amerigo Vespucci. Also presented was an anniversary reading of Jonathan Carver's comments on his visit to the Falls of St. Anthony in November 1766.

Oct. 30, 1967   The meeting was held at the Minnesota Alumni Club where it was voted to change the group's name to "The Associates of the James Ford Bell Library." The meeting was adjourned to the Planetarium of the Minneapolis Public Library where Capt. A. Roland Jones of the Virginia Military Institute was the speaker.

Nov. 12, 1968   An open house was held at the new location of the James Ford Bell Library in Wilson Library. The speaker was Dr. Arthur C. Aufderheide of Duluth. He was physician and photographer to the Plaisted Polar Expedition in the spring of 1968.

Nov. 13, 1969   The meeting was held at the James Ford Bell Library. John Parker spoke about his research on the life and travels of Jonathan Carver. A new exhibit was opened titled "The Discoverers: Narratives of Travel and Exploration." The Society for the History of Discoveries also met here at this time.

Nov. 17, 1970   Neil Christian and Don Kelsey sang songs of the North and songs of the sea at the meeting held at the James Ford Bell Library. The new exhibit was "The 300th Anniversary of the Hudson's Bay Company."

Nov. 8, 1971   Prof. W. Roger Buffalohead described the American Indian Studies program at the University of Minnesota. "The Discovery of Minnesota," a slide/tape show was also presented. A new exhibit was opened titled "Indians of North America through Five Centuries."

Oct. 30, 1972   The group "Musica Antiqua" provided music from the years 1450–1550. Books from the first century of printing were on exhibit.

Nov. 20, 1973   The Library's 20th Anniversary was recognized. Prof. William McDonald of the Classics Dept. presented slides and comments on his archaeological work in Greece. Publications issued by the Library during the last two decades were on exhibit.

Nov. 7, 1974   Karen Eastman presented a slide show of birds from remote parts of the world. An exhibit on circumnavigation was on
display.

Nov. 5, 1975   The highlight of the meeting was the announcement of
a new acquisition. Carla Marzoli, the Italian bookseller who ob-
tained it for us, was here as Pierre Biard's *Relation de la Nouvelle
France*, Lyon, 1616, was shown. The exhibit was "Women's
Dress."

Nov. 8, 1976   The first annual Auction was held at the time of the annual meeting.

Nov. 7, 1977   The second annual Auction was held.

Oct. 27, 1978   A 25th Anniversary party was held at the James Ford
Bell Library. *The World for a Marketplace* by John Parker, published by the Associates to celebrate the Library's 25th anniversary,
was unveiled. Special food and champagne were served. Three
special exhibits were on display.

Oct. 24, 1979   An Auction and Book Fair was held at the Earle Brown
Center on the St. Paul Campus.

Oct. 17, 1980   The second combined Book Fair and Auction was held
at the Earle Brown Center.

Nov. 21, 1981   The third Auction and Book Fair was held at the YWCA
in Minneapolis.

Nov. 23, 1982   The speaker was John Parker who shared experiences
from his recent trip to China. The new exhibit was titled "Windows into China: Early Accounts by Western Travelers." It was
also "T.R. Anderson Night." Dick and LaJean Anderson were honored for their library-building activities. An Auction and Book Fair
was held on Oct. 16th at the YWCA.

Nov. 14, 1983   At this annual meeting forthcoming activities to celebrate Columbus and his discoveries were presented. An Auction
was held on Oct. 15th.

Oct. 12, 1984   The meeting was held at the Minneapolis Institute of
Arts. The Christopher Columbus portrait done by artist Leonardo
Lasansky was unveiled. A party followed, during which the music
was provided by "The Musical Offering" and wine and cheese
refreshments were served.

Nov. 5, 1985   The annual meeting began with an afternoon of volunteer work at the Library by some of the Associates followed by dinner at a nearby restaurant. The meeting concluded back at the Li-

brary during which events of the current year were reviewed including Columbus Day activities, the Dutch map program and recent outstanding acquisitions.

Nov. 14, 1986   An Auction was held featuring art work and antiques as well as books.

Dec. 8, 1987   The annual meeting was held. An exhibit of books purchased with Associates' funds was displayed.

Dec. 5, 1988   The annual meeting was held at the Library. Mariann Tiblin, the University Library's Scandinavian bibliographer, presented "An Introduction to the Tell G. Dahllöf Collection of Swedish America." This collection documents 350 years of Swedish- American relations. On Oct. 14th and 15th a play, "The Discovery of the New World by Christopher Columbus" by Lope de Vega, written in 1614, was presented at the theater in Coffman Union. The Society for the History of Discoveries met here at this time and attended the play, too. On Nov. 19th and 20th an Auction in conjunction with a two-day Antique Fair was held in Willey Hall at the University of Minnesota.

Dec. 11, 1989   Professor Carla Phillips described plans for a Columbus-related exhibit and program she is directing. An exhibit of items purchased by gift funds was on display.

THE ASSOCIATES OF THE JAMES FORD BELL LIBRARY

The Associates of the James Ford Bell Library was organized in December, 1963. The following individuals and institutions have been, or currently are, members of the Associates.

Abbe, Ernst C., Mr.
Adams, Charles M., Mr. and Mrs.
ADC Telecommunications
Agee, Rucker, Mr.
Akre, Nancy, Ms.
Albanese, Philip, Mr.
Alden, Dauril, Prof.
Aldrich, Stephen
Allison, Cecil, Mrs.
Al-Tammar, Fahad
Alvin, Stephen R.
American Antiquarian Society,
     Worcester
American School of Classical
     Studies, New York
Amesbury, William H., Mrs.
Amon Carter Museum Library, Fort
     Worth
Amtmann, Bernard, Mr.
Amundson, Gregg R., Mr.
Andersen, Elmer L., Mr. and Mrs.
Elmer L. and Eleanor J. Andersen
     Foundation
Anderson, Bernice, Ms.
Anderson, Carlyle E., Mr. and Mrs.
Anderson, David G.

Anderson, Einer R., Mr.
Anderson, Elizabeth, Ms.
Anderson, James H., Mr.
Anderson, Leland, Mr.
Anderson, Steve B., Mr. and Mrs.
Anderson, T. R., Mr. and Mrs.
Anderson, William, Dr. and Mrs.
Andren, J. B., Mr. and Mrs.
Andrews, Jr., Sewall D., Mr. and
    Mrs.
Anello, Tony, Mr.
Anoka County Library, Anoka
Anson-Cartwright, Hugh, Mr.
Antenne, Robert V.
Antiquarian Bookman, Newark
Apache Foundation
Arader III, W. Graham, Mr.
Arey, S.L., Dr. and Mrs.
Aris, Rutherford, Mr. and Mrs.
Arkway, Richard B.
Arneson, Jr., Theodore J., Mr.
Arnevik, Lennie, Mr. and Mrs.
Athwin Foundation
Augsburg College, Sverdrup Li-
    brary, Minneapolis
Axtell, James, Professor
Bagger, Hans, Mr.
Baker Library-Dartmouth College
Baker Library-Harvard Business
    School
Baker, Robert Orr, Mr. and Mrs.
Baker, Zachary M., Mr.
Bakken Library
Ball, Ernest W., Mrs.
Ballen Booksellers
Barckley, Gwendolyn R.
Barrett, W.J., Mr.
Barry, Jr., Robert J., Mr.
Barth, Thomas
Bartholomew, John, Mr.
Battell, F. C., Mr. and Mrs.
Bauer, Mary K., Mrs.
Bean, Atherton, Mr.
Beaven, Miranda
Beech, Thomas P., Mr.
Begle, Howard E., Mr.

Belisle, Germain, Mr.
Bell, Cecil H., Mr. and Mrs.
Bell, Charles H., Mr. and Mrs.
Bell, Clare E., Miss
Bell, Ford, Mr.
Bell, Ford J., Mr. and Mrs.
James Ford Bell Book Trust, Min-
    neapolis
James Ford Bell Foundation, Min-
    neapolis
Bell, Peter B., Mr.
Bell, Samuel H., Mr. and Mrs.
Bell, Jr., Samuel H., Mr.
Bell, Virginia L., Ms.
Benedict, Williston R., Mr.
Bennett, Russell, Mr. and Mrs.
Bentley, Jerry and Jean
Berg, Howard O., Mr.
Berman, Alden, Mr. and Mrs.
Berman, Morris, Mr.
Berninghausen, D. K., Mr. and Mrs.
Bernstein, Samuel, Mr.
Berrisford, Sr., Paul D., Mrs.
Berrisford, Paul D., Mr. and Mrs.
Berry, Roger B., Mr.
Bertram, Howard, Mrs.
Bibliotheek der Rijksuniversiteit-
    Leiden, The Netherlands
Bibliothèque Nationale, Paris,
    France
Bigelow Foundation
Bishop's University Library, Lennox-
    ville, Quebec, Canada
Bixby, William Kirker, Mr. and Mrs.
Blackburn, Charles H.
Blackmore, Josiah, Mr.
Blakely, Patricia, Ms.
Blegen, Theodore C., Mr. and Mrs.
Bleiweiss, Roy, Mr.
Bodleian Library, Oxford, England
Bogen, Bogie, Mr.
Bogson, Maybelle, Miss
Bohling, Raymond, Mr. and Mrs.
Bohn, Dorothy C., Ms.
Bohstedt, Claudia, Ms.
Bond, Elizabeth M., Miss

The Book Collector, London,
England
The Boston Athenaeum
Boston Public Library
Boswell, Roy V., Mr. and Mrs.
Bowman, Daniel C.
Bowman, Frank W., Mrs.
Boyd, J. Hayden, Mrs.
Boyle, Robert P., Mr.
Braasch, W. F., Dr.
Brandow, William, Mr. and Mrs.,
and Family
Branin, Joe
Brashear, Paul
Braun, Betsy
Bray, Edmund C., Mr. and Mrs.
Bredesen, W.P., Mr. and Mrs.
Brinckman, Roderick, Mr.
The British Library, London,
England
The British Library, Map Library,
London, England
Brogan, James W., Mr. and Mrs.
Bromsen, Maury A., Mr.
Brooks, Jeannette, Ms.
Brown, Donald C., Mr.
Brown, Elizabeth, Ms.
John Carter Brown Library,
Providence
Brown & Bigelow
Buffalo and Erie County Public Li-
brary, Buffalo
Buirge, Raymond E., Dr. and Mrs.
Bumpus, Haldane and Maxwell,
Ltd.
Burchell, Howard B., Mr.
Burrus, S. J., Ernest J., Rev.
Arizona State Museum
Burus, Paul, Dr. and Mrs.
Butler, Albert F., Mr. and Mrs.
Butler, Pierce, Mr. and Mrs.
Canadian Plains Research Center,
Regina, Saskatchewan
Carbonneau, Denis, Mr.
Carlson, Doug, Mr. and Mrs.
Carpenter, Kenneth, Mr.

Carroll, Maezie, Miss
Case, Benton, Mr. and Mrs.
Catz, Rebecca, Dr.
Centro de Estudios Orientales,
Ciudad Universitaria, Mexico
Chapin Library, Williams College
Chase, Harry and Joan
Chase, Naomi, Ms.
Chellis, Robert D., Mrs.
Chernofsky, Jacob L., Mr.
Cherryhomes, Dan and Jackie
Chiesa, Carlo Alberto, Mr.
Child, Rollin B., Mr. and Mrs.
Christianson, J. R., Dr.
Clapp, Maxine B., Ms.
William A. Clark Library
Cohen, Jacob G., Mrs.
Cokato Historical Society
Coleman, Patrick K., Mr.
Collins, D.B., Mr.
Colman, Robert, Mrs.
Columbia University, New York
Conley, Tom, Mr.
Cook, Andrew S.
James Cook University of North
Queensland, Queensland, Aus-
tralia
Cooper, William H., Mr. and Mrs.
Cope, Esther S., Miss
Corey, Steven, Dr.
Cornell University Libraries, Ithaca
Coyne, J. E., Mr.
Cox, James A., Mr.
Cozzetto, Peter R.
Crabtree, Nate L., Mrs.
Crampton, C. Gregory, Mr.
Crandall, G. M., Mrs.
Crounse, Agnes, Miss
Cummings, James, Mr.
Dahlquist, Sally and Eric
Dalrymple, John S., Mrs.
Damms Antikvariat, Oslo, Norway
Daniels, Carol and Richard Jacker
Daniels, John H., Mr. and Mrs.
Davies, K. G., Prof.
Davies, R. A., Mr.

Davis, Charles R., Mr.
Davis and Orioli, London, England
Dayton, Bruce B., Mr. and Mrs.
Dayton, G. N., Mrs.
The DeGolyer Foundation Library,
    Dallas
De Hoog, Jac M.
De Jong, Kersen J., Mr.
Dekker, Alexander, Mr.
Denny, Jr., Charles M., Mr. and
    Mrs.
De Young, Dirk, Mr.
Diffendal, Barbara E., Ms.
Diffie, Bailey W., Mr.
Dillingham, Gaylord, Mrs.
Diracles, James C., Mr.
Dodge, Timothy, Mr.
Dolid, William A., Mr. and Mrs.
Donahue, James L., Dr. and Mrs.
Donnelley, Gaylord, Mr.
Dorsey and Whitney
Douglas, Marjorie Stoneman, Mrs.
Douthwaite, Julia
Doyle, Donald M., Mr.
DuBois, Robert, Mr.
Dulany, Mary, Ms.
Duncan, Judith Anne
Dunnavan, C. Curtis, Mr.
Durgin, James H., Mrs.
Du Rietz, Rolf, Mr.
Duxbury, Susan
Eastman, Whitney, Mr. and Mrs.
Eck, E. Norman
Edblom, T. Thomas, Dr. and Mrs.
Edward Eberstadt & Sons
Ehrlich, Izzy, Mr.
Elliott, Richard M., Mrs.
Emmer, Pieter C.
Erasmus Antiquariaat en Boek-
    handel, Amsterdam, Hol-
    land
Estelle, Robert F., Mr.
Etzwiler, Marion G., Ms.
Ewe, Caroline, Miss
The Explorers Club, New York
Fagerlie, Joan, Ms.

Fair, Anthony, Mr.
Falk, Marvin W.
Famodu, Tunde, Mr.
Fanning, Rebecca-Christopher
    Miller & Co.
Farrar, Fredric, Mr. and Mrs.
Feldman, Stephen
Fennema, Judith, Ms.
Ferguson, Van, Mr.
Field, Wayne, Mr.-Rembrandt En-
    terprises, Inc.
Fikes, Jr., Robert, Mr.
Finch, Bob
Fish, James, Mr. and Mrs.
Fisher, Raymond H.
Fladger, Ellen, Ms.
Fleming, John F., Mr.
Florida State University, Robert
    Manning Strozier Library,
    Tallahassee
The Folger Shakespeare Library,
    Washington, D. C.
Fondersmith, John
Foss, Theodore N.
Foss, William F., Mr. and Mrs.
Four Oaks Foundation, New York
Fransen, Joean, Mrs.
Fredrickson, A.G., Mr.
Free Library of Philadelphia,
    Philadelphia
Freedman, Lee, Mr.
Freilich, Marvin S., Dr. and Mrs.
Froelich, M.E.
Frost, Douglas, Mr.
Fry, Percy Keating, Mr. and Mrs.
Furber, Holden, Professor
Galloway, J.H., Mr.
Galusha, Jr., Hugh, Mr. and Mrs.
Gayl, Jane H., Mrs.
General Mills
Georgia State University Library,
    Atlanta
Geraghty, James F., Mr.
Gerard, Lyle, Mr. and Mrs.
A. Gerits & Sons
Giesecke, E.W., Col. and Mrs.

Gilbert, Bennett, Mr.
Gilbertson, Irvyn, Mrs.
Gilje, Paul A.
Gillis, Frank J., Mr. and Mrs.
Goetz, Mary Rose and Frederick
Goff, Frederich R., Mr.
Goldstein, Erwin M., Mr.
Goldstein, Priscilla P.
Goldstein, Thomas and Helga
Goldstone, Adrian H., Mr.
Golob, Martin, Mr. and Mrs.
Goodsell, James Nelson, Dr.
Goodspeed, George T., Mr.
Gordan, John D., Mr. and Mrs.
Gould, Abbott J., Mr. and Mrs.
Gould, Howard, Mr. and Mrs.
Grace, Charles M., Mr.
Graubard, Mark, Mr. and Mrs.
Grauer, Ben, Mr.
Griep, Roland, Mr. and Mrs.
Grinager, Greg
Grinnell College Library, Grinnell,
    Iowa
Groetzinger, Walker, Mrs.
Growth Ventures, Inc.
Gunderman, Michael, Mr.
Guthorn, Peter J., Dr.
Guthrie, Marguerite, Miss
Guthrie, Murray K., Mr. and Mrs.
Haber, Philip B., Mr.
Habermann, Margaret J., Mrs.
Hagelin, Ove
Haglin, Preston, Mrs.
Hagstrum, Jean H.
Hahn, Betty Jean, Ms.
Haines, Helen, Miss
Hale, Grace, Miss
Hamer, Sidney, Mr. and Mrs.
Hamilton, Jr., Russell G., Mr.
Hanafy, Abdalla A., Dr.
Hancock, John Carl
Hanke, Lewis, Mr.
Hann, Charles, Mr. and Mrs.
Hansen, Clark B., Mr.
Hansen, Helen, Miss
Harley, J. B., Dr.
Lathrop C. Harper, Inc.

Harris, Patty Carver, Ms.
Hart, Henry, Dr.
Hartley, Alan H.
Hartung, David, Mr.
Hartwell, David
Hartwell, Lucy
Harvard University, Houghton Li-
    brary, Cambridge
Harvard University Library, Cam-
    bridge
Friends of the Harvard University
    Library
Hasselmo, Nils
Hasselquist, Maynard B., Mr. and
    Mrs.
Hattendorf, John B., Dr.
Hauser, Walter, Mr. and Mrs.
Haverstock, Sr., Henry W.
Hawkins, Ross
Haymond, Morey W., Dr.
Heath, Oscar V.
Heath, Richard and Betty
Heaton, Herbert, Prof. and Mrs.
Heersema, Margaret M., Mrs.
Heilbrun, Georges, Mr.
Heiman, Willy, Mr.
Hein, Jeanne, Ms.
Helgeson, Henry A., Mr.
Heller, Walter and Emily
Henau, Brigitte PF
Henderson, Jeanette, Miss
Hertzberger, Menno, Mr.
Herz, M.E.
Herz, Wolfgang A.
Heyerdahl-Jensen, Kirsti M., Ms.
Hill, Jonathan A., Mr.
Louis and Maud Hill Family Foun-
    dation, St. Paul
Friends of the Hill Monastic Manu-
    script Library, Collegeville
Hirabayashi, Martin, Mr.
Hispanic Society of America, New
    York
Hitchman, Robert, Mr.
Hofherr, J. Douglas
Hohlen, Dave R., Mr.
Holdgrafer, George C., Mr.

Holland, Clement, Mr.
Hollenhorst, Jr., Robert, Dr. and
  Mrs.
Holloway, R.J.
Holum, Katharine, Ms.
Holzheimer, Arthur, Mr.
Hoover, Roy O., Mr. and Mrs.
Hopp, Ralph, Mr. and Mrs.
Hosmer, James B., Mr.
Houghton, Arthur A., Mr.
Houle, George A., Mr.
Howe, John
Howell, Warren R., Mr. and Mrs.
Hoyle, Robert J. and Karen Nelson
Hruza, W. J., Dr.
Hubbs, Ronald M., Mr.
Hughes, John B., Mr. and Mrs.
Hunegs, Michael L., Mr.
Hunt, Roy A., Mr.
Huntington, Seth G., Mr.
Henry E. Huntington Library & Art
  Gallery, San Marino
Hurwitz, Michael Randall, Mr. and
  Mrs.
Husband, Richard L.
Husby, Scott, Mr.
Hushcha, Sally Ames Wheaton, Ms.
Husted, K. Wallace, Mr. and Mrs.
Hyde, Robert C., Mr.
Immler, Frank
Ingvaldsen, R.E., Mr. and Mrs.
Iowa State University Library, Ames
Israel, B. M., Mr. and Mrs.
Israel, Nico, Mr. and Mrs.
Jackson, Melvin H., Mr.
Jackson, Norris D., Mr. and Mrs.
Jacobs, Alden F., Mr.
Japs, Patricia K., Ms.
Jeffrey, William O., Mrs.
Jenkins, John, Mr.
Jensen, Khin Khin and Vernon, Drs.
Jenson, John R., Mr.
Jerabek, Esther, Miss
Jessup, Paul F.
Johnson, Alberta C., Ms.
Johnson, Annabelle J., Miss

Johnson, Bruce L., Dr.
Johnson, C. L., Mr.
Johnson, Carol A., Ms.
Johnson, Donald Clay
Johnson, Gustave F., Mr. and Mrs.
Johnson, Hildegard B., Professor
Johnson, Howard W., Mr.
Johnson, Peter T., Mr.
Johnson, Russell and Winifred
Johnston, Charles J., Mr. and Mrs.
Johnston, Sheila, Ms.
Jones, Ruth E., Miss
Jones, Waring, Mr. and Mrs.
Kaatz, Steven, Dr.
Kaewer, Barbara A., Ms.
Kagan, Gerald, Mr.
Kahn, Helen R.
Kaimowitz, Jeffery H.
Kaplanoff, Mark D.
Kasper, Lynn Rossetto
Keller, Kenneth H.
Keller III, Thomas A., Mr.
Kelley, James E., Mr.
Kellogg, Martin, Mr. and Mrs.
Kelly, Charles A., Mr.
Kelly, Richard, Mr.
Kennedy, Roger G., Mr.
Kenworthy, Paul R.
Keys, Thomas E., Mr.
Kimbrough, Joseph, Mr.
King, Reatha Clark
King III, Willis L., Mr.
Kingsley, James, Mr. and Mrs.
Kirkpatrick, Wallace A.
Kittleson, J. Harold, Mr.
Klein, Anne, Ms.
Knauth, Lothar, Mr.
Koffler, Henry, Mr. and Mrs.
Korn, Bertram, Dr.
Koshalek, Richard, Mr. and Mrs.
Kraus, H. P., Mr.
Kreidberg, Irving B., Mr. and Mrs.
Kreie, William, Mr. and Mrs.
Kuhn, Jr., John F., Dr.
Lada-Mocarski, V., Mr. and Mrs.
Laird, William P., Mr. and Mrs.

Laguna, Asela, Mrs.
Lamb, Ursula, Professor
Lan, Richard, Mr.
Lande, Laurence M., Dr.
Lanegran, David, Mr. and Mrs.
Lang, William H., Mr. and Mrs.
Larkin, John E., Dr. and Mrs.
Larson, Eugene, Mr.
Larson, Wendy, Mrs.
Lasansky, Leonardo
La Trobe University
Lauerman, Fred, Mr.
Lauria, Arthur, Mr.
Laurie, James K., Mr. and Mrs.
Lavelle, John T., Mr. and Mrs.
Leach, Stowell D., Mr. and Mrs.
Lee, Carlton R., Mr.
Lee, Jeffrey Alan, Mr.
Leiden University
Lenker, John C., Mr.
Lensing, Harold H., Mr.
Leslie, Frank P., Mr. and Mrs.
Lester, Richard G., Dr. and Mrs.
Levinson, Harry A., Mr. and Mrs.
Lewellen, Frances, Miss
Lewman, Jr., John H., Mr. and
    Mrs.
Library Company of Philadelphia,
    The
Lien, Leland N., Mr. and Mrs.
Lighter, Willard C., Mr.
Lillestrand, Robert, Mr. and Mrs.
Lincoln, Jane F., Mrs.
Lincoln, Margaret M., Miss
Lind, Melva, Dr.
Lindley, Grace, Ms.
Little, Jr., Philip, Mr.
Lively, Tom C., Mr.
Livingston, Larry W., Mr.
Lloyd, Stacy B., Mr.
Lobdell, Lucille, Miss
Lockhart, Donald M., Mr.
Loome, Karen and Thomas
Love, John P., Mr.
Low, Jr., William G., Mrs.
Löwendahl, Björn
Lownes, Albert E., Mr.

Lundeen, Cathy, Ms.
Lundstrom, Linden J., Mr. and Mrs.
Maack, Mary Niles, Ms.
Macalester College
MacDonnell, Thomas P., Mr.
MacGregor, Bruce, Mr. and Mrs.
MacGregor, Clark, Mr. and Mrs.
MacInnis, Donald E., Mr.
Magis, Jean-Jacques, Mr.
Magnetic Controls Co.
Magrath, C. Peter, Mr. and Mrs.
Magraw, R.M., Dr.
Maguire, J. Robert, Mr. and Mrs.
Malec, Andrew
Malkerson, Lester A., Mr. and Mrs.
Mankato State College Library
Mann, Ruth J., Miss
Map Library, University of Min-
    nesota
Mapline, The Newberry Library
Marchell, Betty, Mrs.
Mardock, Lori
Marin, Tina M. de
Markoff, Marjorie
Marvel, Josiah
Marzoli, Carla C., Mrs.
Mason, Charlene
Massey, Linton R., Mrs.
Mathson, Robert O.
McAlister, Lyle N., Professor
McCarthy, Jane, Miss
McClelland, Jr., J. M., Mr. and
    Mrs.
McComb, John H. and Ruth Eckert,
    Drs.
McCorison, M.S., Mr. and Mrs.
McCormack, Patricia A., Ms.
McCusker, John J.
McGarvey, E. H., Mrs.
McGill University Libraries
McGrath, Daniel F., Mr. and Mrs.
McGreehan, Jean
McGregor, Della, Miss
McIntyre, J. Lawrence, Mr. and
    Mrs.
McJunkin, David, Mr.
McKee, Ruth V., Miss

McKenna, James Brian, Mr.
McKnight, William L., Mr. and
    Mrs.
McKnight Enterprises
McKnight Family Endowment
    Almoner's Fund, The
McLean, Austin and Sue
McNeely, Donald, Mr. and Mrs.
McNulty, Robert J., Mr. and Mrs.
McWilliams, David Jackson, Mr.
Meagher, Gary and Jackie
Mellon, Paul, Mr.
Menard, Russell, Mr.
Mendel, Bernardo, Mr.
Meyer, Blanche, Miss
Meyer, Richard K., Mr. and Mrs.
Meyer, Ruth, Mrs.
Midwest China Study Resource
    Center
Miller, Creighton S., Mr.
Miller, Lisa K., Ms.
Miller, Rich, Mr. and Mrs.
Mills, Walter A., Mrs.
Milwaukee Public Library
Minneapolis Foundation
Minneapolis Institute of Arts
Minnesota Historical Society
Minnich, Dwight, Mr. and Mrs.
Mitchell, Mary Louise, Ms.
Mitchell, William F., Mr. and Mrs.
Molitor, Jr., Paul, Mr.
Moore, Davis W., Mr.
Moore, William J., Mr. and Mrs.
Moorhead State College
Moos, Malcolm, Dr. and Mrs.
Morey, Janeen, Ms.
Morgan, Samuel H., Mr. and Mrs.
Morrill, J. L., Mr. and Mrs.
Mott, Gordon B., Mr.
Mott, Ralph O., Mr. and Mrs.
Muck, Thomas R. and Bernadette
    Pyter
Mundus Novus Foundation
Murphy, Jr., Joseph E.
Murphy, Terrence J., Rev. Msgr.
Museum of the American China
    Trade

Myre, Charles D.
Myren, Frederick S.
Nason, John W., Mr.
National Library of Australia,
    Canberra
National Library of Canada, Ottawa
National Library of Scotland
Neale, Charles T., Mrs.
Nebenzahl, Kenneth, Mr. and Mrs.
Nelson, Dorothy K.
Nelson, Eleanor, Miss
Nelson, J. R., Mr. and Mrs.
Nelson, William K., Mr. and Mrs.
Nesheim, William, Mr.
Newberry Library, The
Carol Newman Library, Virginia
    Polytechnic Institute and State
    University
Newman, Henry Shaw, Mr.
Newman, Kenneth M., Mr.
Newman, Michael, Mr. and Mrs.
New York Public Libraries
Nicholes, Eleanor L., Dr.
Nielsen, Carl N., Mr.
Nissen, Harlan J., Mr.
Nordley, Eva, Ms.
Norman & Co., Jeremy
Norris, Donald C., Mr. and Mrs.
Nunis, Jr., Doyce B., Mr.
Nyegaard, Claes, Mr.
O'Connor, Patrick J., O'Connor &
    Hannan
Odevall, Bengt, Mr.
Odland, Norine, Miss
Offenbacher, Emil, Mr.
Oftelie, Brad and Lynn Balfour
Olmstead County Historical Society
Olsson, Nils William, Mr. and Mrs.
Olsten, Jann L., Mr.
O'Shaughnessy, Lawrence, Mr. and
    Mrs.
Ostrem, Walter M., Mr.
Owen, Kenneth M., Mr.
Ozolins, Karl L., Mr.
Pankake, Marcia, Ms.
Pankey, Charles H., Mr.
Parady, Rex Dennis, Mr.

Parker, John and Patricia A.
Parker, Paul L., Mr. and Mrs.
Parker, Sarah, and Gary Lee
Parr, Charles McKew, Mr.
Patchen, Paul J., Dr. and Mrs.
Patterson, Hyrum S., Mr. and Mrs.
Peacher, William G., M.D.
Pearson, M.N., Professor
Perpich, Rudy, Governor
Penrose, Boies, Mr.
Perrin, Leslie N., Mr. and Mrs.
Perry, H. O., Mr. and Mrs.
Pesat III, Adolphe A., Mr.
Pesek, Cyril P., Mr. and Mrs.
Peters, Ferdinand F., Mr. and Mrs.
Peterson, Harold P., Mr.
Pfeiffer, Gordon A., Mr. and Mrs.
Phelps, E. J., Mr.
Philadelphia Rare Books Company
Philippon, Lucien R., Mr.
Phillips, Carla Rahn
Phillips, Della G., Miss
Phillips, Josephine E., Miss
Phillips, Jr., W.D.
Piper, Jr., H. C., Mr. and Mrs.
Plank, Raymond, Mr.
Platt, Stanley K., Mr. and Mrs.
Plattes, C. W., Mr. and Mrs.
Polzer, Charles W., Father
Porter, Philip W., Mr.
Postma, Johannes, Mr. and Mrs.
Pouncey, Lorene, Miss
Power-Ross, Robert W., Mr. and
     Mrs.
Pratt, Dallas, Dr.
Princeton University Library
Pringle, Sandy M., Mr.
Printy, David L., Mr. and Mrs.
Provost, Bob and Mary
Provost, Foster
Public Archives of Canada
Puffer, K.E.
Pyter, Thomas C., Mr. and Mrs.
Quinn, C. P., Mr. and Mrs.
Quinn, David and Alison
Quinn, Mary E., Miss
Radaeli, Francesco, Mr.

Ramer, Richard C., Mr.
Rand, Sidney A., Mr. and Mrs.
Randolph-Macon College, Walter
     Hines Page Library
Ranschburg, Otto H., Mr.
Rapoport, Joseph, Mr.
Rawlings, E. W., General and Mrs.
Reed, John R., Mr. and Mrs.
Reed, Lachlan A., Mr. and Mrs.
Regan, John J., Dr. and Mrs.
Reichner, Herbert, Mr.
Reiersgord, Thomas E., Mr. and
     Mrs.
Reister, Raymond A., Mr. and Mrs.
Remington, Reg and Philip
Remley, R. D., Mr. and Mrs.
Renaud, Armand A., Mr.
Rendell, Kenneth W., Mr. and Mrs.
Reuben, Walter, Mr.
Rice, John G., Mr.
Richards, Bergmann, Mr. and Mrs.
Richardson, Jessie F., Ms.
Riedel, Jane E.
Riley, Elizabeth, Miss
Risvold, Floyd E., Mr. and Mrs.
Roberts, Valerie L., Ms.
Robertson, Stewart, Mr.
Robinson, Cedric L., Mr.
Robinson, Walter G., Mr. and Mrs.
Roddis, Louis H., Dr.
Rogers, Francis M., Professor and
     Mrs.
Ronan, Charles E., Father
Rosenkilde and Bagger, Copenhagen
Rosenthal, Bernard M., Mr. and
     Mrs.
Rosenthal, Robert, Dr.
Rosenwald, Lessing J., Mr.
Roy, Curtis L., Mr. and Mrs.
Rozentals, Magdalene, Ms.
Rubinstein, Joseph, Mr.
Ruffner, Fred G., Mr.
Rulon-Miller, Rob
Rumble, D. B., Mrs.
Ryland, Stephen L., Mr.
St. Cloud State University
Saint John's University

Salloch, William, Mr. and Mrs.
Samuelson, Lydia, Miss
Savage, Thomas C., Mr. and Mrs.
Savelle, Max, Professor
Sawyer Ltd., Charles J., London
Scheetz, Nicholas B.
Scheler, Lucien, Mr.
Schouten International, Inc.
Schuman, Henry, Mrs.
Schutz, Wallace J., Mr.
Schwappach, Kirsten
Schwartz, Stuart B., Professor and
    Mrs.
Schwartzberg, Joseph E., Mr. and
    Mrs.
Schweitzer, Robert J., Mr. and Mrs.
Schwenk, William F. and Nina M.,
    Drs.
Scott, Barry, Mr.
Scott, Mary L., Ms.
Seriin, Lillian, Miss
Shanahan, Thomas J., Rt. Rev.
    Msgr.
Shannon, James P., Dr.
Shapiro, S. R., Dr.
Shaughnessy, Thomas N.
Shepard, Roger B., Mr. and Mrs.
Shepherd, William G., Mr. and
    Mrs.
Shippee, Warner B.
Sibley, Marjorie H., Ms.
Silha, Otto A., Mr. and Mrs.
Silver, Joel, Mr.
Silverson, Charles T., Mr. and Mrs.
Simler, Lucy
Simms, Douglas W.
Simon, Ron, Mr.
Sinnen, Jeanne, Ms.
Sitter, James
Skelton, R. A., Mr.
Slater, Gerald, Dr.
Slater, Milton R., Mr.
Slessarev, Vsevolod, Mr.
Slifer, Rosejeanne, Miss
Sloane III, T. O'Conor, Mr.
Sloss, Jr., Henry E., Mr. and Mrs.
Smiley, H.D., Dr.

Smith, Bill and Jean
Smith, Eldred, Mr. and Mrs.
Smith, Jacqueline A., Mrs.
Smith, Josephine L., Mrs.
Smith, Jr., Lloyd and Beatrice
Smith, Merrily A., Ms.
Smith, Robert W., Mr. and Mrs.
Smith, Susan Margot, Ms.
Smith, Thomas R., Mr.
Smith, Wakelee, Mr.
Sodergren, Linnea, Ms.
Sokol, Christopher J.
Solomon, J. J., Mr. and Mrs.
Sonier, Robert S., Mr. and Mrs.
Soule, James I., Mr.
Southern Illinois University, Lovejoy
    Library
Southwest Mission Research Center,
    Tucson
Spears, John E., Mr.
Spencer, William M., Mr. and Mrs.
Spikes, W. F., Mr.
Stafford, R. W., Mr.
Stanford, Edward B., Mr. and Mrs.
Stassen, Harold E., Mr.
Steiner, George R., Mr. and Mrs.
Steinke, Cynthia, Ms.
Stenerud, Gene
Stern, Harry L.
Stevens, Son & Stiles, Henry
Stokes, Claire Zigmund
Stones, Alison, Professor
Stott, James L., Mr. and Mrs.
Stransky, Tom and Kathy
Streeter, Frank S., Mr.
Streeter, Thomas W., Mr.
Strickler, J. H., Dr. and Mrs.
Strickler, John C., Mr. and Mrs.
Strouse, Norman H., Mr. and Mrs.
Robert Manning Strozier Library
Stuart, R. Douglas, Mr. and Mrs.
Stucker, Carol, Mrs.
Sulerud, Ralph, Mr. and Mrs.
Sullivan, Virgil and Christine
Swanson, Edward
Swanson, Loren E., Mr.
Sweatt, Harold W., Mr. and Mrs.

Swenson, David J.
Swets & Zeitlinger BV
Szewczyk, David M., Mr. and Mrs.
Tanenbaum, Charles J., Mr.
Taylor, Henry C., Mr.
Taylor, Thomas W., Mr.
Telles da Sylva, José Antonio, Mr.
Terrell, Burnham and Julie
Tezla, Kathy, Ms.
Thieme, Otto
Thomson, J. Cameron, Mr.
Thorne, Samuel, Mr.
Thueson, James D., Mr. and Mrs.
Tiblin, Mariann, Ms.
Tilton, John E., Mr. and Mrs.
Tinker, Harry A., Mr.
Tió, Aurelio, Mr.
Tomlinson, Regina Johnson, Mrs.
Tracy, James
Tree, Roland, Mr.
Trendota, Kristina, Miss
Trenerry, Walter N., Mr. and Mrs.
Treude, Mai
True, David O., Mr.
Tsangeos, Michael, Mr.
Tufford, Nancy
Turnbull, Andrew, Mr.
Turnbull, M. D., Mrs.
Turner, Patricia
Ueland, Arnulf, Mr. and Mrs.
Universitetsbiblioteket, Uppsala
University Archives, University of
Minnesota, Minneapolis
University of Adelaide, Barr Smith
Library, South Australia
University of Alaska, Elmer E. Ras-
muson Library, Fairbanks
University of Alberta Library, Ed-
monton, Alberta
University of Arizona, Main Library,
Tucson
University of British Columbia,
Main Library, Vancouver,
British Columbia
University of California, General Li-
brary, Berkeley

University of California, Univer-
sity Research Library, Los
Angeles
University of California Library,
Santa Barbara
University of Chicago Library,
Chicago
University of Chicago Library Soci-
ety, The Joseph Regenstein Li-
brary, Chicago
University of Dublin, The Library,
Trinity College, Dublin
University of Houston Libraries,
Houston
University of Illinois at Urbana-
Champaign, The Library,
Urbana
University of Illinois Library
Friends, Urbana
University of Iowa Libraries, Iowa
City
University of Kansas, Kenneth
Spencer Research Library,
Lawrence
University of Kansas Libraries,
Lawrence
University of London Library,
London
University of Miami, Otto G.
Richter Library, Coral Gables
University of Michigan, William L.
Clements Library, Ann Arbor
University of Minnesota-Duluth Li-
brary, Duluth
University of Minnesota Libraries,
Minneapolis
University of Nebraska Libraries,
Lincoln
University of Newcastle-Upon-Tyne
Library, Newcastle-Upon-Tyne
University News Service, University
of Minnesota, Minneapolis
University of Oklahoma Libraries,
Norman
University of Oregon Library,
Eugene

University of Pittsburgh, Hillman Library, Pittsburgh

University of San Francisco

University of South Africa Library, Pretoria

University of South Carolina, McKissick Memorial Library, Columbia

University of South Carolina, Thomas Cooper Library, Columbia

University of Virginia, Alderman Library, Charlottesville

University of Waterloo, The Library, Waterloo, Ontario

Urness, Carl, Mr.

Urness, Carol, Ms.

Urness, Dorothy, Ms.

Urseth, William A., Mr. and Mrs.

U.S. Communications

Valente, Mario, Dr.

Van der Boom, H. E., Mr. and Mrs.

Van Grasstek, L., Mr. and Mrs.

Van Norman, Jr., C. E., Mr.

Van Valkenburg, Horace, Mr.

Vaughn, William S., Mr.

Vellekoop, J.L., Mr.

Verner, Coolie, Professor

Verrilli, Rocco A., Dr.

Vick, Judy, Miss

Vietor, Alexander O., Mr.

Vigevani, Enrico, Dr.

Von Blon, Philip, Mr. and Mrs.

Voyageur Press

Vries, Dirk de

Wagner, Stuart L., Mr.

Wakefield, Lyman, Mr. and Mrs.

Wakefield, Ray and Magrit

Walden, Barbara, Ms.

Wallace, Birgitta, Ms.

Walrath, Ronald, Mr.

Walters, Joe A.

Warwick, Warren J. and Henrietta H.

Washburn, Wilcomb E., Dr.

Wayne State University, Purdy Library

Webster, Roderick S., Mr. and Mrs.

Weeks, John, Mr. and Mrs.

Weiner, Robert, Dr.

Weiss, Janet and Gerhard

Wenberg, Stanley J., Mr. and Mrs.

Wenger, Larry B.

Werkgroep voor de Geschiedenis van de Europese Expansie, Rykuniversiteit te Leiden

Westbrook, Nicholas and Virginia

Westgard, Rolf E., Mr. and Mrs.

Westrem, Scott D.

Wheat, Renville, Mr.

Whitehead, Ralph and Marie

Whitney, Irene Hixon

Whitney, Wheelock, Mr. and Mrs.

Wilcox, William, Mr. and Mrs.

Williams, John Alexander

Wilson, O. Meredith, Mr. and Mrs.

Witt, M. M., Mr.

Wolf, Eric W.

Wolf, Walter A.

Wolter, John A., Mr. and Mrs.

Woo, Howard F., Mr. and Mrs.

Woodbury, Elizabeth, Mrs.

Woodward, David, Mr. and Mrs.

Woolverton, Deborah, Ms.

Wormser, Carola Paine, Mrs.

Wreden, William P., Mr.

Wright, Louis B., Dr.

Wulling, Emerson G., Mr.

Wyllie, John Cook, Mr.

Ylvisaker, Marguerite, Dr.

Zeitlin, Jacob, Mr. and Mrs.

Zeitlin and Ver Brugge

Ziegeweid, Joseph E.

Zissler, Ellen W., Mrs.

Zobel, Larry and Vicki

Zwisohn, Jane

A Letter from the Editor

Dear Jack,

Your surprise book is almost ready for the printer. Apparently you don't suspect that anything special is afoot. With luck the secret of the book will be kept until April 29, 1991, when you give the James Ford Bell Lecture at the Humphrey Institute. A lot of us can hardly wait to deliver this surprise!

Because of the way the paging went, Irv tells me that I can add this letter to you. For once I am at a loss for words. I would like to compose some grand summary statement of thanks and congratulations to you, or even conclude with an apt quotation. When I think back on this book I am reminded that you once said: "Never look ahead or behind. Look down and keep hoeing." Seeing a much-handled, nearly blood-stained stack of galley proofs and a cleaner but bruised set of page proofs on my desk, I have to say that I like this book. Many friends — and your family — helped make this book possible.

In the fall of 1988 you told me you would retire in May, 1991. That should not have surprised me, but it did. I needed to have time to finish research projects and to plan an appropriate gift. The idea of anything other than a book never crossed my mind. I requested and received a sabbatical from July 1, 1989 to June 30, 1990. The book was discussed with Joe Branin, Director of Social Sciences/Humanities Libraries, and it was part of my sabbatical, but not on the official form you saw! I enjoyed taking it from an idea to reality.

On March 1 the Directors received a letter outlining parts one to three of the book, rather as they appear. Dick Anderson was

one of the most enthusiastic supporters of the idea, Jack. By mid-
April selections from your writings were being typed onto disks,
and I was only sorry that I couldn't ask your advice. At this time
I also developed a case of "disk-mania" which has continued to
the present. Disks were stored at Marge and Irv's house, at Jessie
Richardson's house, in John Jenson's office and in a couple of
places in the Library. I even began to take them with me when
I left town, having heard too many stories about lost disks.

The Directors had a secret meeting at the St. Paul Athletic
Club on 18 May 1989. It was still difficult to visualize the book.
Bill Laird, Bernie Muck, Charlie Hann, Betty Savage, Irv, and
I met. We thought about a book of perhaps seventy-five pages,
though we did discuss a bigger book. The minutes show we asked,
"Can we tackle a big book?" More selections from your writings
were added to the disks, but during the first part of my sabbatical
I traveled quite a lot so little else got done on the book. Suddenly
it was 1990. In February I visited the University Archives, reading about the early history of the James Ford Bell Library. I found
the records fascinating. I hope you will write a more complete
history of the Library.

Then came the time to send out the March letter. We worried
about the secret coming out. To our surprise, it seems that five
hundred people can keep a secret better than five. The letters
started coming in. It was obvious that we had a big book on our
hands. In the section on the Associates we wanted to include
Mary's history and Vicki's chronology, plus a list of all Associates.
I was back at my desk, and the intrigue was more pronounced.
We needed a typesetter, a printer and a binder. Sometimes a
caller would hang up if you answered the phone. There were
some long lunches, involving "business" and "legal matters." You
taught an Elderhostel in September; we finished the list of Associates. When you took Mondays off at the beginning of fall quarter
because you were teaching an evening class, we made telephone
calls and did more typing and proofreading.

Irv and I have had fun. We were spurred on by fine food and
continual encouragement supplied by Marge. In general, Irv is
responsible for how the book looks, as I am for what is in it — but
we worked together. We were helped by many people. Typists
and proof readers included Norma Boe, Dorothy Bohn, Arnie
Fredrickson, John Jenson, Jessie Richardson, Sara Shannon, Ka-

ren Sheldon, Mary Whitehead. At Hopf and Hopf, Barbara Steele and Bob Krautbauer helped; Don Leeper at Stanton Publication Services and Tony Schmidt and crew at Viking Press also aided us. At Midwest Editions Lance Johnson was wonderful to us. Cynthia Steinke, Assistant University Librarian, helped with administration, and Ellory Christianson kept track of our account. The Directors of the Associates, Rutherford Aris, Judith Fennema, Charles Hann, Maynard B. Hasselquist, William P. Laird, Melva Lind, Robert O. Mathson, Bernadette Pyter Muck, Curtis L. Roy, Mrs. Thomas C. Savage, Mrs. Robert J. Schweitzer, Jr., and William A. Urseth have been supportive in all kinds of ways.

Thank you, Jack, for being our inspiration in this and in many other efforts.

Sincerely, Carol Urness   6 January 1991